P 70

CAPITAL EXPENDITURE ANALYSIS

Suk H. Kim, Associate Professor
Department of Accounting and Finance
University of Detroit
Detroit, Michigan 48221

Henry J. Guithues, Professor
Department of Finance
St. Louis University
St. Louis, Missouri 63108

Copyright © 1980 by

University Press of America, Inc.

P.O. Box 19101, Washington, D.C. 20036

ISBN: 0-8191-1463-4 (Perfect)

ISBN: 0-8191-1462-6 (Cloth)

Library of Congress Catalog Card Number: 80-6070

TABLE OF CONTENTS

iii

PREFACE

Capital Expenditure Analysis is a field with the greatest promise of growth. Recent records suggest that it will continue to grow at an accelerated pace. Enrollment at colleges and universities in this discipline has expanded rapidly. The reason is not hard to find. Capital budgeting decisions play a vital role in assisting most large companies to achieve their various goals. Efficient management of capital expenditures has become even more essential with the increasing recognition that the ultimate success of company operations depends on sound capital budgeting decisions.

The basic purpose of this text is to provide the college student with all the traditional capital budgeting topics and theoretical topics such as portfolio theory and the capital asset pricing model. The text is organized to serve the needs of upper-level undergraduate and graduate students enrolled in a capital budgeting course. This book will equip the student with the right balance of theory, tools, and practical applications. Thus, it can also be used as a reference text for case-oriented courses in finance or as a valuable source of basic reference material for the practitioner in the field of finance. Throughout this book, only a basic knowledge of algebra and basic statistics is assumed.

Our overriding goal is to provide the student with all the basic tools and techniques of capital expenditure analysis without losing them in a complex treatment of theoretical concepts. This book introduces, develops, and exemplifies virtually all areas of capital expenditure analysis. It has enough detail that the student will be able to understand what is important and what to look for in the field of capital expenditure analysis. Specifically, it shows how capital budgeting tools and techniques can be used to achieve the firm's primary goal of maximizing stockholder wealth.

The special feature of this text, however, is its conciseness and clarity. By stressing these qualities, we hope to motivate the student to seek out additional knowledge and courses. We have indeed found through our first-round class testing of this manuscript that the text has stimulated in our students an increased interest in advanced financial management electives. Given the opportunity we express the opinion that similar results should be obtained by other faculty and institutions who may elect to test the effectiveness of the text.

The text is divided into four major parts. Part One develops the goal of the firm to be used in the capital budgeting process, covers the tax environment in which these capital budgeting decisions are to be made, and discusses the time value of money which is basic to investment decisions. With the use of the tax environment and the time value of money, Part Two evaluates investment projects under certainty. Chapters 4 and 5 describe traditional evaluation techniques which may be used to evaluate individual projects. Chapters 6 and 7 cover mathematical programming models which can be used to evaluate multiple projects simultaneously. Part Three discusses capital budgeting under uncertainty. Chapter 8 describes risk analysis for individual projects, Chapter 9 deals with risk analysis for multiple projects, and Chapter 10 discusses the required rate of return. Part Four describes somewhat specialized topics of capital budgeting such as leasing and multinational capital budgeting. Although this part deals with special applications of capital budgeting, it draws upon the principles developed in earlier parts.

This text contains the end-of-chapter problems which allow the student to apply the concepts and analytical techniques in realistic situations. The Instructor's Manual is available to instructors who adopt the text.

We wish to thank those individuals who have provided the constructive advice critical to the successful development of this text. We owe a big debt of gratitude to our friend, Dean Sam Barone (University of Detroit) for his assistance, support, and encouragement. Several students at the University of Detroit deserve special acknowledgment for their contributions: James Bennett, Dorothy Churukian, Judy Dyki, Beverly Kupiec, and Kathy Rakowski. We wish to express our special thanks to Patricia L. Rogers, who typed the final draft of the manuscript with speed, accuracy, and proficiency. Finally, we would like to devote this book to our wives, Lisa Kim and Florence Guithues, who always encourage us to maintain high professional standards and support our academic pursuits.

Suk H. Kim
Detroit, Michigan

Henry J. Guithues,
St. Louis, Missouri

PART ONE: INTRODUCTION

Chapter 1   An Overview of Capital Expenditure
               Analysis

Chapter 2   Cash Flow Analysis and Taxation

Chapter 3   Mathematics of Finance

CHAPTER 1

AN OVERVIEW OF CAPITAL EXPENDITURE ANALYSIS

IMPORTANCE OF CAPITAL INVESTMENT DECISIONS

Capital budgeting decisions involve the allocation and commitment of funds to investment projects whose returns are expected to extend beyond one year. Such investments usually require very large sums of money and are made in expectation of benefits to be realized over an extended period of time. Thus, the rational use of capital resources is critical for the future well-being of the company and the national economy as a whole. Moreover, once capital investment decisions are made, they are not easily reversible. Most used plant and equipment have a limited market. In certain areas production methods are rapidly outmoded by increasingly higher levels of technology.

Figure 1-1 presents U.S. business expenditures on new plant and equipment from 1947 to 1979. This figure shows that (1) U.S. businesses increased their expenditures for new plants and equipment approximately 10 per cent per year for the last three decades and (2) in recent years such expenditures have been greater than $100 billion per year. This rapid growth in capital expenditures has significantly contributed to the improving U.S. standard of living through higher levels of Gross National Products and increased disposable personal income. Efficient management of capital expenditures has become even more essential with the increasing recognition that the ultimate success of company operations depends on sound capital budgeting decisions.

CAPITAL BUDGETING PROCESS

Figure 1-2 examines the capital budgeting process in the form of a highly simplified flow chart.1 A long-term investment decision process may be described as a system which is a set of interrelated parts. There are many steps and elements in the entire process of planning capital expenditures.

Figure 1-1   Business Expenditures on Plant and
              Equipment

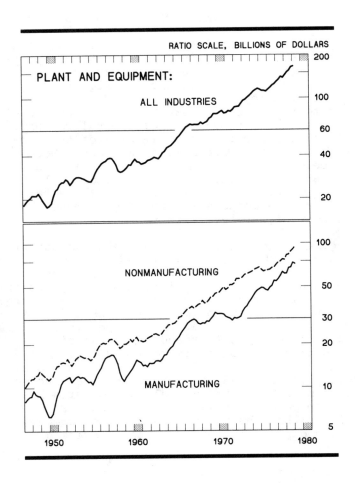

Source: Board of Governors of the Federal Reserve
           System, 1979 Historical Chart Book, p. 16.

Figure 1-2 Capital Budgeting Process

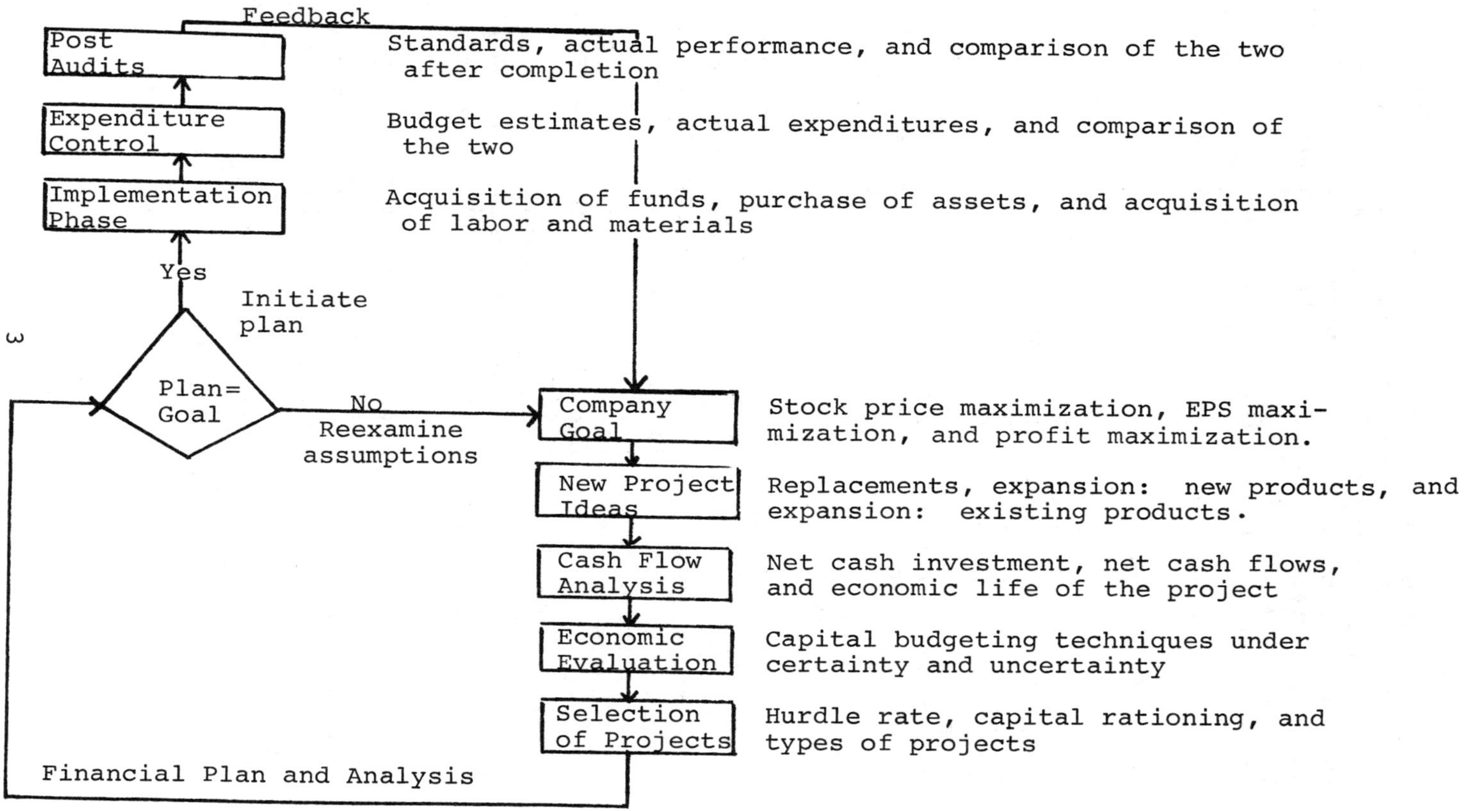

Feedback

Standards, actual performance, and comparison of the two after completion

Budget estimates, actual expenditures, and comparison of the two

Acquisition of funds, purchase of assets, and acquisition of labor and materials

Stock price maximization, EPS maximization, and profit maximization.

Replacements, expansion: new products, and expansion: existing products.

Net cash investment, net cash flows, and economic life of the project

Capital budgeting techniques under certainty and uncertainty

Hurdle rate, capital rationing, and types of projects

Post Audits

Expenditure Control

Implementation Phase

Yes

Initiate plan

Plan= Goal

No
Reexamine assumptions

Company Goal

New Project Ideas

Cash Flow Analysis

Economic Evaluation

Selection of Projects

Financial Plan and Analysis

3

Each element or part is a subsystem of the total
capital budgeting system, and it is closely con-
nected by a variety of other subsystems. Thus,
the entire capital budgeting process may be viewed
as an integral unit of many parts which are directly
or indirectly interrelated. The capital budgeting
process can be divided into eight phases: goal, new
project ideas, cash flow analysis, evaluation, selection, implementation, control, and auditing.

Company Objective

The establishment of long-range objectives is
the first step in the capital budgeting process.
These objectives set the stage for the development,
evaluation, and selection of proposals for plant
expansion, equipment replacements, new product
development, and the like. It is important to
recognize that the primary goal of the firm is
to maximize stockholder wealth. The market value
of the firm's common stock reflects stockholder
wealth because the effects of all financial decisions are thereby included.

The market price of the firm's stock represents the present value of the firm as viewed by
its owners. More specifically, it reflects the
market's evaluation of the firm's prospective
earnings stream over time, the riskiness of this
stream, the dividend policy of the firm, and quality aspects of the firm's future activities. Growth
of sales, stability, and diversification represent
quality aspects of the firm's future activities.
A large, stable, and diversified volume of sales
gives the firm a cushion against business setbacks
such as recessions and changes in consumer preferences.

Because investors want to maximize their own
wealth, they like the firm to adopt policies that
maximize its stock price. Essentially, the market
price of the stock is a performance index of the
firm's progress. Hence, the greater the price of
the stock, the better management's performance from
the standpoint of investors. If stockholders are
not satisfied with management's performance, they
may sell all or part of their holdings for reinvestment in other securities. This action will

place downward pressure on the market price of the firm's stock.

New Project Ideas

A system should be established to stimulate ideas for capital expenditures and to identify good investment opportunities. This is because the availability of good investment opportunities provides the foundation for a successful investment program. Moreover, good investment opportunities do not just appear. A continuous stream of attractive investment opportunities comes from hard thinking, careful planning, and frequently large outlays for research and development.

Aside from the actual generation of ideas, the second step in the capital budgeting process is to classify projects according to certain common characteristics. Such classifications are established (1) to provide categories useful in summarizing the financial totals for a group of projects and (2) to help identify the types of project and necessary decisions.[2] Although project classification practices vary from company to company, capital investment projects are frequently grouped according to the following four categories: replacements, expansion: new products, expansion: existing products, and others such as pollution control equipment.

The replacement of obsolete or worn-out assets is intended to reduce operating expenses or to preserve production efficiency. If the replacement of an existing machine with a new machine enables the firm to produce the same product at a lower cost, the firm must analyze the incremental costs and benefits associated with this change.

A growing firm often finds it necessary to acquire fixed assets that will be used to produce a new product. This type of expenditure is expected to result in incremental sales revenue. To support the expected increase in sales, the firm must increase its costs for labor and material, maintenance, and advertising. Expenditures to increase the output of existing products are often alternatives to replacements. Such expenditures

5

may be suitable solutions to problems of both capacity and cost. Suppose that an existing machine is inadequate to meet the increasing demand for an existing product and that it is also very expensive to operate. If the existing machine is replaced with one that has greater productive capacity, the firm may be able to solve the cost and capacity problems simultaneously.

If a company has identified many investment opportunities of different types, it is necessary to screen and review all of them so that a limited number of projects are chosen for more complex and quantitative analyses. For the manager, such a screening process is a matter of judgment exercised without complete data and particularly without the cash flow estimates.

Cash Flow Analysis

All investment opportunities surviving this screening test require cash flow estimates. The after-tax cash outflows and inflows associated with each project must be estimated to evaluate investment alternatives. There are two important concepts to note in cash flow analysis: (1) cash flows are different from profits or income and (2) cash flows must be estimated on an incremental basis.

Cash flows are not necessarily identical with accounting profits because generally accepted accounting principles treat certain noncash expenditures, such as depreciation charges, as operating expenses rather than as benefits. The concept of cash flows has certain advantages over the concept of profits. First, only cash flows affect the firm's ability to pay bills or buy assets. Second, the cash basis of accounting makes it easier and more objective to measure the benefits of an investment project. It is also important to recognize that only incremental future cash outflows and inflows are relevant in capital expenditure analysis. For example, general office expenses or sunk costs are treated as irrelevant costs because they are not changed by the acceptance of the project.

To determine the attractiveness of an investment project, we must have three elements: the net cash investment, the net cash flows, and the economic life of the project.

The net cash investment refers to the net cash outlay associated with a specific project: the amount of the initial investment required by the project less any cash inflows that occur in the process of placing the asset into service. The initial investment usually consists of the purchase price of the new asset, the transportation costs, the installation costs, and any other costs incurred to put the asset into service. The cash inflows include the proceeds from the trade or sale of existing assets, the tax saving from the sale of the assets, and the investment tax credit.

The net cash flows are net economic benefits caused by an investment project. The benefits expected from the project must be measured on an incremental after-tax basis. The net cash flows are used here to mean the differences between incremental after-tax cash inflows and outflows. Incremental cash inflows include operating savings, increased sales revenues, and salvage value. Incremental cash outflows include labor and material costs, maintenance costs, and other costs directly related to the project. These cash inflows and outflows are normally transformed into an after-tax basis.

The economic life of the project is the time period during which we can expect to obtain the benefits from the project. It is very important to distinguish the economic life of a project from its physical life. For example, a machine with a physical life of ten years may have to be replaced after only two or three years because of the change in the nature of the business or advance in technology.

Economic Evaluation

Once cash flow estimates have been made, the company begins the formal process of evaluating investment projects. The method of analysis must take into account the tradeoff between net cash investment and net cash flows. This evaluation process proceeds in two stages: capital budgeting analysis under certainty and risk analysis. Both

7

analyses are made to rank and select the available investment opportunities.

Many techniques have been developed for project evaluation under conditions of certainty. They range from simple rules of thumb to sophisticated mathematical programming models. The five most commonly used methods for an economic evaluation of individual projects are payback, average rate of return, net present value, profitability index, and internal rate of return. Each of these methods measures the rate of return on a uniform basis for all projects under consideration. A project or a set of projects will be chosen at this stage if the following three assumptions hold: First, the company has a definite cutoff point which all projects must meet; second, all cash outflows and inflows from each project are known with absolute certainty; and third, the company's investment programs are not constrained by any lack of funds. Mathematical programming models--linear programming, integer programming, and goal programming--may be used to evaluate multiple projects simultaneously under conditions of limited funds.

There has to be some kind of method of adjusting project estimates for risk for at least two reasons. First, only a few of the financial variables are normally known in advance with a fair degree of accuracy. Second, investors and businessmen are basically risk averters. If we do not know in advance exactly which of future events will occur, we will have to determine the risk-return tradeoff in order to choose more attractive projects. There are a number of techniques that may be used to evaluate individual projects under conditions of uncertainty: risk-adjusted discount rate, certainty equivalent, probability theory, decision trees, computer simulation, and sensitivity analysis. Portfolio risk analysis--Markowitz approach and capital asset pricing model--may be used to analyze the riskiness of multiple projects.

Selection

The final selection of projects depends on the kinds of capital budgeting decisions. Basically, there are three kinds of capital budgeting decisions:

8

the accept-reject decision, the mutually exclusive choice decision, and the capital rationing decision.

The selected method must successfully pass the accept-reject decision. If projects under consideration are mutually independent and not subject to capital rationing constraints, the company must accept all projects whose expected rate of return exceeds its hurdle rate in order to maximize stockholder wealth. The hurdle rate may be based on the cost of capital, the opportunity cost, and scme other arbitrary standard. However, it is important to recognize some possibility that (1) certain projects may compete with each other and (2) available projects may exceed available funds. Mutual exclusiveness and capital rationing constraints are the two cases where otherwise profitable projects are rejected. Investment proposals are said to be mutually exclusive if the acceptance of one project means the rejection of all the other projects. Capital rationing refers to an upper ceiling on the size of capital expenditures during a given period of time.

Implementation

Authorization to expend funds for the accepted projects may be obtained by submission of individual capital expenditure requests in accordance with formal procedures set forth by the Budget Director. These procedures typically cover the use of standard forms, the channels for submission and review, and the authority requirements and limits for approval. For instance, they may require the approval of the Chairman of the Board for requests of $100,000 or more, of the President for requests of $100,000-$50,000, and of the appropriate Division Manager for requests of less than $50,000. Once funds have been authorized to implement the projects, the firm must acquire the funds, purchase the assets, and begin operating the projects. This phase usually requires relatively little attention from the financial manager if all prior phases in the capital budgeting process have been correctly performed. However, if the necessary funds or assets are not available at the specified cost, the company may be forced to reevaluate all projects.

Expenditure Control

There is a specific phase of the capital budgeting process during which the practical cost control of a project becomes important. This is the time between the approval of the project and the completion of the project. The expenditure control of a project in process is designed to increase the probability that it is completed within the established guidelines. The control also allows management to pinpoint the problem areas of a project so that it can take corrective action. In the case of cost overrun, there are three possible courses of action: (1) to complete the project with added cost, (2) reanalyze its economic worth, or (3) abandon it.

Post-Audits

Because capital expenditure decisions are made on the basis of assumptions, estimates and actual results may differ. Thus, when a project is completed, the firm should perform a post-audit on the entire project to determine its success or failure. Post-audits are an important device to obtain knowledge which aids in present project analysis and to identify further investment opportunities. They are also important to determine some corrective action necessary to bring a project up to its full potential and to assign responsibility for mistakes and mismanagement in project implementation.

The results of post-audits enable the firm to compare the actual performance of a project with established standards. If the capital budgeting process used by a firm has been successful, the system is likely to be reinforced. If the system has been unsatisfactory, it is likely to be revised or replaced.

SCOPE OF THE TEXT

This book consists of four major parts. Part One develops the goal of the firm to be used in the capital budgeting process, covers the tax environment in which these capital budgeting decisions are to be made, and discusses the time value of money which is basic to investment decisions. With the use of the tax environment and the time value of money, Part Two evaluates investment projects under certainty and Part Three analyzes them under uncertainty. Part Four describes somewhat specialized topics of capital budgeting such as leasing and multinational capital budgeting. Although this part deals with special applications of capital budgeting, it draws upon the principles developed in earlier parts.

FOOTNOTES

1. For a good discussion of the capital budgeting process, see Stephen R. Archer, G. Marc Choate, and George Racette, Financial Management (New York: John Wiley and Sons, 1979), Chapter 12; Suk H. Kim, "Making the Long-Term Investment Decision," Management Accounting (March 1979), pp. 41-49; and Reginald L. Jones and H. George Trentin, Budgeting: Key to Planning and Control (New York: American Management Association, 1971), Chapter 8.

2. John H. Kempster, Financial Analysis to Guide Capital Expenditure Decisions, Research Report 43 (New York: National Association of Accountants, 1967), p. 41.

CHAPTER 2

CASH FLOW ANALYSIS AND TAXATION

A project's cash flows are usually computed on an after-tax basis. Thus, financial managers certainly cannot ignore the tax consequences of capital investment decisions and must take into account the tax liabilities generated by each project. Because tax treatments are not alike for all business corporations, tax consideration is essential to draw valid conclusions about the economic worth of each project.

The federal government employs fiscal policy to influence the level of economic activity. Fiscal policy deals with the manipulation of government receipts and expenditures for the expressed purpose of achieving the full employment without inflation. Because taxes constitute the primary receipt of the federal government, they are an important element of fiscal policy. The federal government uses three principal methods to change its tax receipts: (1) changing methods permitted for computing tax-deductible depreciation, (2) changing tax rates, and (3) providing for an investment tax credit for expenditures on new plant and equipment. Each of these factors is discussed in this chapter.

DEPRECIATION

Depreciation charges are usually treated as tax-deductible expenses. The three depreciation methods generally used are straight-line, double declining-balance, and sum-of-years'-digits. The choice of the depreciation method can have a considerable effect on a company's tax liabilities and cash flows. The straight-line depreciation method results in a uniform deduction from revenue each year. The double declining-balance and sum-of-years'-digits methods allow the company to allocate a larger proportion of the asset's cost during its early life and smaller proportion of its cost during its later years. Thus, these two depreciation methods are forms of accelerated depreciation.

13

The accelerated depreciation methods are based on the hypothesis that depreciation charged under these methods results in a more accurate matching of expense with revenue. Assets usually produce large revenues during their early years of use and smaller revenues during their later years of use. Hence, these two methods permit the company to match larger depreciation charges with larger revenues during the early years of use and to match smaller depreciation deductions with smaller revenues during the later years of use. The increasing maintenance expenses are offset by the falling depreciation charges so that the company can achieve a better matching of expense and revenue.

Example 2-1   Assume that a machine is purchased for $15,600. It has an estimated useful life of five years and an estimated salvage value of $600 at the end of five years. Table 2-1 compares the three depreciation methods in terms of the annual depreciation charges over the five-year period.

Table 2-1   Comparison of Depreciation Methods for a Five-Year, $15,600 Machine with an Estimated Salvage Value of $600

Year	Straight Line	Double Declining Balance	Sum-of-Years'-Digits
1st	$ 3,000	$ 6,240	$ 5,000
2nd	3,000	3,744	4,000
3rd	3,000	2,246	3,000
4th	3,000	1,348	2,000
5th	3,000	2,022	1,000
Total	$15,000	$15,600	$15,000

Straight Line

The straight-line depreciation method assumes that depreciation is a function of time. The cost of an asset less its estimated salvage value is allocated in an equal amount each year over its useful life. With this method, a uniform annual depreciation charge of $3,000 is computed as follows:

14

$$\text{Annual Charge} = \frac{\text{Cost} - \text{Salvage Value}}{\text{Asset Life}} = \frac{\$15,600 - \$600}{5 \text{ Years}}$$

$$= \$3,000$$

Double Declining-Balance

Under the declining-balance method of depreciation, the same depreciation rate is applied each year to the undepreciated value of the asset at the end of the previous year. For tax purposes, the annual depreciation rate may not exceed twice the straight-line rate, which is sometimes called the double declining-balance method. There are two important factors to remember in this method. First, salvage value is not deducted from the cost of an asset in determining the annual depreciation charge. Second, the cost of the asset is not fully depreciated at the end of its useful life. Thus, the remaining undepreciated cost at the end of the second-to-last year is included in the last year's depreciation. Because the straight line rate is 20 per cent per year, the double declining-balance rate would be 40 per cent. This rate is applied to the full purchase price of $15,600. The third column of Table 2-1 shows annual depreciation charges computed under this accelerated method.

Sum-of-Years'-Digits

Under the third depreciation method, a firm applies a varying fraction each year to the cost of the asset less its salvage value. The denominator of the fraction is the total of the years' digits representing the asset's useful life, and the numerator is the number of remaining years of the asset's useful life. The sum of the digits as the denominator may be computed as follows:

$$\text{Sum of Digits} = N\left(\frac{N + 1}{2}\right) \qquad (2\text{-}1)$$

where N is the estimated useful life of the asset. For example, if an estimated useful life of the asset is five years, the sum is $15 = 5\left(\frac{5 + 1}{2}\right)$. The numerator of the fraction is changed each year to represent the years of useful life remaining at

15

the beginning of the year in which the depreciation computation is made. For example, if a machine has an estimated useful life of five years, the numerator for the first year would be 5, the numerator for the second year would be 4, and so on. The last column of Table 2-1 shows annual depreciation charges computed under this method.

CORPORATE INCOME TAX

The tax law of 1978 provides a five-step progressive structure:

Taxable Income	Tax Rate
$0 to $25,000	17%
$25,001 to $50,000	20%
$50,001 to $75,000	30%
$75,001 to $100,000	40%
Over $100,000	46%

Example 2-2 Assume that a corporation has gross income of $700,000, operating expenses of $150,000, and a depreciation charge of $50,000.

The company's income tax, earnings after taxes, and net cash flow are computed as follows:

	Earnings	Cash Flow
Gross Income	$700,000	$700,000
Expenses	150,000	150,000
Depreciation	50,000	
Taxable Income	$500,000	
Taxes		
0.17($ 25,000) = $ 4,250		
0.20($ 25,000) = 5,000		
0.30($ 25,000) = 7,500		
0.40($ 25,000) = 10,000		
0.46($400,000) = 184,000	210,750	210,750
Earnings After Taxes	$289,250	
Net Cash Flow		$339,250

The company's average tax rate is its total tax ($210,750) divided by its taxable income ($500,000) or 42.15 per cent. The marginal tax rate is the

16

rate at which any additional income is taxed. Because the company's taxable income exceeds $100,000, its marginal tax rate is 46 per cent.

The company's earnings after taxes are $289,250 and its net cash flow is $339,250. The benefits of an investment project are expressed in terms of cash flows rather than in terms of income because cash is what is central to all decisions of the company. Only cash receipts can be reinvested in the firm or used to pay dividends. The importance of cash flows becomes even more apparent when we recognize the fact that insolvency means the firm's inability to meet its maturing debt obligations. Moreover, under the cash basis of accounting, revenues are recognized when payments are received; expenses are recognized when payments are made. Hence, the use of cash flows to measure the benefits of the project does not require a sophisticated theoretical accounting system.

Carry-Backs and Carry-Forwards of Operating Losses

An operating loss is the excess of deductible expenses over gross income. If a corporation incurs an operating loss for any year, the corporation may carry the loss back three years and carry it forward seven years or it may carry the loss forward ten years. The choice of a process depends largely on whether the company has had profits in those three years immediately prior to the loss. If this is the case, the company must carry the loss back in order to expedite the refund of tax payments.

The purpose of this provision is to allow corporations to average their operating results, which fluctuate widely from year to year. However, some profitable firms use the carry-back and carry-forward feature as a means of reducing their taxable income by merging with other firms that have considerable losses.

Capital Gains and Losses Taxes

Profits from the sale of capital assets and all other income defined as ordinary income constitute corporate taxable income. Capital assets (for example, security investments) are defined as

17

those assets that are not held primarily for resale and that are not acquired in the ordinary course of business. Gains and losses from transactions involving capital assets are capital gains and losses.

If a corporation holds a capital asset less than 12 months, the gain or loss from its sale or exchange is classified as a short-term capital gain or loss. If a corporation holds a capital asset longer than 12 months, the gain or loss from its sale or exchange is a long-term gain or loss. The short-term capital gains or losses are combined to determine the net short-term capital gain or loss. By the same token, long-term capital gains and losses are combined to determine the net long-term capital gain or loss. The total net capital gain or loss is obtained by merging the net short-term capital gain or loss with the net long-term capital gain or loss.

Short-term capital gains are added to the firm's ordinary income and taxed at regular corporate income tax rates. However, long-term capital gains are taxed at a maximum of 28 per cent.

Example 2-3 Assume that a corporation has taxable income of $500,000, including the following:

Long-Term Capital Gain		$180,000
Long-Term Capital Loss		(30,000)
Net Long-Term Capital Gain		$150,000
Short-Term Capital Gain	$120,000	
Short-Term Capital Loss	(170,000)	
Net Short-Term Capital Loss		(50,000)
Total Net Long-Term Capital Gain		$100,000

The firm's income tax of $192,750 is obtained as follows:

Long-Term Capital Gain	$100,000
Ordinary Income	400,000
Taxable Income	$500,000

18

Tax Rate

28% of		$100,000 (Capital Gain)	$ 28,000
17% of	1st	$ 25,000	4,250
20% of	2nd	$ 25,000	5,000
30% of	3rd	$ 25,000	7,500
40% of	4th	$ 25,000	10,000
46% of		$300,000	138,000
			$192,750

If the entire taxable income of $500,000 were ordinary income, the firm's tax liability would be $210,750. Hence, preferential tax treatment of long-term capital gains enables the firm to save $18,000 ($210,750 - $192,750). Of course, if the firm's taxable income is less than $50,000, regular tax rates (17 per cent of 1st $25,000 and 20 per cent of 2nd $25,000) will apply.

Net capital losses cannot be deducted from ordinary income; they may be deducted only from capital gains. The tax law states that the net capital loss may be carried back three years and carried forward five years. If the net capital loss is not entirely used to offset capital gains for the three preceding years, the excess may be carried to the five successive years. Any loss remaining after the fifth year following the loss is no longer available to the company as a deduction.

Sale of Depreciable Assets

The gain or loss from the sale of a depreciable asset or its exchange is usually added to or subtracted from ordinary income.

Example 2-4 A corporation purchased a machine for $40,000 five years ago. The machine had an estimated useful life of ten years and no expected salvage value at the time of purchase. The company has depreciated the machine on a straight-line basis and sells it for $10,000.

The accumulated depreciation of the machine is $20,000 because the annual depreciation of the machine under the straight-line method was $4,000 ($40,000 ÷ 10). Thus, the company incurs a $10,000

19

loss on the sale of the machine, which is the excess of its book value over its selling price. The $10,000 loss is subtracted from the firm's ordinary income in order to determine its taxable income after adjusting for the loss.

Should a corporation happen to dispose of a depreciable asset for more than book value, the problem would be a little more complicated. Typically, the excess of selling price over book value is treated as ordinary income. However, the excess of the gain over the accumulated depreciation is treated as a capital gain, which is taxed at a maximum of 28 per cent. To continue with the preceding example, suppose that the firm sells its machine for $44,600, rather than $10,000 with a total gain of $24,600 ($44,600 - $20,000). Of this amount, $20,000 represents the accumulated depreciation and is treated as ordinary income due to the recapture clause of depreciation. The remaining $4,600 is classified as a capital gain. However, capital gains from the sale of depreciable assets seldom occur, because the selling price is unlikely to exceed the original cost of the asset.

INVESTMENT TAX CREDIT

In an effort to stimulate corporate investment and to help stabilize the economy as a whole, the Revenue Act of 1962 introduced the concept of an investment tax credit. The law provided for a credit against the income tax equal to a specified percentage of the cost of new equipment in certain categories. Since then, the investment tax credit has been alternately repealed and reinstated. The major purpose of the investment credit is to encourage businesses to invest in plant and equipment, thus assuring the full employment of resources.

History of the Investment Tax Credit

The Kennedy administration incorporated the concept of an investment tax credit into the tax law of 1962. Because the full impact of the credit is reflected in the year of depreciation, it has a significant effect on both the national economy and investment plans by individual firms.

In general, the investment tax credit has been suspended to combat inflation and reinstated to stimulate the economy. During the economic boom in 1966 the investment tax credit was cancelled, but it was reinstated in March of 1967. The Tax Reform Act of 1969 suspended it again to attack inflation, but the Revenue Act of 1971 reinstated it with minor modifications to combat recession. The tax law of 1971 allowed corporations to reduce their tax bills up to 7 per cent of the cost of net assets whose declared lives exceed seven years. The Tax Reform Act of 1976 temporarily increased the investment credit from 7 per cent to 10 per cent. The Revenue Act of 1978 permanently sets the investment credit rate at 10 per cent.

Present Law

A number of conditions must be met for an asset to qualify for the investment tax credit. The asset must (1) be depreciable, (2) have a declared life of at least three years, (3) be tangible property, and (4) be placed in service for the production of income.

The amount of the allowable investment credit during any taxable year is the sum of (1) the current year's investment credit, (2) any investment credit carry-backs, and (3) any investment credit carry-forwards. The allowable investment credit is a maximum of 10 per cent of the investment in assets whose declared lives exceed seven years. The amount of the current year's investment that is subject to the credit is computed as follows:

Asset's Useful Life	Part to be Counted
0 to 2 years	0
3 to 4 years	1/3
5 to 6 years	2/3
7 and more	all

Example 2-5 A corporation purchased a machine with an economic life of two years for $10,000, a machine with an economic life of four years for $21,000, a machine with an economic life of five years for $30,000, and a machine with an economic life of ten years for $523,000.

21

The amount of the investment that is subject to the credit is computed in Table 2-2. The investment tax credit is 10 per cent of the amount of the investment subject to the credit or $55,000.

Table 2-2 Amount of Investment Eligible for
Investment Credit

Machine	Cost	Declared Life	Portion to be Counted	Amount Subject to the Credit
1	$ 10,000	2 yrs.	0	$ 0
2	21,000	4	1/3	7,000
3	30,000	5	2/3	20,000
4	523,000	10	all	523,000
	Total Investment Subject to Credit			$550,000

However, the tax law limits the amount of credit that a corporation may use to offset its tax liability in any one year. Under the Revenue Act of 1978, corporations will be allowed to claim an investment credit equal to the first $25,000 of their tax bill plus 90 per cent of their tax in excess of $25,000 for 1982 and later years. The increase to the 90 per cent level will be achieved by a 10 per cent increase per year as follows: $25,000 plus 60 per cent of any excess tax over $25,000 for years ending in 1979, $25,000 plus 70 per cent for years ending in 1980, $25,000 plus 80 per cent for years ending in 1981, and $25,000 plus 90 per cent for years ending after 1981. The remaining investment credit may be carried back to the three preceding years, and the balance unused in these three years may be carried forward to the seven succeeding years.

Recapture Clause

If a corporation sells an asset before its declared life expires, it must recompute the investment credit. The difference between the original credit and the recomputed credit must be added to the company's tax bill in the year in which the sale is made. In this case, the asset's actual life is substituted for its estimated useful life. For example, if an asset with an estimated useful life of ten years was purchased in 1977 and sold

22

in 1981, its actual life was four years.

Example 2-6 In 1977 a corporation purchased two
new machines, which cost $10,000 and $30,000.
Each machine had an estimated economic life of ten
years. The corporation claimed the full credit of
$4,000 against its tax bill in 1977, but it sold
the machine of $30,000 in 1981.

Because the company held the machine for four
years, its recomputed investment subject to the
credit is $20,000 (100% of $10,000 + 1/3 of $30,000).
Thus, its recomputed credit is $2,000 ($20,000 X
10%). The excess of the original credit claimed
in 1977 over the recomputed credit is $2,000
($4,000 - $2,000), which must be added to the
firm's 1981 tax liability.

Building-Rehabilitation Expenditures

The 1978 Revenue Act allows corporations to
claim an investment credit for rehabilitating their
buildings that are at least 20 years old. To
qualify for the investment credit, the building
must have a useful life of five years or more and
it must not have been an object of a rehabilita-
tion within the prior 20 years. The cost of acquiring or enlarging a building does not qualify for
the credit.

Energy Tax Credit

The Energy Tax Act of 1978 permits corporations
to claim an additional 10 per cent credit (20 per
cent in total) for a new classification of property
called energy property. Energy property includes
certain property designed to use fuel other than
oil and natural gas or to reduce energy waste in
existing facilities. The law is intended to create
incentives for energy conservation and to promote
commercial conservations from oil and gas to alternatives, such as solar energy. The investment
credit for energy property may be used to offset
100 per cent of tax liability.

EXAMPLES OF CASH FLOW ANALYSIS

Capital expenditure decisions require knowledge

23

of the cash outflows needed to acquire assets and the cash inflows expected from their use. Thus, it is important to indicate how these cash flows may be determined on the basis of sales and cost estimates combined with the relevant tax implications of the transactions under consideration.

Example 2-6 (Replacements) A corporation is planning to replace an old machine with a new and more efficient one. The firm purchased the old machine five years ago at a cost of $20,000, and it has been depreciated on a straight-line basis. The machine had an expected useful life of ten years at the time of purchase and no estimated salvage value at the end of ten years. The firm has found a person willing to buy the old machine for $5,000 and remove it at his own expense. The firm can buy the new machine for $12,000. The new machine has an estimated useful life of five years and no salvage value at the end of five years. An additional $3,000 will be required to transport and install it. The new machine is not expected to change the firm's revenue but is expected to reduce its operating costs from $10,000 to $5,000 per year. It is to be depreciated on a straight-line basis, and the firm's marginal tax rate is 46 per cent.

The net cash investment consists of the purchase price of the new machine, freight and installation costs, tax effects, and the proceeds from the sale of the old machine. If the firm purchases the new machine and sells the old one, it incurs an operating loss of $5,000 (the book value of $10,000 minus the market value of $5,000). The tax saving on the loss is $2,300 ($5,000 X 0.46). Because the new machine has an estimated useful life of five years, the firm can claim an investment tax credit of $1,000 ($15,000 X 0.10 X 2/3). Thus, the net cash investment for the project is

Purchase Price of New Machine		$12,000
Freight and Installation Costs		3,000
Total		$15,000
Less: Tax Saving	$2,300	
Proceeds from Sale of Old Machine	5,000	

Investment Tax Credit	$1,000	8,300
Net Cash Investment		$6,700

The net cash flows are the differences between the cash flows of the firm with and without the new machine. These differences must be estimated on an incremental after-tax basis, and they are the net benefits for the project. The annual depreciation charge is $2,000 on the old machine ($20,000 X 0.10) and $3,000 on the new machine ($15,000 X 0.20). Hence, the incremental depreciation charges associated with the project are $1,000 a year. Because the new machine is expected to reduce the firm's operating expenses from $10,000 to $5,000 per year, it will result in an annual cash saving of $5,000 per year. The expected net cash flow from the acceptance of the project is

Annual Cash Saving	$5,000
Less: Incremental Depreciation Charge	1,000
Incremental Income Before Taxes	$4,000
Less: Taxes at 46%	1,840
Incremental Income After Taxes	$2,160
Add: Incremental Depreciation Charge	1,000
Annual Net Cash Flow	$3,160

Thus, for a net cash investment of $6,700, the firm is expected to produce a net cash flow of $3,160 per year for the next five years.

Example 2-7 (Expansion: New Products) A corporation is considering the introduction of a new product. To produce it, the firm will need to buy a new piece of equipment for $10,000. The equipment has no salvage value on retirement and an expected useful life of four years. The marketing department expects incremental sales revenue to be $11,000 per year, and the production department expects incremental cash outflows to be $6,000 per year. It has been decided to use the double declining-balance method of depreciation. The firm's marginal tax rate is 40 per cent. Determine the profit and net cash flow of the equipment.

The taxable income and income tax of each year are first computed, and then net cash flows for each year are determined. The expected net cash flows from the project are computed as follows:

25

	Year 1	Year 2	Year 3	Year 4
Revenues	$11,000	$11,000	$11,000	$11,000
Less: Operating Exp.	6,000	6,000	6,000	6,000
Depreciation	5,000	2,500	1,250	1,250
Taxable Income	$ 0	$ 2,500	$ 3,750	$ 3,750
Less: Taxes at 40%	0	1,000	1,500	1,500
Earnings After Taxes	$ 0	$ 1,500	$ 2,250	$ 2,250
Add: Depreciation	5,000	2,500	1,250	1,250
Annual Net Cash Flow	$ 5,000	$ 4,000	$ 3,500	$ 3,500

If we ignore the investment tax credit, the firm expects a net cash investment of $10,000 to result in net cash flows of $5,000, $4,000, $3,500, and $3,500 for the next four years.

Example 2-8 (Expansion: Existing Products) A corporation is considering the purchase of a press to replace an old one. The old press with a useful life of eight years was purchased four years ago at a cost of $8,000. It has been depreciated on a straight-line basis. The market value of the old press is negligible due to advance in technology. The new press requires a net cash investment of $10,000 and an expected useful life of four years. It is to be depreciated on the basis of the sum-of-years'-digits method. The new press is expected to expand sales from $15,000 to $17,500 per year. It is also expected to cut labor and maintenance costs from $7,500 to $6,000 per year. The firm's marginal tax rate is 40 per cent. Determine the profit and net cash flows of the project.

The new press will produce an annual sales increase of $2,500 ($17,500 minus $15,000) and an annual cash saving of $1,500 ($7,500 minus $6,000). Given a depreciable value of $10,000 and a useful life of four years, the annual depreciation charges of the new press for the sum-of-years'-digits method are $4,000, $3,000, $2,000, and $1,000 over the next four years. Because the old press is depreciated on a straight-line of $1,000 per year, the additional depreciation charges will be $3,000, $2,000, $1,000, and $0 for the next four years. The net cash flows of the project are

	Year 1	Year 2	Year 3	Year 4
Additional Sales	$2,500	$2,500	$2,500	$2,500
Add: Cash Savings	1,500	1,500	1,500	1,500
Incremental Revenues	$4,000	$4,000	$4,000	$4,000
Less: Additional Dep.	3,000	2,000	1,000	0
Taxable Income	$1,000	$2,000	$3,000	$4,000
Less: Tax at 40%	400	800	1,200	1,600
Earnings After Taxes	$ 600	$1,200	$1,800	$2,400
Add: Additional Dep.	3,000	2,000	1,000	0
Net Cash Flows	$3,600	$3,200	$2,800	$2,400

Interest, Salvage Value, and Taxes

Unlike depreciation charges, interest expenses
involve actual cash outflows. However, interest
expenses are normally excluded from the cash flows
of the project in order to avoid a double-counting
of the cost of funds. The basic purpose of the discounting process to be discussed in the following
chapter is to insure that the net cash flows of accepted projects are sufficient to cover the cost of
funds. Hence, the double counting of interest may
lead to an incorrect decision to reject otherwise
profitable projects.

Up to this point, we have assumed that there
is no salvage value at the end of the project.
If the project is expected to have a salvage value,
it may influence depreciation charges and the net
cash flow in the last year of the project life.
If a new machine has a cost of $10,000 and an ex-
pected salvage value of $2,000 at the end of its
life, the total depreciable value becomes $8,000;
the expected salvage value of $2,000 is added to
the after-tax cash flow for the final year of the
machine's life. It is important to remember that
the salvage value is not taxable, because it is a
return of capital. However, if the machine is sold
for more than the expected salvage value of $2,000,
taxable income arises; if it is sold at a price of
less than the expected salvage value of $2,000, a
deductible operating loss arises.

CHAPTER 3

MATHEMATICS OF FINANCE

Practically every investment project calls for expenditures at different dates, and its yields are obtained at various times. Hence, to compare different projects with different income patterns, one must convert amounts receivable at different times into a common time basis. The concept of compound value or present value refers to the conversion of cash flows over a period of time to a common point in time. The concepts of compound value and present value are used in this conversion process. They are essential to an understanding of such topics as capital budgeting, the cost of capital, lease versus purchase, bond refunding, and mergers. This chapter discusses both compound value and present value.

COMPOUND INTEREST

Interest is said to compound when the interest for each period is added to the principal and the interest for the next period is computed on the total. The time of computation could be the end of a quarter, a year, etc. To treat the matter systematically, let us define the following notations:

S_n = value at the end of n periods (compound value).

P = principal or initial sum of money.

i = interest rate.

n = number of periods.

If a company invests P on a project that earns i per cent per period, the company would have at the end of one period:

$$S_1 = P + Pi = P(1 + i) \qquad (3\text{-}1)$$

If the initial investment and the accumulated interest continue to earn at the i per cent per period, the company would have at the end of two periods:

29

$$S_2 = P(1 + i) + (P(1 + i))i = P(1 + i)^2 \quad (3\text{-}2)$$

Under the same assumptions, the company would have at the end of n periods:

$$S_n = P(1 + i)^n \quad\quad\quad (3\text{-}3)$$

Example 3-1 A person deposits $100 in a savings account that pays 8 per cent interest compounded annually. How much money would the person have at the end of three years?

At the end of three years, the person would have

$$S_3 = \$100(1 + 0.08)^3 = \$125.97$$

When the value of n is relatively small, it is fairly simple to compute the compound value using Equation (3-3). But when the value of n becomes large, it takes a considerable amount of time to determine the compound value by Equation (3-3). To simplify the computation procedure, it is essential to tabulate the value of the compound interest factor $(1 + i)^n$. Table A at the end of this book shows the values of $(1 + i)^n$ covering a wide range of n and i. The interest factor in Example 3-1 is 1.260, which is found in the intersection of the three-year row and the 8 per cent column in Table A. This interest factor would be used rather than raising $(1 + i)$ to the third power.

In Example 3-1 we assumed that interest was compounded on an annual basis. But such contractual arrangements as an installment contract, an interest-payment schedule on savings deposits, or a bond contract may call for semiannual, quarterly, monthly, or even daily compounding periods. If interest is compounded more often than once a year, the compound value of a current lump sum will be greater, because interest will be earned on interest more frequently. The compound value in such instances may be computed as follows:

$$S_n = P(1 + \frac{i}{m})^{mn} \quad\quad\quad (3\text{-}4)$$

where m is the number of times per year compounding occurs.

30

Example 3-2   Using Example 3-1, let us assume that the person deposits $100 in a savings account that pays 8 per cent interest compounded quarterly. How much money would the person receive at the end of three years?

The compound value of $126.8 at the end of three years is computed as follows:

$$S_n = \$100(1 + \frac{0.08}{4})^{4 \times 3}$$

$$= \$100(1 + 0.02)^{12}$$

$$= \$100(1.268)$$

$$= \$126.8$$

If interest were compounded continuously, Equation (3-4) may be changed as follows:

$$S_n = P\left[\lim_{m \to \infty} (1 + \frac{i}{m})^{mn}\right] \qquad (3-5)$$

$$= P\left[\lim_{m \to \infty} \left[(1 + \frac{i}{m})^{m/i}\right]^{in}\right]$$

As m approaches infinity (∞), the term $(1 + \frac{i}{m})^{m/i}$ approaches e, where e is approximately 2.718. The term e is the base of the natural or Naperian logarithm system. Thus, the compound value at the end of n years of an initial deposit P where interest is compounded continuously is

$$S_n = Pe^{in} = Pe^x \qquad (3-6)$$

where x is equal to in. Table 3-1 contains values of e^x.

Table 3-1   Values of e^x

x	e^x	x	e^x	x	e^x
0.01	1.0101	0.08	1.0833	0.35	1.4191
0.02	1.0202	0.09	1.0942	0.40	1.4918
0.03	1.0305	0.10	1.1052	0.45	1.5683

31

x	e^x	x	e^x	x	e^x
0.04	1.0408	0.15	1.1618	0.50	1.6487
0.05	1.0513	0.20	1.2214	0.55	1.7333
0.06	1.0618	0.25	1.2840	0.60	1.8221
0.07	1.0725	0.30	1.3499	0.65	1.9155

Example 3-3   A person deposits $1,000 in a savings account that pays 10 per cent interest compounded continuously. How much money would the person have at the end of three years?

Using Equation (3-6) and Table 3-1, we have

$$S_n = \$1,000e^{(0.10)3}$$

$$= \$1,000e^{0.30}$$

$$= \$1,000(1.3499)$$

$$= \$1,349.9$$

PRESENT VALUE

When investment projects have different cash flows and different lives, the analysis is quite complicated. The concept of present value can be used to simplify this problem. Essentially this concept evaluates the future expenditures and earnings streams in terms of their worth today. When this is done for all projects, one has a common basis from which to make the selection decision. One can describe the concept of present value both in terms of lump sum amounts or annuities.

Present Value of a Lump Sum

The present value of a lump sum represents the current value of a future payment (compound value). Because discounting (finding present values) is simply the reverse of compounding, one can readily transform Equation (3-3) into a present value formula as follows:

$$P = \frac{S_n}{(1 + i)^n} = S_n \left[\frac{1}{(1 + i)^n} \right] \qquad (3-7)$$

32

$$= S_n \times DF_{n,i}$$

where P is the present value of a future lump sum and $DF_{n,i}$ is the present value discount factor or simply the discount factor. Table B at the end of this book shows the values of $DF_{n,i}$ covering a wide range of n and i.

Example 3-4 A firm needs $1,000 at the end of three years. How much money must the firm invest today at 10 per cent interest to have $1,000 three years hence?

To find a discount factor of $DF_{3,10\%}$, look down the 10 per cent column in Table B to the three-year row. We find it to be 0.751. Thus, the present value of $1,000 due in three years, discounted at 10 per cent, is

$$P = \$1,000 \times DF_{3,10\%} = \$1,000 \times 0.751 = \$751$$

When interest is compounded more than once a year, Equation (3-4) can be transformed into Equation (3-8) to determine present values in such cases

$$P = \frac{S_n}{(1 + \frac{i}{m})^{mn}} = S_n \left[\frac{1}{(1 + \frac{i}{m})^{mn}} \right] \qquad (3-8)$$

If the discount rate is 10 per cent compounded semi-annually, the present value of $1,000 to be received at the end of three years is

$$P = \$1,000 \left[\frac{1}{(1 + \frac{0.10}{2})^{2 \times 3}} \right]$$

$$= \$1,000 \left[\frac{1}{(1 + 0.05)^6} \right]$$

$$= \$1,000 \times DF_{6,5\%}$$

$$= \$1,000 \times 0.746$$

$$= \$746$$

To determine discounted present value in terms of continuous compounding, one can transform Equation (3-6) as follows:

$$P = \frac{S_n}{e^{in}} = \frac{S_n}{e^x} \qquad (3-9)$$

The present value of $1,000 to be received at the end of three years with a discount rate of 10 per cent compounded continuously is

$$P = \frac{\$1,000}{e^{(0.10)3}} = \frac{\$1,000}{e^{0.30}} = \frac{\$1,000}{1.3499} = \$741$$

Therefore, the more times a year the discount rate is compounded, the smaller the present value. This relationship is just the opposite of that for compound values. That is, the more times a year the interest rate is compounded, the greater the compound value.

Present Value of an Annuity

An ordinary annuity is a series of equal cash flows that occur at the end of each period over a specified number of periods. The term annuity usually refers to a series of fixed annual receipts or payments, but it may also apply to a receipt or payment schedule with various intervals. An annuity may be made annually, quarterly, or even daily.

The present value of an annuity is the value at the beginning of the term of the annuity. It is the single sum that one must deposit today to provide for a predetermined series of withdrawals at equal time intervals.

The present value of a series of payments is computed as follows:

$$PA = \frac{A_1}{(1 + i)} + \frac{A_2}{(1 + i)^2} + \ldots + \frac{A_n}{(1 + i)^n} \qquad (3-10)$$

where PA is the present value of an annuity and A is the periodic payment or receipt. If the periodic payments are equal and the discount rate stays the same, Equation (3-10) can be reduced

34

as follows:

$$PA = \sum_{t=1}^{n} \frac{A}{(1 + i)^t} = \sum_{t=1}^{n} A \left[\frac{1}{(1 + i)^t} \right] \qquad (3\text{-}11)$$

$$= A \times ADF_{n,i}$$

where $ADF_{n,i}$ is the present value of an annuity discount factor or simply the annuity discount factor. Table C at the end of this book shows the values of $ADF_{n,i}$ covering a wide range of n and i.

Example 3-5 An investment project is expected to produce cash inflows of $800 at the end of each year for the next three years. What is the present value of this cash flows stream at a discount rate of 5 per cent?

The annuity discount factor of three years and 5 per cent is 2.723. Using Equation (3-11), the present value of the $800 three-year annuity is determined as follows:

$$PA = \$800 \times ADF_{3,5\%} = \$800 \times 2.723 = \$2,178$$

In Example 3-5, we assumed that the only unknown variable was the present value of an annuity and that all the other variables were known. However, there are cases in which the size of each periodic payment, the interest rate, or the number of periods must be determined when the present value of an annuity is known. If the present value of an annuity is given, one can algebraically manipulate the value of a variable other than the present value.

If the value of an annuity is not known, the present value of the annuity, the interest rate, and the number of periods are usually given.

Example 3-6 To help your daughter get through the next four years of college, this morning you deposited $13,548 in a bank account that pays 7 per cent interest on the deposit balance. You plan to have no money left in your bank account by the end of four years. How much can you withdraw at the end of each year for the next four years?

35

Because the discount factor ADF$_{4,7\%}$ is found to be 3.387 from Table C, the size of annual withdrawal is

$$PA = A \times ADF_{n,i} \quad \text{or} \quad A = \frac{PA}{ADF_{n,i}} \qquad (3\text{-}12)$$

$$A = \frac{\$13,548}{ADF_{4,7\%}} = \frac{\$13,548}{3.387} = \$4,000$$

If the interest rate of an annuity is unknown, the size of each periodic payment, the present value of the annuity, and the number of periods are usually given.

Example 3-7   Charles borrowed $10,000 today from his sister Susan and agreed to repay in ten equal semi-annual payments of $1,295. The repayment starts six months from today. Charles wants to determine the implicit annual rate of interest.

The implicit annual rate of interest is

$$PA = A \times ADF_{n,i} \quad \text{or} \quad ADF_{n,i} = \frac{PA}{A} \qquad (3\text{-}13)$$

$$ADF_{10,i} = \frac{\$10,000}{\$1,295} = 7.722$$

Look across the ten-year row of Table C until one finds the discount factor 7.722. It is under the 5 per cent column. Because 5 per cent is the six-month interest rate, the implicit annual interest rate of the loan is 10 per cent.

To determine the term of an annuity, the size of each periodic payment, the present value of the annuity, and the interest rate must be known.

Example 3-8   The price of a small building is $60,000. The buyer made a down payment of $10,000 and agreed to pay $6,279 at the end of each year. The annual installment of $6,279 includes principal and 11 per cent compound interest. How long does it take the buyer to pay the principal and the interest?

The amount borrowed, or the present value of a $6,279 annuity at 11 per cent, is $50,000 (price

36

of $60,000 minus down payment of $10,000). The discount factor $ADF_{n,11\%}$ is

$$ADF_{n,11\%} = \frac{\$50,000}{\$6,279} = 7.963$$

In the 11 per cent column of Table C, the discount factor 7.963 is found to be in the 20-year row; the term of the annuity is 20 years.

APPLICATIONS OF PRESENT VALUE

The concept of present value discussed thus far can be used to solve a number of frequently encountered financial problems. Some of these problems are the determination of (1) the present value of an unequal cash-flow stream, (2) bond values, and (3) an amortization schedule.

Present Value of an Unequal Cash-Flow Stream

Many financial decisions are concerned with unequal cash flows. Common stock investments and most capital investment projects involve uneven cash flows.

Example 3-9 A project is expected to produce $500 at the end of one year, $700 at the end of two years, and $1,000 at the end of three years. Compute the present value of these cash flows at a 10 per cent discount rate.

To obtain the aggregate present value of $1,783.7, multiply each periodic receipt by the appropriate discount factor $DF_{n,10\%}$ and then sum these products. Individual discount factors are obtained from Table B. This computation is given as follows:

Year	Cash Flows	X	$DF_{n,10\%}$	= Present Value
1	$ 500		0.909	$ 454.5
2	700		0.826	578.2
3	1,000		0.751	751.0
	Aggregate Present Value =			$1,783.7

Bond Values

When an investment company buys a bond, it acquires two items, a series of periodic interest payments and the maturity value. Because an investment on bonds involves a long-term commitment of funds, the amount of the discount is significant. Thus, the current value or the purchase price of a bond should be the discounted value of all future payments: that is, (1) the present value of the periodic interest payments and (2) the present value of the maturity value. To find this value, one must solve Equation (3-14), which combines Equation (3-11) and Equation (3-7).

$$\text{Bond Value} = A \times ADF_{n,i} + S_n \times DF_{n,i} \qquad (3\text{-}14)$$

$$\qquad\qquad\quad (\text{Eq. } 3\text{-}11) \qquad\quad (\text{Eq. } 3\text{-}7)$$

Remember: (1) Equation (3-11) is used to determine the present value of an annuity or periodic interest payments and (2) Equation (3-7) is used to determine the present value of a future lump sum or the maturity value.

Example 3-10   A particular bond pays interest in the amount of $300 every six months. The bond with a maturity value of $10,000 will mature in ten years. The appropriate discount rate (or yield rate) is 4 per cent. What is the current market value of the bond?

The buyer will receive an annuity of $300 each six months and a sum of $10,000 at the end of ten years. The number of discount periods is 20 (10 X 2) and the semiannual yield rate is 2 per cent (0.04 ÷ 2). Thus, its value of $11,635 is obtained as follows:

$$\text{Bond Value} = \$300 \times ADF_{20,2\%} + \$10,000 \times DF_{20,2\%}$$

$$\qquad\qquad\qquad (\text{Table C}) \qquad\qquad\qquad (\text{Table B})$$

$$= \$300 \times 16.351 + \$10,000 \times 0.673$$

$$= \$4,905 + \$6,730$$

$$= \$11,635$$

Loan Repayments

A long-term debtor may promise to repay a debt by establishing an amortization schedule. The amortization method refers to the retirement of a debt by making a set of equal periodic payments. These periodic payments include both interest and principal.

Example 3-11 Assume that a firm borrowed $2,400 at 16 per cent interest on the unpaid balance for two years and agreed to amortize it by making equal payments at the end of every six months. Determine the size of the semiannual loan payment and prepare the amortization schedule.

To find the size of the semiannual loan payment, we can use the formula for the present value of an annuity:

$PA = \$2,400$; $i = 16\% \div 2 = 8\%$ (per six months);

$n = 2 \times 2 = 4$ (semiannual periods); $ADF_{4,8\%} = 3.312$

(from Table C).

$PA = A \times ADF_{n,i}$, or $A = \dfrac{PA}{ADF_{n,i}}$

$A = \dfrac{\$2,400}{3.312} = \$724.6$

A semiannual payment of $724.6 for two years will pay off a loan of $2,400 and give the lending institution a return of 8 per cent every six months or 16 per cent per year. To see this, we can construct the amortization schedule, as shown in Table 3-2.

Table 3-2   Amortization Schedule

(1) Period	(2) Beginning Balance (2)* − (5)*	(3) Interest (2) X 8%	(4) Semiannual Payment	(5) Principal Repayment (4) − (3)
1	$2,400.0	$192.0	$724.6	$532.6
2	1,867.4	149.4	724.6	575.2
3	1,292.2	103.4	724.6	621.2
4	671.0	53.6	724.6	671.0

*of the previous period. For example, $1,292.2= $1,867.4 - $575.2.

39

PERPETUITIES

A perpetuity is an annuity whose term begins on a definite date but never matures. Hence, a perpetuity is a special form of an annuity. Perpetuities often stem from the establishment of an endowment. Bonds lacking any maturity also are an example of perpetuities. If a project with a net investment of PA at time 0 is expected to earn A at the end of each year forever, its yield is the discount rate r, which equates the present value of all future net cash flows with the present value of the net investment

$$PA = \frac{A}{(1 + r)^1} + \frac{A}{(1 + r)^2} + \cdots + \frac{A}{(1 + r)^n} \qquad (3\text{-}15)$$

When we multiply both sides of Equation (3-15) by $(1 + r)$, we obtain

$$PA(1 + r) = A + \frac{A}{(1 + r)^1} + \frac{A}{(1 + r)^2} + \cdots + \frac{A}{(1 + r)^{n-1}}$$

$$(3\text{-}16)$$

Subtracting Equation (3-15) from Equation (3-16):

$$PA(1 + r) - PA = A - \frac{A}{(1 + r)^n} \qquad (3\text{-}17)$$

As n approaches infinity, $A/(1 + r)^n$ approaches 0. Therefore, we obtain

$$PAr = A \qquad (3\text{-}18)$$

and

$$PA = \frac{A}{r} \qquad (3\text{-}19)$$

Example 3-11 A bond promises to pay interest of $250 per year indefinitely. If the yield (the internal rate of return) of the bond is 10 per cent, its value would be

$$PA = \frac{\$250}{0.10} = \$2,500$$

Thus, an investor requiring a 10 per cent return would be willing to pay $2,500 for a perpetual bond that pays an annual interest of $250.

40

PART TWO: CAPITAL BUDGETING UNDER CERTAINTY

CHAPTER 4

CAPITAL BUDGETING UNDER CERTAINTY

The last three chapters have provided the necessary background for an economic evaluation of investment projects. This chapter begins the formal process of evaluating investment projects under conditions of certainty. The project evaluation process has two basic steps. The first is to rank available investment opportunities. The second is to determine a hurdle rate or a cutoff point that all projects must meet.

Many methods have been developed to guide management in the acceptance or rejection of proposed investment projects. This chapter explores the five most commonly used methods: payback, average rate of return, net present value, profitability index, and internal rate of return. Because the first two methods do not consider the time value of money, they are frequently called unsophisticated techniques. The last three methods are termed discounted cash-flow approaches, which consider the time value of money. Each of these five methods is defined below.

1. Payback   The payback period is the number of years required to recover the original cost of a project by its net cash flows.

2. Average Rate of Return   This rate is the ratio of the average annual profits after taxes to the average net investment.

3. Net Present Value   This value is the present value of the net cash flows minus the present value of the net investment.

4. Profitability Index   This index is the present value of the net cash flows divided by the present value of the net investment.

5. Internal Rate of Return   This rate is the discount rate that equates the present value of the net cash flows to the present value of the net investment.

THE REQUIRED RATE OF RETURN

The second major step in the project evaluation process is to establish the required rate of return (the hurdle rate or the cutoff point). Because we cannot do everything at the same time, we will postpone an extensive discussion of this concept until Chapter 10. But a brief comment on the concept of the hurdle rate is pertinent at this time because it has a direct influence on the investment decision. The choice of a minimum-profitability standard is essential to maximize the price of the common stock. The choice may be based on the cost of capital. If the cost of capital is used as a minimum acceptable level of return, the accepted project must earn at least as much as the cost of the funds invested in the project. If not, investors can find better yields elsewhere on equally risky investment opportunities. Under these circumstances, the investors will sell their shares, which in turn will depress the market price of the stock and increase the cost of capital. The cost of capital should include the cost of debt and the cost of equity, because almost no projects are financed solely from debt or equity. The quantity and the cost of the different forms of capital are not identical.

The selection of a required rate of return may also be based on the opportunity cost. The opportunity cost is defined as the rate of return that the funds could earn if they were invested in the best available alternative project. Those projects that yield less than the opportunity cost will depress the market price of the common stock. On the other hand, those projects that yield more than the opportunity cost will increase the market price of the stock.

SAMPLE PROJECTS AND ASSUMPTIONS

Before we turn to specific capital-budgeting techniques, we will describe a set of four investment projects. These four projects are designed to make it possible to decide that, within selected pairs, one project is clearly better than the other. Table 4-1 shows the net investment and the net cash flows for each of the four projects.

Table 4-1   Net Investment and Net Cash Flows for
            Four Projects

Project	Net Investment	Net Cash Flow Year 1	Year 2
W	$5,000	$5,000	$ 550
X	5,000	2,881	2,881
Y	5,000	5,000	0
Z	5,000	1,881	3,881

To present the analysis in a simple manner, we
make the following assumptions:1

1. All costs and benefits for each project
are certain to occur.

2. The firm has unlimited funds for investment,
and the four projects are mutually independent.
These two assumptions enable the firm to accept
all profitable projects.

3. The net investment is made at the beginning of the first year, and the net cash flows are
obtained at the end of each year.

4. All four projects have the same net investment, and the net cash flows are the earnings
after taxes plus the annual depreciation charges.
These assumptions will be relaxed in later chapters.

EVALUATING PROJECTS BY INSPECTION

We can rank and select certain limited projects
on the basis of intuition. First, if two projects
have equal net cash flows each year through the
last year of the shorter-lived project, we would
definitely prefer the project that continues to
produce earnings in subsequent years. Thus, Project W is more attractive than Project Y. Second,
if the net investment, the total amount of net cash
flows, and the project life are the same for any
two projects, we would definitely prefer the project that has high net cash flows during its early
years. Hence, Project X is more attractive than
Project Z.

43

UNSOPHISTICATED CAPITAL BUDGETING TECHNIQUES

There are two basic unsophisticated techniques that can be used to rank and select investment projects: the payback method and the average rate of return method. They are easy to compute and popular in practice.[2] But these two methods are theoretically incorrect, because they do not consider the time value of money.

Payback Period

The payback period of a project is the number of years required to accumulate net cash flows sufficient to recover its net investment. If the annual net cash flows are equal, the net investment is divided by the annual net cash flows to obtain the payback period. If the annual net cash flows are not equal, we must add the net cash flows in successive years until we find a total of net cash flows equal to the net investment. Thus, the payback period of Project Y is one year ($5,000 ÷ $5,000). For Project Z, $1,881 will be recovered in the first year, and the remaining balance of $3,119 ($5,000 - $1,881) will be recovered in the second year. The payback period of Project Z is one year plus eight-tenths of one year ($3,119 ÷ $3,881) or 1.8 years.

The firm usually sets some maximum payback period and accepts all projects whose payback periods are shorter than this maximum. In terms of preference, the shorter the payback period, the better the project. The calculated payback periods of the four projects described in Table 4-1 and their rankings are shown in Table 4-2.

The payback method has a number of advantages. It is easy to compute and to understand. It also reflects investment liquidity. In other words, the payback period allows us to judge the length of time the funds will be tied up and to isolate projects with shorter payback periods. Although the payback period is easy to determine and popular in practice, its practicability is limited because of its lack of theoretical validity. It ignores the amount and pattern of net cash flows beyond the payback period. For example, consider

44

Table 4-2   The Calculated Payback Periods of
            Four Projects and Their Rankings

Project	Payback Period	Ranking
W	1.0 years	1
X	1.7	3
Y	1.0	1
Z	1.8	4

Projects W and Y, with an equal cost of $5,000 and
an equal payback period of one year. Project W is
the better investment because it is expected to
produce $550 after the payback period. But this
difference is completely ignored by the payback
method, which rates these two projects equally.
Another obvious limitation is that it does not
take into account the time value of money. Suppose that Project A yields $10 in the first year
and $100 in the second year, whereas Project B
earns $100 in the first year and $10 in the second
year. If these two projects have an equal investment of $110, the payback method would rate them
equally. Yet it is clear that most investors
would prefer Project B, because it recovers the
investment more promptly. Additional problems
are that the payback method disregards (1) the
effect of different economic lives and (2) the
profitability of the project.

Average Rate of Return

      There are many possible definitions of the
average rate of return, depending on how benefits
and costs are measured.[3]   The most common definition of the average rate of return, however, is
the ratio of the average annual profits after taxes
to the average net investment. When this method is
used, the average profits are computed before depreciation. Assuming straight-line depreciation, the
annual depreciation charge for Project Z is $2,500
($5,000 ÷ 2). Because the average annual net cash
flows of the project are $2,881 = $(\dfrac{\$1,881 + \$3,881}{2})$,
its average annual profits are $381 ($2,881 - $2,500).
The average net investment is half the original cost
of the project. Project Z has a cost of $5,000.

45

Thus, its average net investment is $2,500 ($5,000÷ 2).
Given the average annual profits and the
average net investment, the average rate of return
for Project Z is

Average Rate of Return = $\dfrac{\$381}{\$2,500}$ = 15%

Ordinarily, management preestablishes some
minimum average rate of return as a cutoff point
and accepts all projects whose average rates of
return are greater than this minimum. In terms
of ranking projects, the greater the average rate
of return, the better the project. The four projects listed in Table 4-1 are ranked by the average
rate of return, as shown in Table 4-3.

Table 4-3 The Calculated Average Rates of Return
for Four Projects and Their Rankings

Proj-ect	Avg. Net Cash Flows	Avg. Depre-cia-tion	Avg. Prof-its	Avg. Net Invest-ment	Avg. Rate of Re-turn	Rank-ing
W	$2,775	$2,500	$275	$2,500	11%	3
X	2,881	2,500	381	2,500	15	1
Y	5,000	5,000	0	2,500	0	4
Z	2,881	2,500	381	2,500	15	1

The average rate of return is easy to determine,
but it has a number of serious shortcomings. It ignores the time value of money. Under the average-
rate-of-return method, profits in the last year
are given the same weight as profits in the first
year. For example, Projects X and Z have the same
average rate of return. But most firms would definitely prefer Project X, because it has a large
portion of total profits in the first year. Other
deficiencies are (1) it uses accounting income
rather than net cash flows, (2) it relies on a
uniform income stream, and (3) it fails to take
advantage of accelerated depreciation.

DISCOUNTED CASH-FLOW APPROACHES

46

Because both the payback and average-rate-of-return methods have the various limitations described above, discounted cash-flow approaches provide a more sophisticated basis for ranking and selecting investment projects. The net-present-value, profitability-index, and internal-rate-of-return methods clearly recognize that money has a time value. These three techniques also use the cash flows of a project over its entire life span. The measurement of cash flows avoids difficult problems underlying the measurement of accounting income.

Net Present Value

The measurement of a project by the net-present-value method requires a determination of the following: (1) an appropriate rate of discount, (2) the present value of the net cash flows expected from the project, and (3) the present value of the net cash investment required by the project. The net present value of the project is the present value of the net cash flows minus the present value of the net cash investment:

$$(4\text{-}1)$$

$$NPV = \left[\frac{A_1}{(1+k)^1} + \frac{A_2}{(1+k)^2} + \ldots + \frac{A_n}{(1+k)^n} \right] - C_o$$

$$= \sum_{t=1}^{n} \frac{A_t}{(1+k)^t} - C_o$$

where Σ = capital Greek sigma which denotes the sum of discounted net cash flows for the entire life of the project

A_t = net cash flows in year t

k = cost of capital used as a discount rate

C_o = present value of the net cash investment

n = life of the project.

With a 5 per cent rate of discount, the net present value of Project Z is

47

$$NPV = \frac{\$1,881}{(1 + 0.05)^1} + \frac{\$3,881}{(1 + 0.05)^2} - \$5,000$$

$$= \$5,311 - \$5,000$$

$$= \$311$$

An easier way to solve the problem is (1) find the appropriate discount factor from Table B at the end of this book, (2) multiply the annual net cash flow by that discount factor, (3) add the present values of all net cash flow items, and (4) subtract the net investment from the present value of the net cash flows. This is given as follows:

Year	Net Cash Flows	Discount Factor at 5%	Present Value of Net Cash Flows
1	$1,881	0.952	$1,791
2	3,881	0.907	3,520
	Present Value of Net Cash Flows		$5,311
	Less: Net Investment		5,000
	Net Present Value		$ 311

The present value of $5,311 for Project Z is the maximum amount that a firm could pay for the project without a loss. To put the matter another way, the present value of the net cash flows expected from Project Z could pay off an investment of $5,000 and its cost of 5 per cent and still leave $311 for the firm.

The net-present-value method tells us to accept all projects whose net present values are positive and to reject all projects whose net present values are negative. If the net present value is zero, the firm would be indifferent between acceptance and rejection. Because the accept-reject decision is based on the zero net present value, the higher the positive net present value, the better the project. Table 4-4 ranks the four projects of Table 4-1 on the basis of the net-present-value method. As shown in the table, Projects W, X, and Z have positive net present values and consequently would be accepted by the firm. But Project Y has a nega-

48

Table 4-4 Net Present Values of Four Projects at
           5% Discount Rate and Their Rankings

Project	Pres. Value of Net Cash Flows	Net Invest- ment	Net Pres. Value	Rank- ings
W	$5,259	$5,000	$259	3
X	5,356	5,000	356	1
Y	4,760	5,000	-240	4
Z	5,311	5,000	311	2

tive net present value and therefore would be rejected. It is also important to•note that Project
X has the highest net present value among the four
projects and thus should be ranked as the best
project.

It is obvious that different rates of discount
would give different net present values. To illustrate, let us rank the same projects using a
20 per cent discount rate instead of 5 per cent.
This ranking is given in Table 4-5. Project Y remains the lowest ranked, but the relative ranking
of Projects W, X, and Z changes with the change in
the rate of discount. The higher the discount rate,
the better the project with a large portion of the
net cash flows in the early years, such as Project W.

Table 4-5 Net Present Values of Four Projects at
           20% Discount Rate and Their Rankings

Project	Pres. Value of Net Cash Flows	Net Invest- ment	Net Pres. Value	Rank- ings
W	$4,547	$5,000	-$453	1
X	4,399	5,000	- 601	2
Y	4,165	5,000	- 835	4
Z	4,260	5,000	- 740	3

Profitability Index

An attempt to make the net-present-value method
more meaningful can be made by introducing the prof-

itability index. The index is obtained by dividing the present value of the net cash flows by the net investment:

$$\text{Profitability Index} = \frac{\sum_{t=1}^{n} \frac{A_t}{(1 + k)^t}}{C_o} \qquad (4-2)$$

Thus, the index uses the same information as the net-present-value method and measures the present value return per dollar of net investment. With a 5 per cent discount rate, the profitability index for Project W is 1.052 ($5,259 ÷ $5,000). Because the index criterion tells us to accept all projects whose indexes are greater than 1, Project W should be accepted. The greater the index, the better the project.

Table 4-6 shows the calculated profitability indexes of the four projects listed in Table 4-1 and their rankings. Because all the projects with positive net present values tend to have profitability indexes greater than 1, the net-present-value and profitability-index methods yield the

Table 4-6 Profitability Indexes of Four Projects and Their Rankings

Project	Pres. Value of Net Cash Flows	Net Investment	Profitability Index	Rankings
W	$5,259	$5,000	1.052	3
X	5,356	5,000	1.071	1
Y	4,760	5,000	0.952	4
Z	5,311	5,000	1.062	2

same accept-reject decisions. Although these two methods rank the four projects in the same order, they can lead to different rankings under certain circumstances. This is because the net-present-value method measures a project's profitability on an absolute scale while the profitability index measures a project's profitability on a relative scale.

Internal Rate of Return

The internal rate of return is the discount rate that equates the present value of the net cash flows to the present value of the net cash investment or that provides a zero net present value:

$$\frac{A_1}{(1 + r)^1} + \frac{A_2}{(1 + r)^2} + \ldots + \frac{A_n}{(1 + r)^n} - C_o = 0$$

$$\sum_{t=1}^{n} \frac{A_t}{(1 + r)^t} - C_o = 0$$

(4-3)

Here we know the value of net investment (C_o), net cash flows $(A_1, A_2, \ldots)$, and project's life (n), but we do not know the value of the internal rate of return (r).

If the net cash-flow stream represents an even series of an annuity, we can calculate the relatively accurate internal rate of return by a relatively simple procedure. What is needed is an annuity discount factor, which can be used to search for the approximate internal rate of return. The annuity discount factor for any project with an even series such as Project X can be found by applying Equation (3-11):

$$PA = A \times ADF_{n,i}, \quad \text{or} \quad ADF_{n,i} = \frac{PA}{A}$$

$$ADF_{2,i} = \frac{\$5,000}{\$2,881} = 1.736$$

Look across the two-year row of Table C at the end of this book to find that the annuity discount factor 1.736 is under the 10 per cent column. This 10 per cent is the internal rate of return for Project X.

When net cash flows are unequal or uneven in each year, it is necessary to use a trial-and-error procedure. The trial-and-error method requires the following steps:[4]

51

1.   Choose an arbitrary discount rate. The cost of capital is a good starting point, because the firm must earn at least as much as the cost of capital. Alternatively, a first estimate of the answer may be obtained by reconstructing the problem using an average net cash flow each year rather than the exact amounts given.

2.   Compute the present value of net cash flows using an arbitrarily selected rate or the first estimate of the answer.

3.   Compare the present value with the net investment. If the present value is higher than the net investment, try a higher rate and repeat the process. If the present value is lower than the net investment, try a lower rate and repeat the process.

4.   Continue this process until you find the rate that equates the present value of net cash flows to the net investment. Or approximate the internal rate of return using linear interpolation.

To illustrate, consider Project Z, which has a net investment of $5,000 and is expected to yield $1,881 at the end of one year and $3,881 at the end of two years. Because the average annual net cash flow of Project Z is
$$\$2,881 = \frac{\$1,881 + \$3,881}{2},$$
the first estimate of the answer for Project Z is 10 per cent. With the discount rate of 10 per cent, the present value of the net cash flows for Project Z is $4,915.54. Because the present value is lower than the net investment of $5,000, we must try a rate lower than 10 per cent. With a discount rate of 8 per cent, the present value of the net cash flows for Project Z is $5,067.82. Because the present value is higher than the net investment of $5,000, we see that the internal rate of return is higher than 8 per cent but lower than 10 per cent. We can continue the trial-and-error procedure until we find the internal rate of return; or we can interpolate between 8 and 10 per cent to approximate the internal rate of return. If we choose the latter method, it is convenient to diagram the data as follows:

52

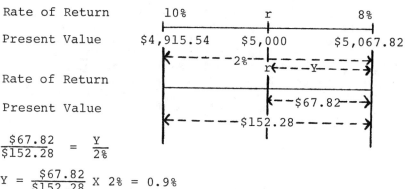

Rate of Return   10%   r   8%

Present Value $4,915.54 $5,000 $5,067.82

$$\frac{\$67.82}{\$152.28} = \frac{Y}{2\%}$$

$$Y = \frac{\$67.82}{\$152.28} \times 2\% = 0.9\%$$

$$r = 8\% + Y = 8\% + 0.9\% = 8.9\%$$

Thus, the internal rate of return for Project Z is approximately 8.9 per cent. It is important to note that interpolation fails to give an exact rate. Although we assumed that the rate difference ratio of Y/2% is equal to the present value difference ratio of $67.82/$152.28, the relationship between a pair of discount rates is not linear with regard to present value.

The 8.9 per cent represents the highest cost of financing that the firm could pay for all the funds to finance Project Z. To put the matter another way, the internal rate of return is the growth rate of a project. In other words, a net investment of $5,000 with an 8.9 per cent growth rate will return $1,881 at the end of one year and $3,881 at the end of two years. This is verified as follows:

Year	Beginning Balance	Interest at 8.9%	Ending Balance	Annual Return
1	$5,000	$445	$5,445	$1,881
2	3,564	317	3,881	3,881

The decision rule compares the internal rate of return with a cutoff point, known as a minimum required rate of return. If the internal rate of return exceeds the cutoff point, the project should be accepted; if not, it should be rejected. The higher the internal rate of return, the better the

project. Table 4-7 presents the internal rates of
return for the four projects described in Table
4-1 and their relative rankings. If the minimum
required rate of return is 5 per cent, Projects
W, X, and Z should be accepted, and Project Y
should be rejected. It should be noted that this
is precisely the same conclusion reached by the
use of the net-present-value method with a discount rate of 5 per cent.

Table 4-7   Internal Rates of Return for Four Proj-
            ects and Their Rankings

Project	Internal Rate of Return	Ranking
W	10.0%	1
X	10.0	1
Y	0.0	4
Z	8.9	3

SUMMARY OF RANKINGS

Table 4-8 summarizes a set of rankings by the
five different techniques for the four projects
listed in Table 4-1. We see that the techniques
produce different rankings for the same set of investment projects. This strongly suggests that the

Table 4-8   Summary of Rankings

| Proj-ect | Capital Budgeting Techniques | | | | |
	Pay-back	Avg. Rate of Return	Net Pres. Value at 5%	Profit-ability In-dex	Inter-nal Rate of Return
W	1	3	3	3	1
X	3	1	1	1	1
Y	1	4	4	4	4
Z	4	1	2	2	3

current choice of methods for the firm to use can
be critical for its future well-being. Because of
the various limitations in the payback and average-

54

rate-of-return methods described in this chapter, we drop these two methods from further consideration.

The current literature in the field of capital budgeting favors the use of the net-present-value and internal-rate-of-return methods because they take into account the time value of money. The rankings of the projects given by these two discounted cash-flow approaches are different. Thus, they could lead to contradictory conclusions in certain situations. In Chapter 5 we shall continue our investigation in an attempt to determine which of the two discounted cash-flow approaches is better.

PROJECTS WITH DIFFERENT LIFE SPANS

When we compare mutually exclusive projects with different life spans, it is often useful to transform the net present value (present value) into an annualized net present value (annualized cost) over the project's life. Although this approach may be used to compare all types of alternative projects, it should not be used to analyze those projects whose cash flows are extremely irregular.

When mutually exclusive projects are under consideration, the financial manager has three basic choices of assumptions.[5] (1) At the end of each project's life, the firm will invest in projects that earn its cost of capital. (2) The firm will make specific assumptions about the reinvestment opportunities that may be available to it in the future. (3) The firm will reinvest in projects of precisely the same characteristics as its current project under consideration. The second assumption is the most practical alternative of the three, but it is the most difficult to implement in practice. The third alternative requires the firm to compute the present value of the first round of the project with no further forecasts about the future. The following numerical examples are based on the third assumption.

Example 4-1   Two mutually exclusive projects have the following characteristics:

| Proj- | Initial | Net Cash Flows | | | |
ect	Cost	Year 1	Year 2	Year 3	Year 4
A	$10,000	$9,000	$7,000		
B	12,000	6,000	4,000	5,500	7,400

The company's cost of capital is 10 per cent.

The net present value is $3,963 for Project A and $5,943 for Project B. If one ignores the difference in project life, Project B is better than Project A. Equation (3-11) can be used to compute the annualized net present value:

$$PA = A \times ADF_{n,i}, \quad \text{or} \quad A = \frac{PA}{ADF_{n,i}}$$

Project A: $A = \dfrac{\$3,963}{ADF_{2,10\%}} = \dfrac{\$3,963}{1.736} = \$2,283$

Project B: $A = \dfrac{\$5,943}{ADF_{4,10\%}} = \dfrac{\$5,943}{3.170} = \$1,875$

Project A is now better than Project B. The superiority of one project over the other, however, really depends on the expected returns from the reinvestment of Project A's cash benefits after year 2 and the rate at which Project B's additional investment of $2,000 could earn.

Example 4-2   Two mutually exclusive projects are under consideration. Project C has a cost of $20,000, an annual operating expense of $4,000, and an economic life of three years. Project D has a cost of $60,000, an annual operating expense of $3,000, and an economic life of eight years. The time value of money is 10 per cent.

The annual equivalent of a $20,000 investment every three years is

$$A = \frac{\$20,000}{ADF_{3,10\%}} = \frac{\$20,000}{2.487} = \$8,042$$

The annual equivalent of a $60,000 investment every eight years is

$$A = \frac{\$60,000}{ADF_{8,10\%}} = \frac{\$60,000}{5.335} = \$11,246$$

The annualized cost is the annual equivalent of each project's initial cost plus its annual operating cost. Thus, the annualized cost is $12,042 ($8,042 + $4,000) for Project C and $14,246 ($11,246 + $3,000) for Project D. Because the annualized cost of Project C is less than that of Project D, Project C should be accepted.

Components of Unequal Lives

There are times when an alternative project may consist of several components of unequal lives. In this case, the company will have to take all of them or none of them. For instance, there may be a building with a life of 20 years costing $1 million. Assume that this building requires a furnace with a life of 15 years costing $200,000 and lighting system with a life of 11 years costing $100,000. With a discount rate of 10 per cent, the total annualized cost is computed as follows:

Cost of Building $= \dfrac{\$1,000,000}{ADF_{20,10\%}} = \dfrac{\$1,000,000}{8.514} = \$117,454$

Cost of Furnace $= \dfrac{\$\ 200,000}{ADF_{15,10\%}} = \dfrac{\$\ 200,000}{7.606} = \$\ 26,295$

Cost of Lighting $= \dfrac{\$\ 100,000}{ADF_{11,10\%}} = \dfrac{\$\ 100,000}{6.495} = \$\ \underline{15,396}$

Total Annualized Cost $=$ $\underline{\underline{\$159,145}}$

If one or more of mutually exclusive projects are made up of several components with different lives, the total annualized cost should be computed for each project so that the decision maker can compare these projects on the basis of a common denominator called an annualized cost. Although we assumed

57

that the above three components can be replaced
for their original cost in later years, we can
make specific assumptions about the replacement
cost. Of course, these additional assumptions
would make the computation process more difficult.

CAPITAL BUDGETING PRACTICES AND EARNINGS
PERFORMANCE

Since the early 1950s the academic community
has tried to convince business that there are
sophisticated techniques to aid in the formulation
of profitable capital expenditure decisions.[6] Although there are some differences in the findings
of the recent studies on capital budgeting practices,
an overview of these studies on capital budgeting
shows an increasing use of discounted cash flow approaches in investment decisions. Despite the
theoretical arguments presented in this chapter
and the increasing acceptance of these techniques
in practice, many firms still rely on such rule-of-
thumb methods as payback. That is, these companies
spend large sums of money without appropriate
analysis.

It has been widely assumed by academicians
that the use of more sophisticated capital budgeting techniques would lead to better earnings performance. However, there are two major factors
which make final conclusions on this point difficult: (1) the lack of follow-up on spending decisions by business firms and (2) the difficulties
of measuring improved earnings attributable to the
use of sophisticated evaluation techniques. Clark,
Hindelang, and Pritchard sum up this point as
follows:

> Yet we can cite some research on the topic.
> George A. Christy, for example, matched
> earnings per share of his surveyed com-
> panies against the capital budgeting tech-
> niques employed. Christy found no sig-
> nificant relationship between profitability
> and the methodology of long-range asset
> management.
>
> By contrast, Suk H. Kim at the University
> of Detroit surveyed 114 machinery companies

and related their average earnings per
share to several variables: the degree
of sophistication in capital budgeting,
size of the firm, capital intensity,
degree of risk, and debt ratio. Kim
found a positive relationship between
profitability and the capital budgeting technique when the latter is considered as a broad process involving
the added variables ignored in the
Christy study.[7]

FOOTNOTES

1. Harold Bierman, Jr. and Seymour Smidt, The
   Capital Budgeting Decision: Economic Analysis
   of Investment Projects (New York: Macmillan
   Publishing Company, 1980), Chapter 2; and
   Charles O. Kroncke, Erwin E. Nemmers, and
   Alan E. Grunewald, Managerial Finance: Es-
   sentials (St. Paul, Minnesota: West Pub-
   lishing Company, 1978), pp. 188-189.

2. Thomas Klammer, "Empirical Evidence of the
   Adoption of Sophisticated Capital Budgeting
   Techniques," Journal of Business (July 1972),
   pp. 387-397; James M. Fremgen, "Capital
   Budgeting Practices: A Survey," Management
   Accounting (May 1973), pp. 19-25; and J.
   William Petty, David F. Scott, Jr. and Mon-
   roe M. Bird, "The Capital Expenditure De-
   cision-Making Process of Large Corporations,"
   The Engineering Economist (Spring 1975),
   pp. 159-172.

3. Abdelsamad claims that there are at least 864
   possible ways of determining the average rate
   of return. See Moustafa H. Abdelsamad, A
   Guide to Capital Expenditure Analysis (New
   York: American Management Association, 1973),
   p. 45.

4. Bernhard Schwab and Peter Lusztig, "A Compara-
   tive Analysis of the Net Present Value and
   the Benefit-Cost Ratio as Measures of the
   Economic Desirability of Investments," Journal
   of Finance (June 1969), pp. 507-511; and H.

Martin Weingartner, "The Excess Present Value Index: A Theoretical Basis and Critique," _Journal of Accounting Research_ (Autumn 1963), pp. 120-121.

5.   Bierman and Smidt, _The Capital Budgeting Decision: Economic Analysis of Investment Projects_, p. 103.

6.   Joel Dean, _Capital Budgeting_ (New York: Columbia University Press, 1955).

7.   John J. Clark, Thomas J. Hindelang, and Robert E. Pritchard, _Capital Budgeting: Planning and Control of Capital Expenditures_ (Englewood Cliffs, N.J.: Prentice-Hall, Inc., 1979), p. 397.
For details of these two studies, see George A. Christy, _Capital Budgeting: Current Practices and Their Efficiency_ (Eugene, Ore.: Bureau of Economic Research, University of Oregon, 1966); and Suk H. Kim, "Capital Budgeting Practices and Their Impact on Overall Profitability," _Baylor Business Studies_ (November, December 1978, January 1979), pp. 49-66.

CHAPTER 5

NET PRESENT VALUE VERSUS INTERNAL RATE OF RETURN

The current literature in the field of capital budgeting favors the use of the net-present-value and internal-rate-of-return methods because they consider the time value of money. Their accept-reject rules are: (1) accept projects whose net present values are greater than or equal to 0 and (2) accept projects whose internal rates of return are greater than or equal to the firm's cost of capital. These two basic rules lead to the same decision if the following conditions hold:[1]

1. Investment proposals under consideration are mutually independent and they are free of capital rationing constraints.

2. All projects are equally risky so that the acceptance or rejection of any project does not affect the cost of capital.

3. A meaningful cost of capital exists to the extent that the company has access to capital at this cost.

4. A unique internal rate of return exists; every project has just one internal rate of return.

In the absence of these assumptions, the capital investment decision becomes more complex and these two discounted cash-flow approaches may lead to the different decisions.

In this chapter we shall examine the sources of possible conflicts in ranking and their resolution. This book will consistently recommend the use of the net-present-value method. The remainder of this chapter will explain why the net-present-value method is superior. This chapter will also show how the internal rate-of-return method could be used correctly in arriving at the same answers as the net-present-value method.

MUTUALLY EXCLUSIVE PROJECTS AND CAPITAL RATIONING

In Chapter 4, we assumed that the investment projects under consideration are mutually independent and that the firm has unlimited funds for investment. Under these two assumptions, the net-present-value and internal-rate-of return methods lead to the same decision. If these two assumptions are removed, however, the two discounted cash-flow methods may give different answers.

To illustrate, we will retabulate the results of the computation for Projects W, X, Y, and Z described in Chapter 4, with respect to the two discounted cash-flow approaches. It is clear from Table 5-1 that the two techniques do not rank the four projects in the same order of preference.

Table 5-1   Selection of Projects When They Are
            Mutually Exclusive and Subject to
            Capital Rationing

Rank	Net Invest-ment	Cum. Net Invest-ment	Net Pres. Value Rank at 5%	Internal Rate of Return Rank
1	$5,000	$ 5,000	X = $356	W = 10.0%
2	5,000	10,000	Z = 311	X = 10.0
3	5,000	15,000	W = 259	Z = 8.9
4	5,000	20,000	Y = -240	Y = 0.0

If Projects Z and W are mutually exclusive, Project Z should be accepted when making a decision on the basis of the net-present-value method. On the other hand, Project W should be accepted over Project Z when making a choice using the internal-rate-of-return method.

When mutually independent projects are evaluated under a capital-rationing constraint, they are listed in the order of preference according to the net present value or the internal rate of return. Then, projects are selected in the descending order from the top of the list until the available funds have been consumed. If the firm has a capital budget of $10,000, the net-present-value criterion tells us to accept Projects X and Z, but the internal-rate-of-return criterion tells us to accept Projects W and X.

Under ordinary circumstances, the two capital
budgeting techniques yield identical decisions.
Under certain circumstances, however, they produce
different rankings, which makes it impossible for us
to avoid the necessity of choosing between the two
methods of evaluating investment alternatives.

There are two situations where conflicts can
arise between the two techniques in the way in which
they rank mutually exclusive projects: (1) net
present value measures the absolute dollar value
while internal rate of return reflects the average
percentage return and (2) the reinvestment assumption. Specifically, conflicts could arise
between net present value and internal rate of
return when:

1. Two projects have substantially different
investments (size disparity).

2. They have the same investment but a large
difference in the time patterns of their net cash
flows (time disparity).

SIZE DISPARITY BETWEEN PROJECTS

The financial manager must frequently evaluate
mutually exclusive projects that require varying
sizes of discounted cash investments. Such conditions may create conflicts in the rankings assigned the various projects by net present value
and internal rate of return. The major reason
for such conflicts is because net present value
measures the absolute magnitude of the excess of
discounted net cash flows over discounted net investment, whereas internal rate of return measures
the discount rate which equates discounted net cash
flows to discounted cash investments.

Example 5-1 Two mutually exclusive projects have
the following cash outflows and inflows:

| Project | Cash Flows | |
	Year 0	Year 1
A	-$3,500	$4,500
B	- 1,000	1,500

Table 5-2 shows the net present values of Projects A and B at the selected discount rates. Figure 5-1 plots the net present values of the two projects for all discount rates from zero to 50 per cent.

Table 5-2   Net Present Values at the Various Discount Rates

| Discount Rate | Net Present Value | |
	Project A	Project B
0.00	$1,000	$500
10.00	591	363
20.00	250	250
28.57	0	167
40.00	-287	71
50.00	-498	0

Figure 5-1   Net-Present-Value Profiles for Projects A and B

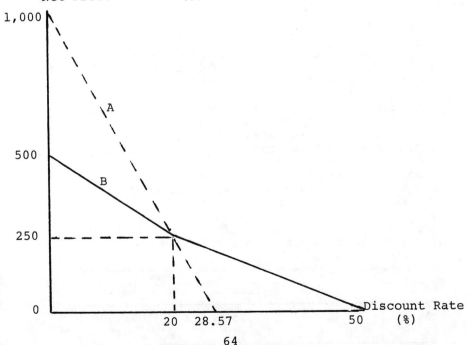

64

Figure 5-1 shows that, as the discount rate increases, the net present value decreases. At the horizontal intercept the net present value is zero. The discount rate that makes the net present value zero represents the internal rate of return. Thus Project A has a 28.57 per cent internal rate of return, and Project B has a 50 per cent internal rate of return. For rates of discount greater than 20 per cent, both the net-present-value and internal-rate-of-return methods rank Project B higher than Project A and thus lead to the same decision. But for rates of discount smaller than 20 per cent, the two techniques lead to conflicting results, because Project A has the higher net present value but the lower internal rate of return.

When the conflict exists between net present value and internal rate of return, which method should we choose? Because the primary goal of the firm is to maximize the value of the firm, the correct decision is to accept the project with the highest net present value. The project with the largest net present value makes the greatest net contribution to the value of the firm. This leads to the conclusion that the net-present-value method is better than the internal-rate-of-return method.

Resolution of Conflicts in Size Disparity

The internal-rate-of-return method may be modified to give the same results as the net-present-value method. To illustrate, we shall determine the internal rate of return on incremental cash flows.

| Project | Cash Flows | | Internal Rate of Return |
	Year 0	Year 1	
A	-$3,500	$4,500	28.57%
B	- 1,000	1,500	50.00
A - B	-$2,500	$3,000	20.00

Thus, as long as the required rate of return is less than 20 per cent, the incremental investment of $2,500 in Project A is justified because the internal rate of return would exceed the required rate of return under this assumption. It is also important to recognize that the net present value on incremental cash flows is positive if the discount rate is less than 20 per cent. Hence, these two techniques would consistently argue that Project A is better than Project B.

The internal rate of return for the incremental project is often called the Fisher's intersection.[2] Recall that there could be a conflict between net present value and internal rate of return if the firm's cost of capital is less than the discount rate at which the intersection in net-present-value profiles occurs. Although there could be zero, one, or multiple intersections between net-present-value profiles, we shall limit our attention to cases where there is one intersection.

Of course, one way of finding the Fisher's intersection is to compute the internal rate of return for the incremental project. We may also solve for the Fisher's intersection (r') directly for Projects A and B:

$$-\$3,500 + \frac{\$4,500}{(1 + r')^1} = -\$1,000 + \frac{\$1,500}{(1 + r')^1}$$

$$\frac{\$4,500 - \$1,500}{(1 + r')^1} = \$2,500$$

$$\frac{\$3,000}{(1 + r')^1} = \$2,500$$

This is precisely the internal rate of return for the incremental investment in Project A.

TIME DISPARITY BETWEEN PROJECTS

In addition to size disparity, management frequently has to analyze mutually exclusive projects where differences exist with respect to the sequence of the time of net cash flows. These time disparities and differing reinvestment assumptions can lead to conflicts in rankings between the two discounted cash-flow approaches.

Reinvestment Assumption

It is frequently claimed that the net-present-value method assumes reinvestment at the firm's cost of capital, whereas the internal-rate-of-return method assumes reinvestment at the internal rate of return. With the net-present-value method, the implied reinvestment rate reflects an approximation of the opportunity cost for reinvestment. With the internal-rate-of-return method, the implied reinvestment rate is not likely to be harmful, but it is not exactly correct.

The firm's cost of capital approximates the opportunity cost for reinvestment. That is, the rate of return that the funds could earn if they were invested in the best available alternative project. Those projects that yield less than the opportunity cost will depress the market price of the stock. In contrast, those projects that yield more than the opportunity cost will increase the market price of the stock.

With the internal-rate-of-return method, the implied reinvestment rate will differ from project to project. For example, a project with a 20 per cent internal rate of return is assumed to reinvest its intermediate cash flows at 20 per cent; a project with a 10 per cent internal rate of return is assumed to reinvest its intermediate cash flows at 10 per cent. Of course, such a reinvestment assumption does not reflect the opportunity cost for reinvestment at all.

Example 5-2 Two mutually exclusive projects have the following features:

Project	Net Invest- ment	Net Cash Flows				Net Pres. Value at 5%	Internal Rate of Return
		Year 1	Year 2	Year 3	Year 4		
C	$7,054	$4,000	$3,000	$2,000	$1,000	$2,026	20%
D	7,054	1,000	2,000	3,000	5,042	2,454	16

Both projects cost $7,054, but Project C produces the largest net cash flow in the first year and Project D produces the largest net cash flow in the last year. Because of these timing differences, the two techniques produce the differences in rankings. Project C has a higher internal rate of return than Project D, but at the 5 per cent discount rate, Project D has a higher net present value than Project C. The internal-rate-of-return method favors projects that have high net cash flows early in the life of the project. Such intermediate cash flows considerably increase the internal rate of return because the technique assumes that they can be reinvested at this higher rate. On the other hand, the net-present-value method assumes reinvestment at the 5 per cent cost of capital, which is much lower than the internal rate of return. Such a low reinvestment rate assesses a smaller penalty for net cash flows received later in the project's life compared to the internal-rate-of-return method.

Figure 5-2 shows the net-present-value profiles for Projects C and D. Fisher's intersection

Figure 5-2 Net-Present-Value Profiles for Projects C and D

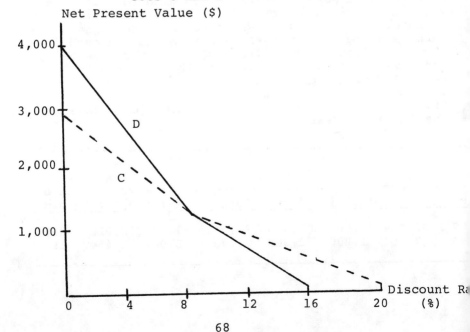

occurs at approximately 9.5 per cent. The conflict between the net-present-value and internal-rate-of-return methods occurs at all discount rates less than this intersection. The resolution of such a conflict can be achieved by computing the terminal value of the project, provided that intermediate cash flows can be reinvested at a specified rate. The terminal value for a project is

$$TV = \sum_{t=1}^{n} S_t (1 + i)^{n-t} \qquad (5-1)$$

where TV = terminal value

S_t = net cash flow that occurs at the end of period t

i = reinvestment rate

n = useful life of the project

The modified net present value (NPV*) would depend on Equation (5-1):

$$(5-2)$$

$$NPV^* = \frac{TV}{(1 + k)^n} - C_o$$

where k = firm's cost of capital

C_o = present value of the net cash investment

The modified internal rate of return would employ Equation (5-2):

$$(5-3)$$

$$\frac{TV}{(1 + r^*)^n} - C_o = 0$$

where r* is the modified internal rate of return.

Example 5-3   For Projects C and D, calculate TV, NPV*, and IRR* at the reinvestment rates of 8 per cent and 11 per cent.

Assuming a reinvestment rate of 8 per cent, the terminal value for Projects C and D are

69

$$TV_C = \$4,000(1.08)^3 + \$3,000(1.08)^2 + \$2,000(1.08)^1$$
$$+ \$1,000(1.08)^0 = \$11,698$$

$$TV_D = \$1,000(1.08)^3 + \$2,000(1.08)^2 + \$3,000(1.08)^1$$
$$+ \$5,042(1.08)^0 = \$11,874$$

If these two projects have equal costs of \$7,054, we can see that Project D is better than Project C at a reinvestment rate of 8 per cent. Proceeding with these terminal values, the modified net present values and internal rates of return for both projects are obtained as follows:

$$NPV*_C = \frac{\$11,698}{(1.05)^4} - \$7,054 = \$2,573$$

$$NPV*_D = \frac{\$11,874}{(1.05)^4} - \$7,054 = \$2,718$$

$$IRR*_C = \frac{\$11,698}{(1 + r*_C)^4} - \$7,054 = 0$$

$$r*_C = 13.5\%$$

$$IRR*_D = \frac{\$11,874}{(1 + r*_D)^4} - \$7,054 = 0$$

$$r*_D = 14.0\%$$

Because $NPV*_D > NPV*_C$ and $IRR*_D > IRR*_C$, Project D is better than Project C at a reinvestment rate of 8 per cent.

Under the assumption that net cash flows can be reinvested at 11 per cent (higher than Fisher's intersection of 9.5%), we obtain the following terminal values:

$$TV_C = \$4,000(1.11)^3 + \$3,000(1.11)^2 + \$2,000(1.11)^1$$
$$+ \$1,000(1.11)^0 = \$12,388$$

$$TV_D = \$1,000(1.11)^3 + \$2,000 (1.11)^2 + \$3,000(1.11)^1$$
$$+ \$5,042(1.11)^0 = \$12,204$$

As with a reinvestment rate of 8 per cent, these
terminal values are sufficient for us to conclude
that Project C is better than Project D at a reinvestment rate of 11 per cent. The modified NPV*
and IRR* will lead to the same conclusion:

$$NPV^*_C = \frac{\$12,388}{(1.05)^4} - \$7,054 = \$3,141$$

$$NPV^*_D = \frac{\$12,204}{(1.05)^3} - \$7,054 = \$2,990$$

$$IRR^*_C = \frac{\$12,388}{(1 + r^*_C)^4} - \$7,054 = 0$$

$$r^*_C = 15.1\%$$

$$IRR^*_C = \frac{\$12,204}{(1 + r^*_D)^4} - \$7,054 = 0$$

$$r^*_D = 14.7\%$$

Because $NPV^*_C > NPV^*_D$ and $IRR^*_C > IRR^*_D$, Project C is
better than Project D at a reinvestment rate of 11
per cent.

Given the net-present-value profiles of two
projects, Fisher's intersection plays a key role
in determining the preferred project because it is
the point at which project preference changes.
Thus, we can conclude that Project D is preferred
at all discount rates less than the Fisher's intersection of 9.5 per cent while Project C is preferred
at all discount rates greater than 9.5 per cent.
These conclusions are consistent with the rankings
by the terminal values, the modified net present
values, and the modified internal rates of return.

Varying Discount Rates

Up to now we have assumed that the firm's cost
of capital and the reinvestment rate stay the same
throughout all future periods. If these rates are
expected to vary from year to year, Equations (5-1),

(5-2), and (5-3) for NPV, TV, and NPV* should be modified as follows:

$$NPV = \sum_{t=1}^{n} \frac{S_t}{\prod_{j=1}^{t} (1 + k_j)} - C_o \qquad (5-4)$$

where $\prod$ = symbol for a geometric sum

$\quad k_j$ = firm's cost of capital in period j

$\quad C_o$ = present value of the net cash investment

$$ \qquad\qquad\qquad\qquad\qquad\qquad\qquad (5-5)$$

$$TV = \sum_{t=1}^{n} S_t \left[\prod_{j=t+1}^{n} (1 + i_j) \right]$$

where i_j is the reinvestment rate that can be earned during period j.

$$NPV* = \frac{TV}{\prod_{t=1}^{n} (1 + k_t)} - C_o \qquad (5-6)$$

Therefore, uneven discount rates present no problems when the net-present-value method is used to evaluate the investment project. This dynamic assumption may be more realistic during a period of rising interest rate and inflation. However, once computed, the internal rate of return remains constant over the entire life of the project.

MULTIPLE INTERNAL RATES OF RETURN

Another problem with the internal-rate-of-return method is that it produces more than one solution under certain circumstances. These circumstances prevail when projects are unconventional. Conventional investments are those that have positive net cash flows over their entire life span. In contrast, unconventional investments are those that have negative net cash flows in any one or more years. When investments are conventional, we compute the internal rate of return for each of the alternative projects and select the project with

the highest internal rate of return. But the
choice is not that obvious when investments are
unconventional, because an unconventional project has more than one internal rate of return.
Normally, one is a real number, and all the others
are either negative or imaginary numbers. The
difficulty of the decision maker in clearly iden-
tifying the correct internal rate of return for
unconventional projects leads us to conclude that
the net-present-value method is better than the
internal-rate-of-return method.

Example 5-4   Assume the following stream of cash
flows corresponding to the "oil pump" proposal
of Lorie and Savage:[3]

Year	0	1	2
Cash Flow	-$400	$2,500	-$2,500

In this example, a new oil pump replaces an existing pump. On an incremental basis, there is an
original outflow followed by net cash flows. Such
incremental net cash flows result from the increasing efficiency of the new pump. If the quantity of
oil is fixed, the new pump will get the oil out of
the ground more rapidly than the pump currently in
use. The earlier exhaustion of this supply with
the use of the higher-capacity pump will result in
final incremental outlay.

    The incremental project will have two internal
rates of return: 25 per cent and 400 per cent.
Figure 5-3 illustrates this unusual situation.

Figure 5-3   Dual Internal Rates of Return

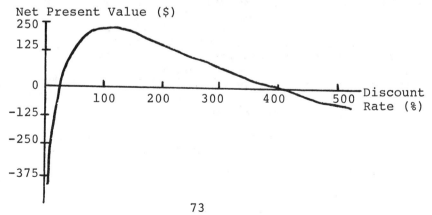

73

As the discount rate approaches zero, the net present value of the project approaches the algebraic sum of all the cash flows, -$400. As a result, the net present value of the project becomes negative at those discount rates close to zero. As the discount rate increases, the present value of the second-year outflow decreases in importance with respect to the first-year cash inflow. Such a decrease causes the net present value of the project to become positive when the discount rate exceeds 25 per cent. As the discount rate continues to increase beyond 100 per cent, the present value of all future net cash flows (year 1 and year 2) tends to diminish relative to the initial outflow of -$400. At a 400 per cent discount rate, the net present value of the project again becomes zero.

The decision criterion based on the internal rate of return is then ambiguous and anomalous. We know that the use of the net present value can solve this dilemma. If the financial manager is not willing to abandon the internal-rate-of-return method even in such situations where it cannot be used, he may be able to adjust the cash flows in a way that the possibility of multiple rates will be eliminated.

There are a number of approaches that do this adjustment. We will discuss two approaches, both of which call for the elimination of the negative cash flow. The first approach requires us to compound forward positive cash flows at the cutoff rate. These compounded cash flows are accumulated forward in time until they eliminate all subsequent negative cash flows. To proceed with Example 5-3, assume that we would accumulate $2,500 at a reinvestment rate of 20 per cent for one year and obtain $3,000. The $3,000 is then added to the $2,500 outlay to obtain a positive cash flow of $500 at the end of two years. We now have a project which has an initial investment of $400 and an expected cash inflow of $500 at the end of two years; the internal rate of return for this project is approximately 12 per cent.

The second approach discounts back the negative cash flows using the cutoff rate until they

74

are at least balanced by positive cash flows of a prior period. With this approach we will discount the $2,500 outlay at 20 per cent for one year and obtain a negative present value of $2,083. The negative cash flow of $2,083 is then added to the first-year cash flow of $2,500 to obtain a positive cash flow of $417. We now have a project which has an initial investment of $400 and an expected cash inflow of $417 at the end of one year; the internal rate of return for this project is 4.25 per cent.

According to Descartes' rule, a project could have as many internal rates of return as the number of sign changes in the direction of annual cash flow.[4] For example, if a project with a cost of $1,000 is expected to produce $6,000, -$11,000 and $6,000 at the end of each year for the next three years, the signs of the cash flow (minus to plus to minus to plus) change three times. Thus, the project has three internal rates of return: 0 per cent, 100 per cent, and 200 per cent. In general, there can be one internal rate of return for each change in sign.

Although multiple reversals of signs are a necessary condition for multiple rates of return, they are not a sufficient condition for such an occurrence. The number of internal rates of return also depends on the magnitude of cash flows. To illustrate, assume that a project has an initial investment of $10,000 and is expected to produce $14,000 at the end of one year and -$1,000 at the end of two years. This project has one internal rate of return (32.5 per cent) despite two reversals of sign.

WHICH METHOD ARE WE TO CHOOSE?

This book advocates the net-present-value method, using the firm's cost of capital to determine the net present value for the following reasons.

1. The net present value is easier to compute than the internal rate of return.

2. If the primary goal of the firm is to maximize the value of its stock, the net-present-

value method leads to the correct decision while the internal-rate-of-return method may lead to the incorrect decision.

3. A single project may have more than one internal rate of return under certain conditions, whereas the same project has just one net present value at a particular rate of discount.

4. Once computed, the internal rate of return remains constant over the entire life of the project. This static assumption is less than realistic during a period of rising interest rates and inflation. Uneven discount rates present no problems when the net-present-value method is used.

5. With the net-present-value method, the implied reinvestment rate reflects an approximation of the opportunity cost for reinvestment. But with the internal-rate-of-return method, the implied reinvestment assumption does not approximate the opportunity cost for reinvestment at all.

Although the net-present-value method is superior theoretically, the internal-rate-of-return method does have certain advantages. The internal rate of return is identical with the yield rate to the maturity of bonds or other securities. Thus, the internal rate of return is directly comparable with the firm's cost of capital. In addition, we do not need to specify a required rate of return in the computations. In other words, it does not require the prior computation of the cost of capital. The prior determination of the cost of capital is frequently cited as one of the advantages for the net-present-value method. But it is, in fact, the method's most controversial and difficult aspect.

FOOTNOTES

1. For details, see Alexander A. Robichek and James C. Van Horn, "Abandonment Value and Capital Budgeting," Journal of Finance (December 1967), p. 577; and John J. Clark, Thomas J. Hindelang, and Robert E. Pritchard, Capital Budgeting: Planning and Control of Capital Expenditures (Englewood Cliffs, N.J.: Prentice-Hall, Inc., 1979), pp. 70-71.

2.   For an extensive discussion of Fisher's
     intersection, see James C.T. Mao, "The
     Internal Rate of Return as a Ranking
     Criterion," The Engineering Economist
     (Summer 1966), pp. 1-13; and Eugene
     F. Fama and Milton H. Miller, The Theory
     of Finance (New York: Holt, Rinehart &
     Winston, Inc., 1972), Chapter 3.

3.   James H. Lorie and Leonard J. Savage, "Three
     Problems in Rationing Capital," The Journal
     of Business (October 1955), p. 237.

4.   See William S. Burnside and Arthur W. Pan-
     ton, The Theory of Equations, Vol. I (New
     York: Dover Publications, Inc., 1960).

CHAPTER 6

MATHEMATICAL PROGRAMMING

It should be clear from Chapter 5 that the net-present-value method gives a better result than the internal-rate-of-return method. However, there are times when the capital budgeting decision is surrounded by many complications which require the use of more sophisticated techniques than the net-present-value method. In the first five chapters, we have examined various types of financial decisions, all of which were designed to maximize stockholder wealth subject to financial and nonfinancial restrictions. The capital budgeting process becomes more complicated as the number of alternatives and the number of constraints increase. This chapter shows how mathematical programming models can be used to facilitate the evaluation of decision alternatives.

CAPITAL RATIONING AND MULTIPERIOD ANALYSIS

When capital rationing constraints are imposed, we rank projects according to the net present value and select them from the top of the list until the available funds have been exhausted. But this technique frequently fails to select projects in a way that the composite net present value of the accepted projects is the greatest among the alternative composite net present values.

Example 6-1 Assume that four projects are under a capital rationing constraint of $12,500. Their costs, present values of net cash flows, and net present values are given in Table 6-1.

Table 6-1 Costs, Present Values of Net Cash Flows, and Net Present Values

Project	Cost	Present Value of Net Cash Flows	Net Present Value	Rank
A	$5,500	$8,500	$3,000	1
B	7,000	9,500	2,500	2
C	4,000	6,000	2,000	3
D	3,000	4,000	1,000	4

Projects A and B have the highest net present value and call for a capital expenditure of $12,500. Thus, these two projects should be accepted according to the net-present-value rule. Their composite net present value is $5,500. Note that Projects A, C, and D also require a total capital expenditure of $12,500, but their combined net present value is $6,000. Therefore, Projects A, C, and D should be accepted over Projects A and B. This limitation becomes even more apparent when many large and small projects are under simultaneous consideration. It may be better to accept several smaller but less profitable projects to fully utilize the capital budget than to accept a larger project which may leave a part of the budget unused.

Another problem arises because the cost of some projects may be spread over several years, thus requiring a multiperiod analysis. If some of the less profitable projects cannot be accepted this year because of capital rationing constraints, it is better to postpone these projects rather than to abandon them once and for all. It is inconsistent to reject a 25 per cent project this year because the budget does not permit but to accept a 10 per cent project next year because the budget will permit. The multiperiod analysis may eliminate this inconsistency.

Capital rationing constraints allow us to select a group of projects that maximize present value subject to a budget constraint. Thus, a capital budget rules out value maximization. Of course, constrained maximization behavior produces a lower value than unconstrained maximization behavior. Mathematical programming models are designed to cope with capital rationing problems, multiperiod problems, and other complications.

MATHEMATICAL PROGRAMMING MODELS

Formulation of Linear Programming Problem

If we have n decision variables and m side constraints, we would have the following type of mathematical formulations:

$$\text{maximize} \quad \sum_{j=1}^{n} f_j x_j \tag{6-1}$$

$$\text{subject to} \quad \sum_{j=1}^{n} d_{ij} x_j \leq e_i \quad \text{(for } i = 1, 2, \ldots, m) \tag{6-2}$$

$$\text{and} \quad x_j \geq 0 \quad \text{(for } j = 1, 2, \ldots, n) \tag{6-3}$$

where d_{ij}, e_i, f_j = given constants

    Σ = Greek letter capital sigma, which means "the sum of"

    x_j = decision variables

    m = number of constraints

    n = number of decision variables

Equation (6-1) is called the objective function; Equation (6-2) represents a set of linear inequalities called side constraints; and Equation (6-3) is the nonnegative condition. These three components constitute a complete statement of mathematical programming. The given linear programming problem is called the primal problem because the optimal solution indicates the primary relationships of the decision variables in the objective function.

Every primal problem has its dual problem. The dual solution to a given primal problem is important because it contains a significant economic meaning and important mathematical properties. To understand better the properties of the dual problem, it is appropriate to find the mathematical relationship in the formulation of the dual problem. If we call Equations (6-1), (6-2), and (6-3) the primal problem, its dual problem consists of Equations (6-4), (6-5), and (6-6):

$$\text{minimize} \quad \sum_{i=1}^{m} e_i y_i \tag{6-4}$$

$$\text{subject to} \quad \sum_{i=1}^{m} d_{ij} y_i \geq f_j \quad \text{(for } j = 1, 2, \ldots, n) \tag{6-5}$$

81

and $\qquad y_i \geq 0 \quad$ (for $i = 1, 2, \ldots, m$) $\quad$ (6-6)

As an illustration, consider the following pair of problems:

$$
\left.
\begin{array}{ll}
\text{maximize} & 8x_1 + 10x_2 + 18x_3 \\
\text{subject to} & 2x_1 + 2x_2 + 4x_3 \leq 32 \\
& 14x_1 + 10x_2 + 6x_3 \leq 50 \\
\text{and} & x_1 \geq 0 \quad x_2 \geq 0 \quad x_3 \geq 0
\end{array}
\right\} \text{ \underline{Primal}}
$$

$$
\left.
\begin{array}{ll}
\text{minimize} & 32y_1 + 50y_2 \\
\text{subject to} & 2y_1 + 14y_2 \geq 8 \\
& 2y_1 + 10y_2 \geq 10 \\
& 4y_1 + 6y_2 \geq 18 \\
\text{and} & y_1 \geq 0 \quad y_2 \geq 0 \quad y_3 \geq 0
\end{array}
\right\} \text{ \underline{Dual}}
$$

The pair of problems shows the following relationships:

1. The jth column of coefficients in the primal problem is the same as the jth row of coefficients in the dual problem.

2. The row of coefficients of the primal objective function is the same as the column of constants on the right-hand side of the dual problem.

3. The column of constants on the right-hand side of the primal problem is the same as the row of coefficients of the dual objective function.

4. The direction of the inequalities and sense of optimization are reversed in the pair of problems.

HISTORICAL DEVELOPMENT

An article published in 1955 by Lorie-Savage was first to point out the inadequacies of tradi-

82

tional project evaluation techniques, especially the internal-rate-of-return method, to cope with capital rationing constraints.[1] They discussed the following three problems:

1. Given a firm's cost of capital and a management policy of using this cost to identify acceptable investment proposals, which group of "independent" investment proposals should the firm accept?

2. Given a fixed sum of money to be used for capital investment, what group of investment proposals should be undertaken?

3. How should a firm select the best among mutually exclusive alternatives?[2]

They overcame problems 1 and 3 by using the net-present-value method rather than the internal-rate-of-return method. They unsuccessfully attempted to overcome problem 2 by means of "generalized Lagrange multipliers." Although they did not develop a mathematical programming technique to deal with capital budgeting problems, the breakdown of their approach opened doors to various mathematical programming techniques for solving capital budgeting problems.

The possibility that the work of Lorie-Savage could be handled in a linear programming model was first recognized by Charnes, Cooper, and Miller.[3] Their basic idea was to include a capital rationing constraint in the firm's financial planning model; optimize total yield using a linear programming model; determine the firm's optimal capital structure by parametric variations of capital rationing constraints; and use marginal values from the dual problem to improve the objective function of its primal problem.

Triggered by these two studies, Weingartner developed a programming model to solve capital budgeting problems under conditions of certainty.[4] His model for finding the optimal combination of independent projects under the capital rationing constraint can be stated as follows:

$$\text{maximize} \quad \sum_{j=1}^{n} b_j x_j \qquad\qquad (6-7)$$

$$\text{subject to} \quad \sum_{j=1}^{n} c_{jt} x_j \leq C_t \quad (\text{for } t = 1, 2, \ldots, T) \qquad (6-8)$$

$$\text{and} \quad 0 \leq x_j \leq 1 \qquad\qquad (6-9)$$

where b_j = net present value of Project j

x_j = fraction of Project j accepted

c_{jt} = net investment outlay required for project j in period t

C_t = capital rationing constraint in period t

n = total number of projects under consideration.

This linear programming model overcomes one of the major limitations of the traditional discounted cash-flow approaches, which is their inability to deal with all combinations of projects simultaneously. This model with a condition of $0 \leq x_j \leq 1$ is used to set a participation limit on every project accepted. Thus, the model indicates precisely what portion of each project should be undertaken to maximize total yield. Weingartner also developed the dual problem to this model and discussed the important economic meanings of both shadow prices and dual slack variables.[5]

The values of the dual decision variables are called shadow prices or imputed costs. This value represents the amount by which management could increase the total net present value by relaxing one unit in the financial constraints. To solve a linear programming problem using the simplex method, all the inequalities (side constraints) must be converted into equalities by adding arbitrary variables called slack variables to the smaller sides of the inequalities.

One problem with this model, however, is its inability to accomplish the elimination of fractional projects from the optimal solution for indivisible projects. This is a serious shortcoming of the model for capital investment projects because they are usually indivisible. Weingartner restated the Lorie-Savage problem as a zero-one integer programming model, which overcomes that difficulty:

maximize $\quad \sum_{j=1}^{n} b_j x_j$ $\qquad\qquad$ (6-10)

subject to $\quad \sum_{j=1}^{n} c_{jt} x_j \leq C_t$ (for $t = 1, 2, \ldots, T$) (6-11)

and $\qquad x_j = (0,1)$ $\qquad\qquad$ (6-12)

This zero-one integer programming model [Equations (6-10), (6-11), and (6-12)], differs in only one aspect from the earlier linear programming model [Equations (6-7), (6-8), and (6-9)]. That is, an integer constraint has been added to the latter programming model, restricting the value of x_j to either 0 or 1. Zero (0) indicates that an investment project is rejected entirely, whereas one (1) indicates that an investment project is accepted entirely. Remember that in the earlier model x_j was an amount between 0 and 1 or fraction of Project j accepted.

Weingartner's restated model may be rewritten as follows:

maximize $\quad \sum_{j=1}^{n} \sum_{t=1}^{T} \dfrac{a_{jt}}{(1 + r)^t} x_j$ $\qquad\qquad$ (6-13)

subject to $\quad \sum_{j=1}^{n} \sum_{t=1}^{T} c_{jt} \leq C_t$ $\qquad\qquad$ (6-14)

and $\qquad x_j = (0,1)$ $\qquad\qquad$ (6-15)

where a_{jt} = cash flow from Project j during period t

$\qquad r$ = rate of discount

The net present value of b_i in the earlier models is replaced with $a_{jt}/(1 + r)^t$, which simply means that cash flow a_{jt} is discounted at r rate. Weingartner then extended his zero-one integer programming model to allow for mutually exclusive projects, contingent projects, multiperiod financial constraints, and other specific factors.

LINEAR PROGRAMMING

Before we turn to the linear programming solution of the capital rationing problem, we shall describe the basic assumptions of linear programming models and their graphic solution.

The major assumptions of linear programming (LP) models are as follows:

1. The decision variables are assumed to be continuous. In other words, they can take on fractional values within a relevant range.

2. The objective function and all the side constraints must be linear. That is, the measure of effectiveness and utilization of each resource must be directly and exactly proportional to the level of each individual activity.

3. The activities must be additive: the whole is equal to the sum of the parts. For example, the effectiveness of a system must equal the sum of the system's component effectiveness.

4. The coefficients of the decision variables and the available resources are known with certainty.

5. There should be a finite number of resource restrictions and available alternative activities. A relative scarcity of productive resources creates the need for optimal decision making in business. The LP problem is the optimal allocation of limited resources among alternative activities to achieve a specific business objective.

6. All the decision variables must have non-negative values.

Example 6-1 Assume that a company intends to buy computers and trucks. A computer requires an investment outlay of $2 in each of periods 1 and 2,

whereas a truck requires an outlay of $3 in period
1 and $1 in period 2. The net present values of
both projects are positive: $50 for each computer
and $60 for each truck. These two investment oppor-
tunities are mutually independent and the firm can
invest in more than one computer or truck. The firm
has $18 to invest in period 1 and $12 in period 2.

If we denote the number of computers and trucks
by the letters x_1 and x_2, we can write out the LP
formulation of this problem as follows:

maximize $50x_1 + 60x_2$

subject to $2x_1 + 3x_2 \leq 18$

                 $2x_1 + 1x_2 \leq 12$

and $x_1 \geq 0$ and $x_2 \geq 0$

The first equation is the objective function, which
is the net present value to be earned from operating
computers and trucks. The next two inequalities
represent the budget constraints in periods 1 and
2. The last line restricts the decision maker to
positive investment; no one can buy negative computers or trucks.

A LP problem can easily be solved by a graphic
method when it has only two decision variables. A
LP problem with three decision variables can also
be solved by a graphic method. Because the LP problem with three decision variables requires three
dimensions to illustrate, its presentation is not
as easy as in the problem with two decision variables.
A graphic method is not possible when a LP problem
involves more than three variables because space can
accommodate only three dimensions.

Let us draw three two-dimensional graphs, with
the purchase of computers shown on the horizontal
axis and the purchase of trucks shown on the vertical axis. Figure 6-1a plots the budget constraint
of period 1; Figure 6-1b plots the budget constraint
of period 2; and Figure 6-1c illustrates the budget
constraints of periods 1 and 2.

Figure 6-1 Feasible Purchasing Policies

a. First-Period Constraint

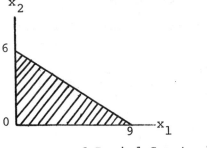

b. Second-Period Constraint

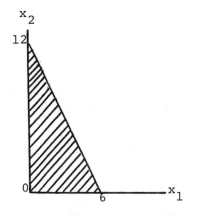

c. Constraints of
    Periods 1 and 2

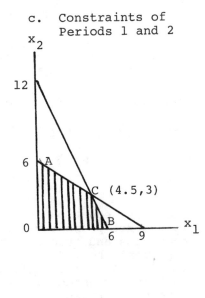

The budget constraint for the first period consists of two parts: an equality part and an inequality part. Thus, the company will spend either
$18 or less than $18 to purchase both computers and
trucks. If the entire budget of $18 is used to pur-
chase only computers, the company will be able to
buy 9 computers. If the entire budget is used to
purchase only trucks, the company will be able to
buy 6 trucks. All the points on the line 69 show
different purchasing programs of computers and trucks
with full utilization of available resources. Together with the nonnegative condition, the inequality
budget constraint for the first period can be represented by the shaded area shown in Figure 6-1a.
Similarly, the shaded area under the second-period

constraint (Figure 6-1b) gives those combinations of computers and trucks which satisfy the second-period constraint.

Because all these constraints must be satisfied simultaneously, they are combined in Figure 6-1c. The shaded area in Figure 6-1c is called the feasible region: it represents all the feasible investment combinations, i.e., those projects which satisfy all the side constraints and the negative condition. Consequently, all points outside the shaded area are not feasible.

The next step is to find a point from the feasible region that maximizes the value of the objective function, i.e., the net present value. To determine the optimal solution, it is important to remember that the optimal solution can only occur at the intersection of two or more constraints or a constraint and either axis; these points are often called the corner points. There are two methods of finding the optimal solution:

1. One could graph the objective function at successively higher values moving farther away from the origin; the optimal solution is found at the point where the objective function is tangent.

2. The coordinates for each corner point are determined algebraically and these values are substituted into the objective function; the corner point with the largest value of the objective function is the optimal solution.

To determine the optimal solution using the first method, let us consider an arbitrary case in which the net present value is $300. Then the objective function is $300 = 50x_1 + 60x_2$. If we set $x_2 = 0$, then $300 = 50x_1 + 60(0)$ or $x_1 = 6$. If we set $x_1 = 0$, then $300 = 50(0) + 60x_2$ or $x_2 = 5$. A straight line P_1 in Figure 6-2 is obtained by connecting two extreme points $x_1 = 6$ and $x_2 = 5$. All points on the line P_1 produce a net present value of $300 with different combinations of x_1 and x_2.

We can draw many new straight lines such as P_2, P_3, and P_4, all of which are parallel to the line P_1. Each of these straight lines represents different combinations of x_1 and x_2 that give the same value for the linear objective function $50x_1 + 60x_2$. The optimal solution occurs at Point C that lies on the highest line P_4 and is in common with the feasible region. Point C is the point at which the objective function is tangent or the point at which the budget constraints of periods 1 and 2 intersect.

Figure 6-2 Optimal Solution

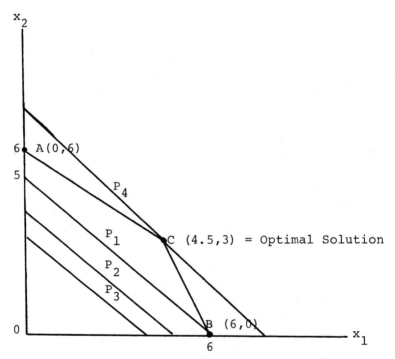

Point C corresponds to an investment in 4.5 computers and 3 trucks, and results in a total net present value of $405. To verify the optimal solution at Point C, we test the objective function $50x_1 + 60x_2$ at each of the three corner points A, B and C.

90

A(0,6):   50(0) + 60(6) = 360

B(6,0):   50(6) + 60(0) = 300

C(4.5,3):50(4.5) + 60(3) = 405

Again, we see that the maximum net present value of $405 is obtained at Point C.

The investment in 4.5 computers and 3 trucks must satisfy the budget constraints.

The First-Period Constraint: 2(4.5) + 3(3) = 18

The Second-Period Constraint: 2(4.5) + 1(3) = 12

Thus, the budget constraints of periods 1 and 2 are fully utilized at Point C.

The full utilization of the budget in both periods indicates that the firm could increase its net present value if additional resources were available for investment in either of the two periods. To illustrate, assume that the company could add $1 to the $18 already available in period 1. Then solve the original problem subject to the constraints:

$2x_1 + 3x_2 \leq 19$

$2x_1 + 1x_2 \leq 12$

This results in a net present value of $422.5, which is an increase of $17.5 over the previous result ($405). Similarly, we can relax the second period constraint by $1 and solve the original problem subject to the constraints:

$2x_1 + 3x_2 \leq 18$

$2x_1 + 1x_2 \leq 13$

The addition of $1 to the second-period budget results in a total net present value of $412.5, which is an increase of $7.5 over the original result ($405).

Lorie-Savage Nine-Project Problem[6]

Let us apply this type of model to the two-period capital rationing problem which was originally considered by Lorie-Savage and later used by Weingartner to illustrate the use of LP to represent the capital rationing problem. Table 6-2 shows the nine-project problem. The present values of the two budget constraints are $50 in period 1 and $20 in period 2. If these nine projects are independent, we can formulate this problem as follows:

Table 6-2 Lorie-Savage Nine-Project Problem

Projects	NPV	Present Value of Outlays	
		Period 1	Period 2
1	$14	$12	$ 3
2	17	54	7
3	17	6	6
4	15	6	2
5	40	30	35
6	12	6	6
7	14	48	4
8	10	36	3
9	12	18	3

$$\text{maximize} \quad NPV = 14x_1 + 17x_2 + 17x_3 + 15x_4 + 40x_5$$
$$+ 12x_6 + 14x_7 + 10x_8 + 12x_9$$

$$\text{subject to} \quad 12x_1 + 54x_2 + 6x_3 + 6x_4 + 30x_5 + 6x_6$$
$$+ 48x_7 + 36x_8 + 18x_9 + s_1 = 50$$

$$3x_1 + 7x_2 + 6x_3 + 2x_4 + 35x_5 + 6x_6$$
$$+ 4x_7 + 3x_8 + 3x_9 + s_2 = 20$$

$$x_1 + s_3 = 1 \quad x_4 + s_6 = 1 \quad x_7 + s_9 = 1$$
$$x_2 + s_4 = 1 \quad x_5 + s_7 = 1 \quad x_8 + s_{10} = 1$$
$$x_3 + s_5 = 1 \quad x_6 + s_8 = 1 \quad x_9 + s_{11} = 1$$

and $\qquad x_j, \ s_i \geq 0 \qquad \left. \begin{array}{l} j = 1, \ 2, \ \ldots, \ 9 \\[4pt] i = 1, \ 2, \ \ldots, \ 11 \end{array} \right\}$

Slack variables s_1 and s_2 represent the unused portion of the budget constraint in periods 1 and 2. Slack variables s_3 through s_{11} represent the per cent of Projects 1 through 9 which are rejected by the company. The sum of x_j and its corresponding slack variable s_{j+2} must be equal to 1.00 or 100 per cent because the entire project must be either accepted or rejected. The solution to this problem is similar in principle to the computer-truck problem, but now requires more calculations. The solution technique called the simplex method examines all feasible sets of projects and chooses the portfolio of projects with a maximum net present value. Such software package as the IBM LINPROG may be used to avoid the tedious calculations required by the simplex method. The solution of the Lorie-Savage Nine-Project Problem by the IBM LINPROG package is shown in Table 6-3.

All variables in the first column of Table 6-3 are called the basic variables, all of which have a value of 1 in one of the rows and blanks everywhere else in the column for that variable. That is, they take on the value shown on the right-hand side (RHS) of the table in the optimal solution. We find the value of the objective function at the corner of the NPV row and the RHS column. Some of the variables in the first row of Table 6-3 (i.e., x_5, x_8, s_1, s_2, etc.) do not appear on the first column of the table. These variables are called the nonbasic variables, all of which do not have a 1 in any one of the rows and blanks everywhere else in the column for that variable. These nonbasic variables take on the value of zero in the optimal solution. The values in the objective-function row are the shadow prices.

Thus, the optimal solution is $x_1 = 1$, $x_2 = 0$, $x_3 = 1$, $x_4 = 1$, $x_5 = 0$, $x_6 = 0.97$, $x_7 = 0.045$, $x_8 = 0$, and $x_9 = 1$, with NPV = \$70.273. This means that we should invest to the extent of 100 per cent in Projects 1, 3, 4, and 9; 97 per cent in Project 6; and 4.5 per cent in Project 7. Substituting these values into the objective function on page 92, we find the net present value from this optimal solution to be \$70.273.

Table 6-3 Optimal Tableau for LP Formulation of Lorie-Savage Nine-Project Problem

Basic Variables	x_1	x_2	x_3	x_4	x_5	x_6	x_7	x_8	x_9	s_1	s_2
x_1	1.0										
x_3			1.0								
x_4				1.0							
x_6		0.455			5.91	1.0				-0.015	0.1818
x_7		1.068			-0.114		1.0	0.75		+0.023	-0.023
x_9									1.0		
s_4		1.0									
s_7		-0.455			1.0						
s_8		-1.068			-5.91					0.015	-0.1818
s_9					0.114			-0.75		-0.023	0.023
s_{10}								1.0			
Z	0	3.41	0	0	29.32	0	0	0.50	0	0.1364	1.864

Table 6-3 Optimal Tableau for LP Formulation of Lorie-Savage Nine-Project Problem

Basic Variables	s_3	s_4	s_5	s_6	s_7	s_8	s_9	s_{10}	s_{11}	RHS
x_1	1.0									1.00
x_3			1.0							1.00
x_4				1.0						1.00
x_6	-0.364		-1.0	-0.273					-0.273	0.969697
x_7	-0.205			-0.091					-0.341	0.045455
x_9									1.0	1.00
s_4		1.0								1.00
s_7					1.0					1.00
s_8	0.364		1.0	0.273		1.0			0.273	0.030303
s_9	0.205			0.091			1.0		0.341	0.954545
s_{10}								1.0		1.00
Z	6.77	0	5.0	10.45	0	0	0	0	3.95	70.273

95

Because slack variables s_1 and s_2 are non-basic variables in the optimal solution, their values are equal to zero. This suggests that their corresponding resources (budget dollars in periods 1 and 2) are completely exhausted in the optimal solution. The shadow price of 0.136 for slack variable s_1 (period 1) indicates that the net present value can be increased by $0.136 if the budget in period 1 is increased from $50 to $51. By the same token, the shadow price of 1.864 for slack variable s_2 (period 2) indicates that the net present value can be increased by $1.864 if the budget in period 2 is increased from $20 to $21. The shadow price for the rejected project shows the amount by which the objective function would decrease if the company were forced to accept the unattractive project. For example, the shadow price of 3.41 for Project 2 indicates that the net present value would decrease by $3.41 if the company were forced to accept Project 2.

INTEGER PROGRAMMING

If investment projects are indivisible, the investment decision process must use integer programming techniques rather than linear programming models. If funds run short, the company could scale down the plans for a proposed new parking lot or building. However, it is generally impossible to buy 5.89 airplanes of a given variety. Where management faces an all-or-none decision problem, the answer must be given to the two possible values--1 for the acceptance of a project in total or 0 for the rejection of the project altogether.

Example 6-2 Assume that a company has $110 to invest in period 1 and $22 in period 2. It has the four projects listed in Table 6-4. All these four projects are indivisible. We can write out the integer

Table 6-4 Net Present Values, Costs, and Budgets for 4 Projects

Project	NPV	Cost in Period 1	Cost in Period 2
x_1	$30	$50	$ 5
x_2	25	60	10
x_3	20	30	10
x_4	10	25	5

programming formulation of this problem on the basis of Equations (6-10), (6-11), and (6-12):

maximize $\quad$ NPV $= 30x_1 + 25x_2 + 20x_3 + 10x_4$

subject to $\quad 50x_1 + 60x_2 + 30x_3 + 25x_4 + s_1 = 110$

$\qquad\qquad\quad 5x_1 + 10x_2 + 10x_3 + 5x_4 + s_2 = 22$

and $\qquad\qquad x_1, \ x_2, \ x_3, \ x_4 = 0 \text{ or } 1$

Solution

It is important to note that there are 16 possible solutions to this particular zero-one integer programming problem. When there are n projects, there are 2^n possible solutions, i.e., an investment program with four projects can have 2^4 or 16 alternative solutions. All these possibilities are divided into three types of solutions: an optimal feasible solution, feasible solutions, and nonfeasible solutions. The optimal solution is the combination of projects which gives the greatest total net present value. The feasible solutions are those that satisfy all the constraints. The nonfeasible solutions are those that fail to satisfy one or more constraints. To find the optimal solution, all the 16 combinations of four projects should be evaluated individually. All these 16 alternative solutions and their total net present values are given in Table 6-5.

Table 6-5   Integer Programming Solution

Combina-tion	Projects x_1	x_2	x_3	x_4	Solu-tion	Total Net Present Value
1	0	0	0	0	FS	$ 0
2	1	0	0	0	FS	30
3	1	1	0	0	FS	55
4	1	1	1	0	NF	–
5	1	1	1	1	NF	–
6	0	1	1	1	NF	–
7	0	0	1	1	FS	30
8	0	0	0	1	FS	10
9	1	0	1	1	OS	60
10	1	0	0	1	FS	40
11	0	1	0	0	FS	25
12	0	1	1	0	FS	45

| Combina- | Projects | | | | Solu- | Total Net |
tion	x_1	x_2	x_3	x_4	tion	Present Value
13	0	1	0	1	FS	35
14	0	0	1	0	FS	20
15	1	1	0	1	NF	-
16	1	0	1	0	FS	50

Note: FS = feasible solutions; OS = optimal solution; and NF = nonfeasible solutions.

Result and Discussion

Table 6-5 shows that there are four nonfeasible solutions, 11 feasible solutions, and an optimal solution. By inspecting the total net-present-value column, we find that Combination 9 gives the largest total net present value. Thus, the combination of Projects 1, 3, and 4 is the optimal solution to this particular investment program. This combination results in a total net present value of $60. Thus, the company must accept Projects 1, 3, and 4; it must reject Project 2.

Some Other Complications

Up to this point, we have assumed that investment projects are mutually independent and they are subject to capital rationing constraints. The integer programming model can be extended to deal with mutually exclusive projects, contingent projects, and many other constraints of these types.

If a set of projects under consideration are mutually exclusive, a nonprogramming computation becomes very difficult in the presence of capital rationing constraints. However, such a set of mutually exclusive projects can easily be handled by the integer programming model:

$$\sum_{j=1}^{J} x_j \leq 1 \qquad (6\text{-}16)$$

where J = number of mutually exclusive projects. It is important to note that at most one project from set J can be accepted. This means that the company could reject the entire set of projects. If it was necessary for the company to accept one project from set J, Equation (6-16) should appear as a strict equality:

$$\sum_{j=1}^{J} x_j = 1 \qquad (6-17)$$

This constraint may be applied to the situation where the company desires to delay a project for one or more years rather than abandon it once and for all. Consider Project A with the following cash flows:

Time	Cash Flows Project A
0	-$1,000
1	+ 800
2	+ 900

The net present value of this project at 10 per cent is $470. If the company wants to delay Project A one or two years, two new Projects A' and A" should be established as follows:

Time	Cash Flows Project A'	Project A"
0	$ 0	$ 0
1	- 1,000	0
2	+ 800	- 1,000
3	+ 900	+ 800
4		+ 900

The net present value to be included in the objective function is $428 for Project A' and $390 for Project A". Because Projects A, A', and A" are mutually exclusive, we can establish the following constraint:

$$x_A + x_{A'} + x_{A''} \leq 1 \qquad (6-18)$$

Contingent projects are a group of projects where the acceptance of one project necessitates the prior acceptance of some other project(s). For

99

example, the acceptance of Project A may be contingent upon the adoption of Project B. This requirement can easily be incorporated into the integer programming model by means of the constraint:

$$x_A \leq x_B \tag{6-19}$$

Because both of these projects are restricted to integer values, we see that only three possibilities are permitted: (1) $x_A = 1$, $x_B = 1$; (2) $x_A = 0$, $x_B = 0$; and (3) $x_A = 0$, $x_B = 1$.

Of course, there are many possible variations to this constraint. For instance, if the acceptance of Project F is contingent upon the adoption of Projects G and H, we should establish the following constraint:

$$2x_F \leq x_G + x_H \tag{6-20}$$

Mutually exclusive projects and contingent projects may be combined to establish some additional constraints. If Projects I and J are mutually exclusive and Project K depends on either Project I or J, two constraints are required to capture the conditions specified:

$$x_I + x_J \leq 1 \tag{6-21}$$

$$x_K \leq x_I + x_J \tag{6-22}$$

If at most three out of Projects L, M, N, and O can be accepted and the acceptance of Project Q is contingent upon the adoption of two projects from the set, two constraints are necessary to relate these conditions:

$$x_L + x_M + x_N + x_O \leq 3 \tag{6-23}$$

$$2x_Q \leq x_L + x_M + x_N + x_O \tag{6-24}$$

Complementary projects are a set of projects where the acceptance of one project increases the cash flows of one or more other projects. For example, the simultaneous acceptance of Projects R

and S will reduce the cost by 5 per cent and increase the net cash flow by 10 per cent. To handle.
this problem, a new project (call it RS) would be
constructed with its cost equal to 95 per cent of
the cost for Project R plus Project S and its net
cash flows equal to 110 per cent of those for Project R plus Project S. In addition, we would need
the following constraint to avoid the acceptance
of Projects R and S as well as Project RS:

$$x_R + x_S + x_{RS} \leq 1 \qquad (6\text{-}25)$$

A minimum accounting rate of return is an important goal to many business firms. The accounting rate of return is an annual dollar profit as a
per cent of project cost. If projects are required
to meet a minimum accounting rate of return for acceptance, we merely add another constraint to the
integer programming model:

$$\sum_{j=1}^{n} \sum_{t=1}^{T} e_{jt} x_j \geq \sigma \sum_{j=1}^{n} \sum_{t=1}^{T} c_{jt} x_j$$

$$\sum_{j=1}^{n} \sum_{t=1}^{T} (\sigma c_{jt} - e_{jt}) x_j \leq 0 \qquad (6\text{-}26)$$

where e_{jt} = expected rate of return from Project j
during period t

σ = minimum accounting rate of return

Example 6-3   Assume that a holding company has six
investment projects under consideration. Their net
present values, cost commitments, and accounting
rates of return are given in Table 6-6. The following additional assumptions exist:

1. The company has $160 to invest in year 1
and $20 in year 2.

2. The company requires the second-year profit to be at least 20 per cent of the first-year cost.

3. Of the set of Projects 11, 12, and 22, at
most two can be accepted.

101

Table 6-6   Net Present Values, Costs, and Profits
for Six Projects

Subsid-iary	Proj-ect	NPV	1st Year Cost	2nd Year Cost	2nd Year Accounting Profits
1	1	$20	$10	$ 3	$ 3
	2	60	80	0	20
2	1	20	10	10	2
	2	15	50	5	7
3	1	25	50	5	10
	2	20	30	5	10

4. Projects 11 and 22 are mutually exclusive, but one of the two must be accepted.

5. Project 12 cannot be accepted unless both Projects 11 and 31 are accepted.

6. The simultaneous acceptance of Projects 22 and 32 will decrease their total costs by 2 per cent and increase their composite net present value by 3 per cent.

7. Project 31 can be delayed for one year. If so, the same costs will be required, but the net present value will drop to $10.

To write out the integer programming formulation of this problem, we need two new decision variables: x_{41} is a decision variable to denote the simultaneous acceptance of Projects 22 and 32 and x_{42} is a decision variable to denote the delay of Project 31 for one year. The complete statement of our integer programming problem is

maximize $NPV = 20x_{11} + 60x_{12} + 20x_{21} + 15x_{22}$

$+ 25x_{31} + 20x_{32} + 36.05x_{41} + 10x_{42}$

subject to $10x_{11} + 80x_{12} + 10x_{21} + 50x_{22}$

$+ 50x_{31} + 30x_{32} + 78.4x_{41} + 0x_{42} \geq 160$

$$3x_{11} + 0x_{12} + 10x_{21} + 5x_{22}$$
$$+ 5x_{31} + 5x_{32} + 9.8x_{41} + 50x_{42} \leq 20$$
$$(.20x10-3)x_{11} + (.20x80-20)x_{12} + (.20x10-2)x_{21}$$
$$+ (.20x50-7)x_{22} + (.20x50-10)x_{31} + (.20x30-10)x_{32} \leq 0$$

or

$$-x_{11} - 4x_{12} + 0x_{21} + 3x_{22} + 0x_{31} - 4x_{32} \leq 0$$

$$x_{11} + x_{12} + x_{22} \leq 2 \qquad \text{Assumption 3}$$

$$x_{11} + x_{22} = 1 \qquad \text{Assumption 4}$$

$$2x_{12} \leq x_{11} + x_{31} \qquad \text{Assumption 5}$$

$$x_{22} + x_{32} + x_{41} \leq 1 \qquad \text{Assumption 6}$$

$$x_{31} + x_{42} \leq 1 \qquad \text{Assumption 7}$$

and
$$x_j = (0,1) \quad j=11, 12, \ldots, 42$$

There are 2^6 or 64 possible solutions to this zero-one integer programming problem. The optimal solution yields a total net present value of \$125 with $x_{11} = 1$, $x_{12} = 1$, $x_{21} = 1$, $x_{22} = 0$, $x_{31} = 1$, $x_{32} = 0$, $x_{41} = 0$, and $x_{42} = 0$. Thus, the combination of Projects 11, 12, 21, and 31 is the optimal solution to this investment program. This combination results in a total net present value of \$125 and no other feasible solution is better than this one.

By substituting the zero-one values of the optimal solution in the equations for the first- and second-year budget constraints, we can obtain an unused portion of the budget for each year as follows:

$$10(1) + 80(1) + 10(1) + 50(0) + 50(1) + 30(0) + 78.4(0)$$
$$+ 0(0) \leq 160$$

$$150 \leq 160$$

$$3(1) + 0(1) + 10(1) + 5(0) + 5(1) + 5(0) + 9.8(0)$$
$$+ 50(0) \leq 20; \quad 18 \leq 20$$

103

Thus, an unused portion of the budget is $10 in the first year and $2 in the second year. These two values are slack variables which are used to convert inequality constraints to equalities.

The existence of unutilized funds may result in a loss to the company. This is because any funds have a certain cost whether they are bonds, common stocks, preferred stocks, or retained earnings. Of course, these unused funds can be used for other business purposes such as the investment in marketable securities. However, it appears reasonable to believe that any unutilized portion of the budget will lose money, because the investment in marketable securities or other uses are not likely to earn more than the cost of the funds.[7] We may establish another constraint to incorporate any unused funds into the model:

$$\sum_{j=1}^{n} \sum_{t=1}^{T} c_{jt} x_j + \sum_{t=1}^{T} U_t = \sum_{t=1}^{T} C_t \qquad (6\text{-}27)$$

where U_t = unused portion of the budget in period t.

Evaluation of the Integer Programming Model

Operation researchers and decision scientists have added the integer programming model to the growing body of quantitative methods for capital expenditure analysis. While the model has not been widely applied, it is a valuable technique to select the best combination of investment projects within definite limits on capital resources and other factors.

This technique has many advantages for capital expenditure analysts. Among these is the optimum utilization of limited capital resources within the business firm. The most efficient utilization of financial and nonfinancial resources can be obtained by finding the optimal solution to a well-structured integer programming problem. If well implemented, it can also result in the improved quality of capital investment decisions. A clear picture of the relationships within the objective function and inequality constraints allow the capital expenditure analyst to better understand the multiplicity of variables involved in capital budgeting and their solutions.

104

One must acknowledge, however, that there are a number of practical problems associated with this technique. The model does not allow for uncertainty in the cash flow estimates. If any of the estimates is changed shortly after a set of projects have been selected using the model, management may have to start computation work all over again which may be very costly in terms of time and money. This is because management is using only one equation to select the best set of projects among many alternative projects.

Another limitation of the model has to do with the assumption that the values of the integer programming decision variables must be additive. This means that multiple conflicting goals cannot be incorporated into the objective function of the model. Although the model has an implicit ability to handle these goals by establishing additional constraints, it does not have an explicit ability to deal with multiple goals. Furthermore, the establishment of additional constraints to cope with multiple objectives could make the model unmanageably complex.

The third shortcoming of this model is the solution to a complex integer programming problem. If a relatively small number of projects are involved, we can quickly find an optimal solution by evaluating all combinations of projects individually. However, when there are a large number of projects under simultaneous consideration, it may take an almost endless number of iterations in searching for an optimal solution. Consider an investment program with 25 projects. There are 2^{25} or 33,554,432 solutions. "Integer programming problems can take up to 100 times longer to solve on the computer than the equivalent LP formulation."[8]

The last limitation is the fact that the integer programming decision variables are discrete. Because the marginality concept (dual problem) does not exist for those variables with discrete distributions, integer programming fails to give the important economic meanings of both shadow prices and dual slack variables.

When we compare the advantages of the integer

programming model with its disadvantages, it appears that its advantages exceed its disadvantages. This model along with standard computer programs can become a powerful management tool to solve complex capital budgeting problems.

FOOTNOTES

1. James H. Lorie and Leonard J. Savage, "Three Problems in Rationing Capital," Journal of Business (October 1955), pp. 229-239.

2. Ibid., pp. 229-230.

3. Abraham Charnes, William W. Cooper, and Mefron H. Miller, "The Application of Linear Programming to Financial Budgeting and the Cost of Funds," Journal of Business (January 1959), pp. 20-46.

4. H. Martin Weingartner, Mathematical Programming and the Analysis of Capital Budgeting Problems (Englewood Cliffs, N.J.: Prentice-Hall, Inc., 1968).

5. Linear programming problems with a condition of $0<x_j<1$ or $x_j>0$ have their dual problems. The values of these dual decision variables are called shadow prices. This value represents the amount by which management could increase the total net present value by relaxing one unit in the financial constraints.

Another important concept of the dual problem is its slack variables. The optimal solution to the dual problem results in the certain values of the dual slack variables. This value must be either zero or positive, because a negative value of either decision variable or slack variable is not allowed in the optimal solution. A zero slack variable indicates that there would be no change in the total net present value, regardless of whether the participation limit of a particular project is increased or decreased. A positive slack variable indicates the relative loss in the objective function for each one-unit increase of the accepted project.

This is because an increase in the participation limit of an accepted project would result in a greater reduction in the total net present value than a possible extra gain from this increase.

6. This section draws heavily upon John J. Clark, Thomas J. Hindelang, and Robert E. Pritchard, Capital Budgeting (Englewood Cliffs, N.J.: Prentice-Hall, Inc., 1979), Chapters 12 and 13.

7. See Lawrence J. Gitman, Principles of Managerial Finance (New York: Harper & Row Publishers, Inc., 1976), p. 301.

8. Clark, Hindelang, and Pritchard, Capital Budgeting, p. 238.

CHAPTER 7

GOAL PROGRAMMING

In Chapter 1 the concept of stockholder wealth maximization was carefully established as the primary goal of the firm. This is why in the succeeding chapters we have focused on the net-present-value method. If the primary goal of the firm is to maximize the value of the firm, the correct decision is to accept the project with the highest net present value. The project with the largest net present value makes the greatest net contribution to the value of the firm. It is also important to remember from Chapter 6 that under conditions of certainty, the firm can maximize stockholder wealth by accepting the combination of projects that gives the greatest total net present value.

However, investors and managers are interested in and motivated by many objectives other than stockholder wealth maximization. They include growth and stability of earnings and dividends per share, market share, sales growth, and diversification. Mathematical programming techniques described in Chapter 6 have an implicit ability to handle these multiple goals by establishing additional constraints. But they do not have an explicit ability to deal with multiple goals because of their assumption that the values of decision variables must be additive. Furthermore, the establishment of additional constraints to deal with multiple goals could make the mathematical programming models unmanageably complex.

In recent years, the goal programming approach has been suggested as a model which is capable of coping with multiple conflicting goals. This approach was originally proposed in 1961 by Charnes and Cooper[1] and further developed by Ijiri[2], Lee[3], and Ignizio.[4] With this technique, the objective function is expressed in terms of deviations from the stated goals. Because multiple goals are often in conflict or are achievable only at the expense of other goals, the solution of the goal programming requires the establishment of a hierarchy of importance among these conflicting goals. Goals of different hierarchy levels mean that the higher-level goals must be satisfied first before the lower-level goals are considered.

Goal programming differs from linear programming to the extent that it does not require the translation of multiple goals into a unidimensional objective criterion. It measures these goals in unlike units and treats them in a sequential and/or simultaneous manner. This technique expresses all goals as constraints in a linear programming format. Additional variables known as deviational variables are then added to these constraints to represent deviations from the predetermined goals.

INTRODUCTION

Just like linear programming, goal programming (GP) has three major components: the objective function, constraints, and the nonnegative condition.

The Objective Function

The objective function of a general GP problem may be mathematically stated as follows:

$$\text{minimize} \quad \sum_{i=1}^{n} \sum_{k=1}^{m} h_i P_{ki} (d_i^+ + d_i^-) \qquad (7-1)$$

where h_i = real number or relative weight assigned to goal i

P_{ki} = kth priority assigned to goal i

d_i^+ = positive deviation from goal i

d_i^- = negative deviation from goal i

Equation (7-1) is simply a minimization function of deviational variables (d_i^+ and d_i^-) with certain preemptive priority factors (p_{ki}) and relative weights (h_i).

Relative or Scalar Weight   The objective function of GP allows for relative or scalar weighting. The scalar weight may be assigned to each goal where there are two or more goals on the same priority level. The scalar weight assigned to a particular goal would indicate the relative importance of that goal. Consider a company that operates two plants,

A and B. The company's goal may be to minimize the overtime operation of both plants as much as possible, but its management may desire to assign different weights to the minimization of overtime operation according to the relative overtime-wage level of the two plants. If the overtime-wage level of Plant A is three times as much as that of Plant B, the management may assign 3 to the minimization of overtime operation for Plant A and 1 to the minimization of overtime operation for Plant B. Thus, goals on the same priority level are weighted to allow for the management's preference between goals.

Preemptive Priority Factors   The objective function of GP also allows for ordinal ranking. To achieve the goals according to their importance, positive and/or negative deviations must be ranked according to the preemptive priority factors. These factors indicate the ordinal rankings of various management goals whereby the goals will be optimized. For example, if p_1 represents the highest priority, all other goals are considered only after this goal is achieved as desired. The preemptive priority factors have the following relationship:

$$p_k >>> np_{k+1} \qquad\qquad (7\text{-}2)$$

Equation (7-2) implies that the multiplication of n, no matter how large it may be, cannot make p_{k+1} greater than or equal to p_k.

Deviational Variables   Notations d^+ and d^- represent deviational variables from the desired goal level. The positive deviation from the goal or the overachievement of the goal is represented by d^+. The negative deviation from the goal or the underachievement of the goal is represented by d^-. If the goal is exactly achieved, both deviational variables will be zero. Because the goal can be either overachieved or underachieved, one of the two deviational variables will always be zero and the other will be equal to the size of the deviation from the goal.

The objective function contains the appropriate deviational variable(s) for each goal and these variables depend on the desired action for that goal.

111

There are five practical variations. First, if management does not want to exceed a maximum level of some goal such as cost, the only deviational variable required in the objective function would be d^+. Second, if it desires to achieve a minimum level of some goal such as profit, the only deviational variable required in the objective function would be d^-. Third, if it wants to achieve a specified level of some goal as close as possible, both overachievement and underachievement of the goal would be penalized. Thus, the deviational variables required in the objective function would be $(d^+ + d^-)$. Fourth, if it desires to overachieve an established minimum level of some goal by the greatest possible amount, the maximization attempt would be carried out in two steps. The first step is to achieve the minimum level and the second step is to overachieve the minimum by the greatest possible amount. Hence, the deviational variables required in the objective function would be $(d^- - d^+)$. Fifth, if it wants to underachieve an established maximum level of some goal by the greatest possible amount, the minimization attempt would be carried out in two steps. The first step is to not exceed the maximum level and the second step is to underachieve the maximum by the greatest possible amount. Thus, the deviational variables required in the objective function would be $(d^+ - d^-)$.

Constraints

A set of constraints may be expressed as follows:

$$\text{subject to} \quad \sum_{j=1}^{J} c_j x_j + \sum_{i=1}^{n} (d_i^- - d_i^+) = g_i \qquad (7\text{-}3)$$

where c_j = coefficient of choice variable j (i.e., product or project)

x_j = choice variable j

g_i = desired level of goal i

There are two types of constraints in GP: economic constraints and goal constraints. The economic constraints are those constraints that cannot be violated because they represent resource limitations or restrictions imposed by the decision maker. The economic constraints in GP are the same as those in linear programming. Thus, such a constraint requires only one deviational variable, either the usual slack variable (d^-) or the surplus variable (d^+). However, if one wishes to include both variables in each economic constraint, it is perfectly permissible.

The goal constraints are those constraints that are flexible because they represent managerial policies and desired levels of various objectives sought by the decision maker. They are always specified as strict equalities and thus each goal constraint must contain both deviational variables.

The Nonnegative Condition

The nonnegative condition takes one of the three forms: $x_j \geq 0$, $1 \geq x_j \geq 0$ and $x_j = (0,1)$. A condition of $x_j \geq 0$ can take on any positive value and is used for most managerial decisions other than investment decisions. A condition of $1 \geq x_j \geq 0$ can take on any value between 1 and 0; it is used to evaluate divisible projects such as security investments. A condition of $x_j = (0,1)$ is used to evaluate indivisible projects such as capital investments; zero (0) represents the rejection of an entire project while one (1) represents the acceptance of an entire project.

GOAL PROGRAMMING MODEL FORMULATION

Model formulation is the process of converting a real-world decision problem into a management science model. The formulation of the model is generally more difficult than the solution because of the great advances in standard computer programs. Thus, before we discuss the details of the goal programming solution, we will discuss the formulation of the model with two numerical examples: a typical managerial problem and a typical capital budgeting problem.

Example 7-1 The Lilly Manufacturing Company specializes in the manufacture of two types of television sets, regular and color. The production of either a regular television or a color television requires an average of one hour in the plant. The plant has a normal production capacity of 130 hours a month. Because the market is highly competitive, the monthly maximum sales volumes are expected to be 90 regular television sets and 60 color television sets. The profit margin from the sale of a regular television is $50 and that from the sale of a color television is $150. The president of the company has set the following goals in order of their importance:

P_1: The most important goal is to avoid any underutilization of normal production capacity so that there will be no lay-offs of production workers.

P_2: The second goal is to sell as many tele-vision sets as possible. Because the profit margin of the color television set is three times as much as that of the regular television set, the presi-dent has three times as much desire to achieve sales for color televisions as for regular televisions.

P_3: The third goal is to minimize the over-time operation of the plant as much as possible.

We can write out the goal programming formula-tion of this problem as follows:

$$\text{minimize} \quad P_1 d_1^- + 3P_2 d_2^- + P_2 d_3^- + P_3 d_1^+$$

$$\text{subject to} \quad x_1 + x_2 + d_1^- - d_1^+ \qquad = 130$$

$$x_1 + d_2^- - d_2^+ \qquad = 60$$

$$x_2 + d_3^- - d_3^+ = 90$$

$$\text{and} \quad x_1,\ x_2,\ d_1^-,\ d_1^+,\ d_2^-,\ d_2^+,\ d_3^-,\ d_3^+ \geq 0$$

where d_1^- = underutilization of normal production capacity (200 hours)

114

d_1^+ = overtime operation of the plant

d_2^- = underachievement of sales goal for color television sets

d_2^+ = overachievement of sales goal for color television sets

d_3^- = underachievement of sales goal for regular television sets

d_3^+ = overachievement of sales goal for regular television sets

x_1 = number of color television sets

x_2 = number of regular television sets

The objective function is to minimize deviations from the goals. In this model the value of the deviational variable associated with the highest pre-emptive priority factor is d_1^-. Thus, it must first be minimized to the fullest possible extent. Once this goal is achieved as desired, we then attempt to minimize the value of the deviational variable associated with the second highest priority factor. Although there are two deviational variables to minimize here, they (d_2^- and d_3^-) are on the same priority level. When no further improvement is possible in the second highest goal, we then attempt to minimize the overtime operation of the plant (d_1^+).

The first constraint relates to the operational capacity restriction. Because this goal was given the lowest priority, it is quite possible that the production of both television sets may take more than the set production capacity of 130 hours. The second and third constraints relate to the sales goal. Because the company cannot sell more than the stated numbers (60 color televisions and 90 regular televisions), positive deviations from the goals are not essential, even though we included them in the constraints.

Example 7-2 Assume that a company is evaluating four projects with the characteristics listed in Table 7-1.

115

Table 7-1   Characteristics of Four Projects

Project	NPV	Cost in Year 1	Cost in Year 2	Skilled Workers	Profit in Year 1	Profit in Year 2	Profit in Year 3
x_1	$40	$ 70	$25	10 men	$15	$17	$20
x_2	27	40	18	5	10	15	5
x_3	60	90	30	15	30	25	15
x_4	49	85	25	12	25	23	10
Amount Available		$120	$60	25 men			
Desired Goal	$95				$40	$30	$25

116

The president of the company has set the following goals in order of their importance:

P_1: The first goal is to achieve a minimum profit of $40 in year 1.

P_2: The second goal is to achieve a minimum profit of $30 in year 2.

P_3: The third goal is to achieve a minimum profit of $25 in year 3.

P_4: The fourth goal is to overachieve an established minimum net present value of $95 by the greatest possible amount.

We can write out the GP formulation of this problem as follows:

Objective function:

minimize $\quad P_1 d_4^- + P_2 d_5^- + P_3 d_6^- + P_4 (d_7^- - d_7^+)$

Economic constraints:

subject to
$$70x_1 + 40x_2 + 90x_3 + 85x_4 + d_1^- = 120$$
$$25x_1 + 18x_2 + 30x_3 + 25x_4 + d_2^- = 60$$
$$10x_1 + 5x_2 + 15x_3 + 12x_4 + d_3^- = 25$$

Goal constraints:

subject to
$$15x_1 + 10x_2 + 30x_3 + 25x_4 + d_4^- - d_4^+ = 40$$
$$17x_1 + 15x_2 + 25x_3 + 23x_4 + d_5^- - d_5^+ = 30$$
$$20x_1 + 5x_2 + 15x_3 + 10x_4 + d_6^- - d_6^+ = 25$$
$$40x_1 + 27x_2 + 60x_3 + 49x_4 + d_7^- - d_7^+ = 95$$

Nonnegative condition:

$$1 \geq x_j \geq 0 \text{ and } d_i^-, d_i^+ \geq 0$$

GOAL PROGRAMMING SOLUTION FOR CAPITAL BUDGETING PROBLEMS

117

The objective of a goal programming solution is to achieve a given set of goals to the fullest possible extent. The solution must be achieved within the given constraints and according to the management's priority for the goals. GP problems are solved in the same manner as linear programming problems. Two basic solution methods are the graphical method and the simplex method. A GP problem can be solved by a graphical method when it has only two or three choice variables. More complex problems with more than three choice variables can be solved by the simplex method or computerized algorithms.

Example 7-3   Assume that a company has $60 to invest in year 1. Its two projects under consideration have the characteristics listed in Table 7-2.

Table 7-2   Characteristics of Two Projects

Project	Cost in Year 1	NPV	Profit in Year 1	Profit in Year 2
x_1	$ 50	$21	$20	$22
x_2	80	90	8	14

The president of the company has set the following goals in order of their importance:

p_1: The first goal is to achieve a minimum profit of $12 in year 1

p_2: The second goal is to achieve a minimum profit of $16 in year 2

p_3: The third goal is to overachieve the minimum net present value of $15.

We can write out the GP formulation of this example as follows:

minimize $p_1 d_2^- + p_2 d_3^- + p_3 (d_4^- - d_4^+)$

subject to $50x_1 + 80x_2 + d_1^- = 60$

$20x_1 + 8x_2 + d_2^- - d_2^+ = 12$

118

$$22x_1 + 14x_2 + d_3^- - d_3^+ = 16$$

$$21x_1 + 90x_2 + d_4^- - d_4^+ = 15$$

and $\quad 1 \geqslant x_j \geqslant 0$ and $d_i^-,\ d_i^+ \geqslant 0$

The shaded area in Figure 7-1 represents the initial feasible region. It is obtained by drawing the lines which represent the first-year budget constraint and the nonnegative condition of $1 \geqslant x_j \geqslant 0$. These constraints will be satisfied as long as the company invests in the combination of projects x_1 and x_2 within the shaded area. Figures 7-2 through 7-4 plot the three goal constraints. The region with the deviation to be penalized is eliminated as we move from one priority to the next lower priority. To maximize the total net present value, first plot the third goal with a net present value of \$15 in Figure 7-4 and then move as far above the line for the third goal as possible. The optimal solution of $x_1 = 0.415$ and $x_2 = 0.49$ is obtained at the point at which the first-year budget constraint and the second-goal constraint intersect.

MODIFIED GOAL PROGRAMMING

Up to this point our discussion focused on the minimization of the deviations from the stated goals. Under certain assumptions, however, we can modify the GP model in a way that the objective function represents the maximization of the deviations from the stated goals.[5]

The modified GP model requires four basic assumptions. First, all goals must be on the same priority level. This assumption effectively removes all the preemptive priority factors from the GP model. Second, goals on the same priority level must be weighted to allow for the management's preference among goals. That is, the relative importance of each goal must be specified by the management. Third, the relative importance of each goal or its scalar weight must be made on a comparable basis among all other goals. Fourth, the unit denominations of the deviational variables must be made on a comparable basis in the objective function.

119

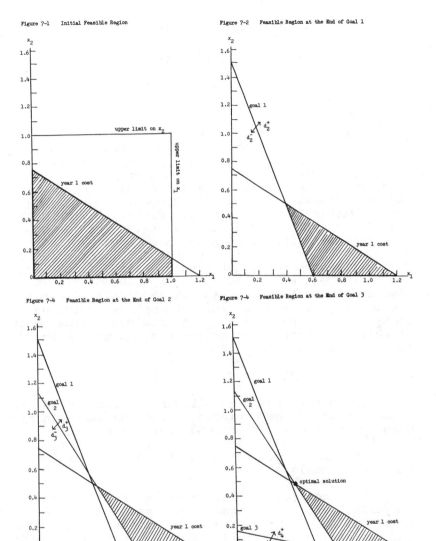

Figure 7-1   Initial Feasible Region

Figure 7-2   Feasible Region at the End of Goal 1

Figure 7-4   Feasible Region at the End of Goal 2

Figure 7-4   Feasible Region at the End of Goal 3

120

Because the first two assumptions have been discussed in the preceding sections of this chapter,
there is no point to rediscuss them. But the last
two assumptions require further elaboration. The
third assumption is designed to determine those constraints which do not permit both negative and positive deviations. To illustrate, assume that the company desires to minimize an established maximum payback period and to maximize an established minimum
net present value. It is important to note that the
company wants to overachieve both of these goals.
Let us further assume that the overachievement of
the minimum net present value (d_1) is four times as
important as the overachievement of the maximum payback period (d_2). We then can state the objective
function of this GP example as follows:

$$\text{maximize} \quad 4d_1^+ + d_2^- \qquad\qquad (7\text{-}4)$$

It should be emphasized that the two deviational
variables d_1^- and d_2^+ are excluded from Equation (7-4)
because the company is interested only in the overachievement of the goals.

The fourth assumption is designed to assure
that after the scalar weights are added to the objective function, a true weighting of goals is obtained. Consider the preceding example. The net
present value is expressed in dollars, while the
payback period is stated in years. They must be
expressed in comparable terms. However, a $1 in-
crease in net present value is hardly comparable to
a one-year decrease in payback period. To overcome this problem, the deviation from the maximum
payback period may be specified in sixths of a
year, while the deviation from the minimum net
present value may be stated in thousands of dollars. The combination of these unit denominations
with our scalar weights yields an objective function that a $4,000 increase in the net present
value is equal to a two-month decrease in the payback period.

The modified GP model maximizes the deviational
variables and sets all goals equal to zero. Thus,
Equations (7-1) and (7-3) are modified as follows:

$$\text{maximize} \qquad \sum_{i=1}^{n} h_i (d_i^+ - d_i^-) \qquad\qquad (7\text{-}5)$$

$$\text{subject to} \qquad \sum_{j=1}^{J} c_j x_j + \sum_{i=1}^{n} (d_i^- - d_i^+) = 0 \qquad (7\text{-}6)$$

where h_i = scalar weight assigned to goal i

$\quad\quad c_j$ = coefficient of choice variable j

$\quad\quad x_j$ = choice variable j

Example 7-4 The financial manager must evaluate the three indivisible projects listed in Table 7-3.

Table 7-3 Characteristics of Three Projects

Project	Initial Cost ($)	NPV ($100)	Average Rate of Return (%)	Payback Period (month)
x_1	300	150	30	60
x_2	240	135	36	30
x_3	270	90	24	15

The multiple goals of net present value, average rate of return, and payback are weighted as 50 per cent, 30 per cent, and 20 per cent, respectively. The financial manager has an absolute fund limitation of $600.

We can write out the GP formulation of this problem as follows:

$$\text{maximize} \qquad 50 d_2^+ + 30 d_3^+ - 20 d_4^+$$

$$\text{subject to} \qquad 300 x_1 + 240 x_2 + 270 x_3 + d_1^- = 600$$

$$150 x_1 + 135 x_2 + 90 x_3 - d_2^+ = 0$$

$$30 x_1 + 36 x_2 + 24 x_3 - d_3^+ = 0$$

$$60x_1 + 30x_2 + 15x_3 - d_4^+ = 0$$

and $\quad x_j = (0, 1)$ and $d_i \geq 0$

It is important to note that there are 2^3 or 8 possible solutions. If implicit enumeration is used to solve this problem, all possible feasible solutions must be determined to find the combination of goals that gives the greatest objective function value. All the possible feasible solutions and their objective function values are given in Table 7-4. The values of the deviational variables are obtained by substituting the values of the project variables for each feasible solution into the appropriate constraints. These values are then substituted into the objective function to determine the objective function values. By inspecting the objective function value column, we find that the combination of Projects 1 and 2 is the optimal solution to this particular investment program.

Table 7-4   Integer Goal Programming Solution

Feasible Solutions	Initial Cost	d_2	d_3	d_4	Objective Function Value
x_1	$300	$150	$30	$60	7,200
x_2	240	135	36	30	7,230
x_3	270	90	24	15	4,920
x_1, x_2	540	285	66	90	14,430
x_1, x_3	570	240	54	75	12,120
x_2, x_3	510	225	60	45	12,150

FOOTNOTES

1.   A. Charnes and W.W. Cooper, Management Models and Industrial Applications of Linear Programming (New York: John Wiley & Sons, Inc., 1961).

2.   Y. Ijiri, Management Goals and Accounting for

Control (Chicago: Rand-McNally, 1965).

3. Sang M. See, Goal Programming for Decision
    Analysis (Philadelphia: Auerbach Publish-
    ing Co., 1972).

4. James P. Ignizio, Goal Programming and Ex-
    tensions (Lexington, Mass.: Lexington
    Books, 1977).

5. This section draws heavily upon Jerome S.
    Osteryoung, Capital Budgeting (Columbus,
    Ohio: Grid Publishing, Inc., 1979), pp.
    264-273.

PART THREE   CAPITAL BUDGETING UNDER UNCERTAINTY

CHAPTER 8

RISK ANALYSIS

To develop the key concepts and techniques of capital budgeting in a systematic manner, the riskiness of projects was not treated explicitly in the preceding chapters. Very few financial variables are known with certainty. Investors and financial managers are basically risk averters. This chapter considers the basic concept of risk and a number of approaches to risk analysis for individual projects.

THE BASIC CONCEPT OF RISK

In the preceding chapters, we assumed that cash flows are known with certainty. If we could always describe a project as a unique set of cash flows, it would be possible to make relatively simple and straightforward capital budgeting decisions. The shortcomings of such an assumption are obvious. It is extremely difficult to specify unique cash flows because we have an imperfect ability to predict future events that will affect the cash flows. If we do not know in advance exactly which of these events will occur, we have to estimate a number of possible cash flows for each period in the future.

The most appropriate classification of decisions may be based on the amount of information at the decision maker's disposal. Decision problems can be classified into certainty, risk, and uncertainty, depending on the amount of information available. Decisions are made under risk when the decision maker knows all the available alternatives and can assign probabilities to the set of possible consequences for each alternative. Decisions are made under uncertainty when the decision maker knows all the available alternatives but does not have enough information to assign probabilities to the set of possible consequences for each alternative. Thus, a distinction can be made between risk and uncertainty, but this distinction is ignored for our purposes; risk and uncertainty are used interchangeably in this chapter.

Example 8-1 Assume that Projects A and B have an

equal cost of $600 at time 0 and expected net cash flows of $500 in each of the next three years. Let us further assume that the probability distributions of net cash flows on these two projects were those shown in Figure 8-1.

Figure 8-1 Comparison of Probability Distributions

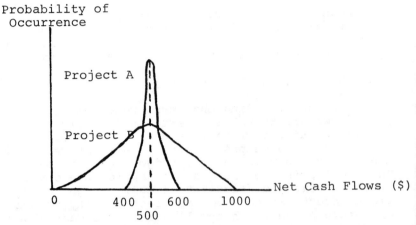

Without the introduction of risk, we would rank these two projects equally. Although Projects A and B have the same expected value, they have different variabilities of their possible returns. In general, the narrower the probability distribution, the less the deviation of actual outcome from the expected value. Project A has a narrower probability distribution than Project B. Hence, Project B is the riskier investment.

INTRODUCTION TO RISK ANALYSIS

Standard probability theory can be used to evaluate investment risk. This approach is based on the assumption that the investor identifies a large number of possible payoffs for a project and that he assigns a probability to each of these possibilities. A probability represents the likelihood that an event will occur; it can take on any value between 0 and 1. A probability of 1 means that an event is certain to occur. A probability of 0 means that an event will not occur. The sum of the probabilities for a set of mutually exclusive

126

and completely exhaustive events must be equal to 1.

Under conditions of uncertainty, we must analyze two factors for capital budgeting decisions, the expected value for a project and its risk. The expected value of a probability distribution is defined as follows:

$$\bar{R}_t = \sum_{i=1}^{n} R_{it} P_{it} \qquad (8\text{-}1)$$

where $\bar{R}_t$ = expected value of cash flows in period t

$\qquad R_{it}$ = return associated with the ith event in period t

$\qquad P_{it}$ = probability of the ith event in period t

The risk may be described by the dispersion of alternative returns around the expected value. The conventional measure of dispersion is the standard deviation, which is defined as follows:

$$\sigma_t = \sqrt{\sum_{i=1}^{n} (R_{it} - \bar{R}_t)^2 P_{it}} \qquad (8\text{-}2)$$

where σ_t is the standard deviation in period t.

Example 8-2 Assume that Project C has the following probability distributions of net cash flows in year 1:

Possible Event	Probability of Each Event	Net Cash Flow for Each Event
Boom	0.10	$1,100
Normal	0.80	1,000
Recession	0.10	900

The expected value of Project C and its standard deviation are computed as follows:

$$\bar{R}_1 = (\$1,100)(0.10) + (\$1,000)(0.80) + (\$900)(0.10)$$

$$= \$1,000$$

$$\sigma_1^2 = (\$1,100 - \$1,000)^2(0.10) + (\$1,000 - \$1,000)^2(0.80)$$

$$+ (\$900 - \$1,000)^2(0.10) = \$2,000$$

$$\sigma_1 = \sqrt{\sigma_1^2} = \$44.73$$

Another absolute measure of dispersion is the semivariance. It is similar to the variance but considers only deviations below the expected value. Because most businessmen are primarily concerned with negative deviations, the semivariance is very appealing to them. The semivariance is defined as:[1]

(8-3)

$$SV_t = \sum_{x=1}^{k}(R_{xt} - \bar{R}_t)^2 P_{xt}$$

where SV_t = semivariance in period t

   x = index set which includes all values of the random variables less than the expected value

   k = number of outcomes which are less than the expected value

Thus, the semivariance of Project C is

$$SV_1 = (\$900 - \$1,000)^2 0.10$$

$$= \$1,000$$

A measure of relative dispersion is the coefficient of variation, which is the standard deviation divided by the expected value. In other words, it shows the amount of risk per dollar of expected value. The coefficient of variation for Project C is 0.04473 ($44.73 ÷ $1,000). In general, the coefficient of variation is a better measure of risk than the standard deviation for projects whose returns are stated in dollars. The standard deviation should be used to measure risk only for those

128

projects whose returns are stated as percentages.

RISK ANALYSIS: CORRELATION OF CASH FLOWS OVER TIME

In this section, we consider ways to measure the importance of risk in capital budgeting under varying assumptions as to cash-flow behavior. Interperiod cash flows can be completely independent, perfectly correlated or mixed. The expected value of possible net-present values for a project is

$$(8-4)$$

$$\overline{NPV} = \sum_{t=1}^{n} \frac{\bar{R}_t}{(1 + k)^t} - C_o$$

where $\overline{NPV}$ = expected value of possible net-present values for a project

$\bar{R}_t$ = expected value of net cash flows in period t, which is computed by Equation (8-1)

k = discount rate

C_o = present value of the net cash investment

It is important to recognize that Equation (8-4) is used to calculate the expected value of a project regardless of correlation of interperiod cash flows.

Assumption of Independence

With independence of cash flows over time, successive periods' cash flows are not related in any systematic manner. Such an independent condition may exist in highly competitive markets where trade names and advertising do not exist. Given the assumption of independence of cash flows for various future periods, the standard deviation of the entire project is

$$(8-5)$$

$$\sigma = \sqrt{\sum_{t=1}^{n} \frac{\sigma_t^2}{(1 + k)^{2t}}}$$

where σ = standard deviation of possible net present

129

values for a project

σ_t = standard deviation of possible net cash flows in period t, which is computed by Equation (8-2)

Example 8-3 Assume that Project D has an initial cost of $3,000 and the firm's cost of capital is 10 per cent. Project D has the following net cash flows:

Period 1		Period 2	
Probability	Cash Flow	Probability	Cash Flow
0.20	$4,000	0.40	$4,000
0.20	3,000	0.30	3,000
0.50	2,000	0.10	2,000
0.10	1,000	0.20	1,000

The expected value of net cash flows is $2,500 in period 1 and $2,900 in period 2. The expected NPV of Project D at 10 per cent is

$$\overline{NPV} = \frac{\$2,500}{(1.10)^1} + \frac{\$2,900}{(1.10)^2} - \$3,000$$

$$= \$1,668$$

The standard deviation of net cash flows is $922 in period 1 and $1,136 in period 2. Under the assumption of mutual independence of net cash flows over time, the standard deviation of Project D is

$$\sigma = \sqrt{\frac{(\$922)^2}{(1.10)^2} + \frac{(\$1,136)^2}{(1.10)^4}}$$

$$= \sqrt{\$1,583,578}$$

$$= \$1,258$$

Assumption of Dependence

In the previous section, we assumed that net cash flows from one future period to another are completely independent. For most investment proj-

ects, however, this assumption of complete independence is very questionable. An extremely un-
favorable or favorable outcome in the early life
of a project affects its later outcome. Under the
assumption that net cash flows are perfectly correlated over time, the net cash flow in period t
depends entirely on what happened in previous
periods. That is, given the outcome of cash flows
in period 1, all subsequent cash flows are predetermined. Such a perfect correlation among cash
flows would exist in monopolistically competitive
markets where strongly recognized brand names,
high-pressure advertising, and limited entry exist.
If perfect correlation is assumed, the standard
deviation of a project is computed as follows:

$$\sigma = \sum_{t=1}^{n} \frac{\sigma_t}{(1 + k)^t} \tag{8-6}$$

To illustrate, consider Project D in Example
8-3. Because the standard deviation of net cash
flows for the project was $922 in period 1 and
$1,136 in period 2, the standard deviation of the
entire project is

$$\sigma = \frac{\$922}{(1.10)^1} + \frac{\$1,136}{(1.10)^2}$$

$$= \$1,776$$

Assumption of Mixed Correlation

A project can have mixed correlation where
some parts of its annual cash flows are perfectly
correlated and other parts are independent. One
method for dealing with the problem of mixed correlation is with a series of conditional probability
distributions. Given the assumption of mixed correlation of cash flows over time, the standard
deviation of a project is

$$\sigma = \sqrt{\sum_{i=1}^{n} (NPV_i - \overline{NPV})^2 P_i} \tag{8-7}$$

where NPV_i = net present value associated with series
i of net cash flows

131

$$\overline{NPV} = \text{expected net present value}$$

$$P_i = \text{probability of the ith series}$$

Example 8-4   Assume that in year 1, Project E with a
cost of $300 has a 0.5 chance to earn $200 and a 0.5
chance to earn $100. Given a net cash flow of $200
in year 1, the probabilities are 0.4 that the project will yield $400 in year 2 and 0.6 that it will
yield $300. If a net cash flow of $100 is given in
year 1, the probabilities are 0.4 that the project
will produce $200 in year 2 and 0.6 that it will
produce $100.

Table 8-1 shows that there are four possible
cash-flow series. Once the probabilities have been

Table 8-1   Illustration of Conditional Probability
Distribution

| Year 1 | | Year 2 | | Joint | |
Initial Probability P(1)	Net Cash Flow	Conditional Probability P(2/1)	Net Cash Flow	Proba- bility P(1,2)	Cash Flow Series
0.5	$200	0.4	$400	0.2	1
		0.6	$300	0.3	2
0.5	$100	0.4	$200	0.2	3
		0.6	$100	0.3	4

assigned to the possible net cash flows, the next step
is to determine the probability of each series or the
joint probability. A joint probability is the likelihood that two or more events will occur simultaneously
or successively. Thus, the probability of 0.2 for
series 1 represents the joint probability that Project E will earn $200 in year 1 and that it will earn
$400 in year 2. Column 5 of Table 8-1 carries out
this computation for all four possible cash-flow
series.

The use of conditional probability distributions
allows us to consider the correlation of cash flows
over time. In Example 8-4, the cash flow in year 2
depends on what happened in year 1. However, the cor-

relation of cash flows over time is not perfectly correlated. This is because given a cash flow in year 1, the cash flow in year 2 can vary within a range.

From Table 8-1, we can compute the possible net present values for all series. With a discount rate of 5 per cent, these net present values are computed as follows:

$$NPV_1 = \frac{\$200}{(1.05)^1} + \frac{\$400}{(1.05)^2} - \$300 = \$253$$

$$NPV_2 = \frac{\$200}{(1.05)^1} + \frac{\$300}{(1.05)^2} - \$300 = \$162$$

$$NPV_3 = \frac{\$100}{(1.05)^1} + \frac{\$200}{(1.05)^2} - \$300 = -\$23$$

$$NPV_4 = \frac{\$100}{(1.05)^1} + \frac{\$100}{(1.05)^2} - \$300 = -\$114$$

The expected NPV is computed in the same manner as before:

$$\overline{NPV} = \$253(0.2) + \$162(0.3) - \$23(0.2) - \$114(0.3)$$

$$= \$60$$

The standard deviation of Project E is computed by Equation (8-7):

$$\sigma = \sqrt{(\$253-\$60)^2(0.2) + (\$162-\$60)^2(0.3) + (-\$23-\$60)^2(0.2) + (-\$114-\$60)^2(0.3)}$$

$$= \$145$$

Standardizing the Dispersion

The expected net present value and the standard deviation give us a considerable amount of information by which to measure the risk of the investment project.

133

If probability distributions of continuous random variables are characterized by symmetrical, bell-shaped curves, they are called normal distributions. The normal distribution plays an important role in the area of statistical inference. Because the expected net present value ($\overline{NPV}$) and the standard deviation (σ) determine the location and spread of the distribution, we use the normal distribution in terms of areas under the normal curve.

The proportions of possible net present values falling within 1, 2, and 3 standard deviations of the expected net present value are

$\overline{NPV} \pm 1\sigma$ includes 68.27 per cent

$\overline{NPV} \pm 2\sigma$ includes 95.45 per cent

$\overline{NPV} \pm 3\sigma$ includes 99.73 per cent

These relationships are also illustrated graphically in Figure 8-2. Although the distribution theoretically ranges from minus infinity to plus infinity, an interval of three standard deviations on both sides of the expected net present value gives the practical limits of the distribution.

Figure 8-2 The Normal Curve

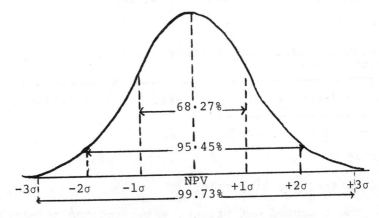

If alternative net present values are normally distributed, we are able to compute the probability that the project would provide a net present value of more or less than a specified amount. Table 8-2 shows the proportion of the total area which lies between the expected net present value and any other outcome NPV. To use the table, first take NPV - $\overline{NPV}$ and divide it by σ as follows:

$$z = \frac{NPV - \overline{NPV}}{\sigma} \qquad (8\text{-}8)$$

where z is the number of standard deviation units the random variable NPV is above or below the expected net present value. Thus, the entire table represents a standardized normal distribution with $\overline{NPV}$ = 0 and σ = 1. Table 8-2 shows entries only for positive z values. However, because the normal distribution is symmetrical about the expected net present value, the table can be used for net present values on either side of the expected net present value.

Example 8-5 Assume that the expected net present value of Project F is $700 and its standard deviation is $1,000. If the returns from this project are normally distributed, what is the probability that the net present value will fall between $0 and $2,200?

First, we compute deviations of these two net present values from the expected net present value of $700 in units of the standard deviation:

If NPV = $0 $z = \dfrac{\$0 - \$700}{\$1,000} = -0.7$

If NPV = $2,200 $z = \dfrac{\$2,200 - \$700}{\$1,000} = 1.5$

For the net present value of $0, look down the z column of Table 8-2 to 0.7 and across the column headed .00; the area is 0.2580. Similarly, for the net present value of $2,200, the area is 0.4332. Because these net present values fall on both sides of the expected net present value, the areas between the expected net present value and each net

135

Table 8-2 The Normal Distribution

z	.00	.01	.02	.03	.04	.05	.06	.07	.08	.09
0.0	.0000	.0040	.0080	.0120	.0160	.0199	.0239	.0279	.0319	.0359
0.1	.0398	.0438	.0478	.0517	.0557	.0596	.0636	.0675	.0714	.0753
0.2	.0793	.0832	.0871	.0910	.0948	.0987	.1026	.1064	.1103	.1141
0.3	.1179	.1217	.1255	.1293	.1331	.1368	.1406	.1443	.1480	.1517
0.4	.1554	.1591	.1628	.1664	.1700	.1736	.1772	.1808	.1844	.1879
0.5	.1915	.1950	.1985	.2019	.2054	.2088	.2123	.2157	.2190	.2224
0.6	.2257	.2291	.2324	.2357	.2389	.2422	.2454	.2486	.2517	.2549
0.7	.2580	.2611	.2642	.2673	.2703	.2734	.2764	.2794	.2823	.2852
0.8	.2881	.2910	.2939	.2967	.2995	.3023	.3051	.3078	.3106	.3133
0.9	.3159	.3186	.3212	.3238	.3264	.3289	.3315	.3340	.3365	.3389
1.0	.3413	.3438	.3461	.3485	.3508	.3531	.3554	.3577	.3599	.3621
1.1	.3643	.3665	.3686	.3708	.3729	.3749	.3770	.3790	.3810	.3830
1.2	.3849	.3869	.3888	.3907	.3925	.3944	.3962	.3980	.3997	.4015
1.3	.4032	.4049	.4066	.4082	.4099	.4115	.4131	.4147	.4162	.4177
1.4	.4192	.4207	.4222	.4236	.4251	.4265	.4279	.4292	.4306	.4319
1.5	.4332	.4345	.4357	.4370	.4382	.4394	.4406	.4418	.4429	.4441
1.6	.4452	.4463	.4474	.4484	.4495	.4505	.4515	.4525	.4535	.4545
1.7	.4554	.4564	.4573	.4582	.4591	.4599	.4608	.4616	.4625	.4633
1.8	.4641	.4649	.4656	.4664	.4671	.4678	.4686	.4693	.4699	.4706
1.9	.4713	.4719	.4726	.4732	.4738	.4744	.4750	.4756	.4761	.4767
2.0	.4772	.4778	.4783	.4788	.4793	.4798	.4803	.4808	.4812	.4817
2.1	.4821	.4826	.4830	.4834	.4838	.4842	.4846	.4850	.4854	.4857
2.2	.4861	.4864	.4868	.4871	.4875	.4878	.4881	.4884	.4887	.4890
2.3	.4893	.4896	.4898	.4901	.4904	.4906	.4909	.4911	.4913	.4916
2.4	.4918	.4920	.4922	.4925	.4927	.4929	.4931	.4932	.4934	.4936
2.5	.4938	.4940	.4941	.4943	.4945	.4946	.4948	.4949	.4951	.4952
2.6	.4953	.4955	.4956	.4957	.4959	.4960	.4961	.4962	.4963	.4964
2.7	.4965	.4966	.4967	.4968	.4969	.4970	.4971	.4972	.4973	.4974
2.8	.4974	.4975	.4976	.4977	.4977	.4978	.4979	.4979	.4980	.4981
2.9	.4981	.4982	.4982	.4983	.4984	.4984	.4985	.4985	.4986	.4986
	.4987	.4987	.4987	.4988	.4988	.4989	.4989	.4989	.4990	.4990

present value must be added. Thus, the combined
area is 0.6912 or 69.12 per cent. In other words,
there is a 69 per cent chance that the actual net
present value of Project F will fall between $0
and $2,200. This is illustrated in Figure 8-3.

Figure 8-3 Area Under a Normal Curve: Example 8-5

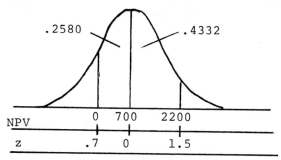

Example 8-6 What is the probability that the actual net present value of Project F will be 0 or
greater?

   In Example 8-5, we found that 25.80 per cent
of the area under the normal curve falls between a
net present value of $0 and the expected net pres-
ent value of $700. We also noted that Project F
has more than 50 per cent chance to achieve a positive net present value. Thus, there is a 75.80 per
cent chance that the actual net present value of
the project will be 0 or greater. This is illustrated in Figure 8-4.

Figure 8-4 Area Under a Normal Curve: Example 8-6

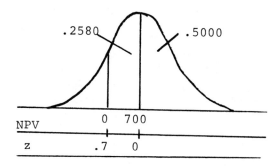

137

The table of areas under a normal curve thus indicates the probabilities for any part of the curve. When there are doubts about how to apply this table, a diagram such as Figures 8-3 and 8-4 can be drawn to picture the areas needed. It is also important to note that the concepts discussed here can be adapted to other techniques described in Chapter 4. For example, we may be able to compute the expected value of Project F and its standard deviation in terms of the internal rate of return instead of the net present value. Then we can apply the same concepts to determine the probability that the project would give an internal rate of return more or less than a specified amount.

Interpretation: Combining Expected Value and Risk

Up to this point, we described ways of quantifying risk for the project. It does not enable us to make accept/reject decisions. However, our preceding discussion can be used to rank certain projects.

Example 8-7 Three pairs of mutually exclusive projects have the following:

Pair	Project	Expected NPV	Standard Deviation
1	G	$1,000	$400
	H	1,000	700
2	I	900	400
	J	600	400
3	K	500	300
	L	300	210

For pair 1, Projects G and H have an equal expected NPV of $1,000, but Project G has the smaller standard deviation. This leads us to conclude that Project G is better than Project H. For pair 2, Projects I and J have an equal standard deviation of $400, but Project I has the higher expected NPV. Thus, Project I is better than Project J. For pair 3, both the expected NPV and the standard deviation are greater for Project K than for Project L. Under

138

these circumstances, we are not sure which project
is better. To eliminate this problem, we must adjust the standard deviation for differences in project size. The coefficient of variation does this
job. The coefficient of variation is 0.60 ($300 ÷
$500) for Project K and 0.70 ($210 ÷ $300) for Proj-
ect L. Because Project K promises the greater expected NPV for a lower degree of risk, Project K is
better than Project L.

UTILITY THEORY

A more difficult problem arises when both the
expected NPV and the coefficient of variation for
a project exceed those for another project. Suppose that the expected NPV of Project M is $1,500
and its coefficient of variation is 0.60. In contrast, the expected NPV of Project N is $2,000 and
its coefficient of variation is 0.85. The expected
NPV and the coefficient of variation are greater
for Project N than for Project M. Hence, we are
not sure which project is better. To overcome this
and other problems, we need a utility curve for the
investor that reflects his attitude toward risk and
return.

Because preferences are basically subjective,
the precise specification of a decision maker's
utility function must overcome many operational
difficulties. Moreover, individual utility curves
are likely to change over time. Nevertheless, we
can divide decision makers into three broad categories based on their risk preferences: risk-tak-
ing, risk-indifferent, and risk-averse. Figure
8-5 shows the utility functions for these three
types of decision makers.

Risk takers have increasing marginal utilities
for potential increases in income. They feel that
their first $10 has the lowest subjective value
and successive increments of $10 have successively
increasing subjective value. Risk-indifferent decision makers have constant marginal utilities and
thus their utility curves are linear. Risk averters
have diminishing marginal utilities for increases in
income. They feel that their first $10 has the high-
est subjective value and successive increments of $10
have successively decreasing subjective value. Hence,
we can anticipate a different utility curve for each

139

Figure 8-5   Relationship Between Income and
             Utility

Income

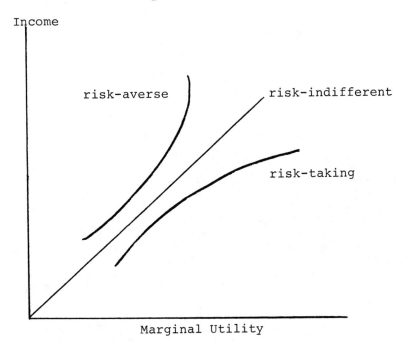

Marginal Utility

individual decision maker.   However, because the
great majority of managers are risk averters, the
value of each additional dollar decreases as risk
increases.   As a result, the expected value or the
risk premium must increase at an increasing rate
as risk increases at a constant rate.

Example 8-8   Suppose that there are five mutually
exclusive projects that are equally desirable in
the eyes of an investor.   The five projects have
the following coefficients of variation and expected NPVs:

Proj-ect	Coefficient of Variation	Expected NPV	Marginal Expected NPV
0	0	$ 0	$ 0
P	1	30	30

140

Project	Coefficient of Variation	Expected NPV	Marginal Expected NPV
Q	2	$ 70	$ 40
R	3	120	50
S	4	180	60

The marginal expected NPV is the amount of additional expected NPV necessary to compensate the investor for each additional unit of risk. It should be noted that the marginal expected NPV increases at an increasing rate as the coefficient of variation increases at a given rate.[2]

These five projects are plotted in Figure 8-6. Line I represents the investor's least acceptable risk-return indifference curve. The investor is indifferent between any combination of expected NPV and coefficient of variation on that line. In other words, an indifference curve refers to those combinations of expected NPV and coefficient of variation that produce a fixed level of utility. Each successive curve to the left of Line I represents a higher level of expected utility; Line II represents a higher level of expected utility than Line I. Furthermore, each decision maker has a whole family of nonintersecting utility curves.

Figure 8-6 Risk-Return Tradeoff Curve for a Particular Investor

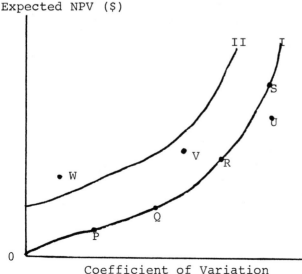

Expected NPV ($)

Coefficient of Variation

141

Because Line I is the investor's least acceptable indifference curve, all projects to the right of Line I are rejected, while all projects to the left of Line I could be accepted. Although Project U has a positive expected NPV, it is rejected because this value is not sufficient to compensate the investor for the degree of risk. If Projects W and V are mutually exclusive, the investor would select Project W over Project V. Although Project V has a higher expected NPV than Project W, the additional expected NPV is insufficient to compensate the investor for the additional risk of Project V over Project W. Because the utility curve allows us to rank projects, it can be used to evaluate mutually independent projects under a capital rationing constraint. Thus, the utility theory can be used to make the accept/reject decision, the mutually exclusive choice decision, and the capital rationing decision.

COMPUTER SIMULATION MODEL

The concept of computer simulation in capital budgeting under conditions of uncertainty was first reported by David B. Hertz in 1964.[3] He established probability distributions about nine separate variables to determine the expected value and risk. Hertz assumed that these nine variables are independent. Although this is an important assumption for simulation analysis, dependency exists among variables. For example, the firm's sales volume may affect the market price of a product and its cost. As more units are produced, both the cost and unit price are likely to fall.

Simulation involves one or more trial runs of a process to learn about its possible alternative consequences before taking a particular course of action. Basically, the method is used to determine the expected value of a project and its risk by empirical procedures rather than by theoretical analysis.

To apply the technique to the evaluation of major investment projects, we must list all of the key variables and assign a probability distribution to each variable. For example, the marketing department may estimate (1) S = initial unit sales volume of the industry, (2) G = annual percentage

142

growth rate of market demand, (3) M = percentage market share, and (4) P = selling price per unit. The engineering department may estimate (5) V = variable cost per unit, (6) F = fixed cost, (7) C_0 = cost of a new project, and (8) n = life of the project. The accounting department may supply (9) T = tax rate, and (10) D_t = depreciation charge in year t. The problem of the financial manager is to determine the expected value of the project and its risk.

If a probability distribution can be assigned to each of these variables, we can write a computer program to simulate what is likely to occur. Essentially, the computer selects one value at random from each probability distribution for each variable. This and other values selected from the other probability distributions are combined to calculate one possible net present value of the project. The annual net cash flows of a project and its net present value can be computed as follows:

$$R_t = \left[S(1 + G)^t M(P - V) - F - D_t \right] (1 - T) + D_t \qquad (8\text{-}9)$$

$$NPV = \sum_{t=1}^{n} \frac{R_t}{(1 + k)^t} - C_0 \qquad (8\text{-}10)$$

Example 8-9 Assume that the computer selected these specific values for Project Q:

S = 350 units	V = $30	k = 10 per cent
G = 0 per cent	F = $800	C_0 = $1,000
M = 20 per cent	T = 50 per cent	n = 5 years
P = $50	D_t = $200	

Because the growth rate is equal to 0, the annual net cash flow will remain constant for the next five years. Thus, the net present value of the project is

$$R_1 = \left[\$350(1 + 0.00)^1 (0.20)(\$50 - \$30) - \$800 - \$200 \right]$$

$$(1 - 0.50) + \$200 = \$400$$

143

$$NPV = \sum_{t=1}^{5} \frac{\$400}{(1.10)^t} - \$1,000$$

$$= \$516$$

The annual net cash flow of $400 and the net present value of $516 obtained for this particular combination of values are the results for just one computer trial run. The computer proceeds to select other sets of values; each time, we obtain a set of values for these variables and the net present value of the project for that set. Table 8-3 and Figure 8-7 show a frequency distribution of net present values generated by a hypothetical trial of such a simulation model involving 200 computer runs.

Table 8-3 Frequency Table of Simulated Net Present Values

NPV ($)	Mid-NPV		Frequency	Probability
0-200	100		20	0.10
201-400	300		40	0.20
401-600	500		80	0.40
601-800	700		40	0.20
801-1000	900		20	0.10
		Total	200	1.00

Figure 8-7 Frequency Polygon of Simulated Net Present Values

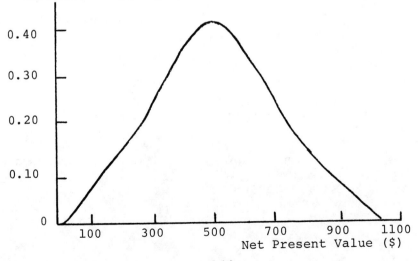

144

Estimates of the probabilities for the various net present values in the last column of Table 8-3 represent the relative frequencies. For example, the project has a 10 per cent probability for a net present value of $200 or less and a 30 per cent chance for a net present value of $600 or more. From a frequency distribution such as Table 8-3, it is possible to calculate an expected NPV and standard deviation of possible net present values:

$$\overline{NPV} = \$100(0.10) + \$300(0.20) + \$500(0.40) + \$700(0.20) + \$900(0.10) = \$500$$

$$\sigma^2 = (\$100 - \$500)^2(0.10) + (\$300 - \$500)^2(0.20) + $$
$$(\$500 - \$500)^2(0.40) + (\$700 - \$500)^2(0.20) + $$
$$(\$900 - \$500)^2(0.10)$$

$$= \$48,000$$

$$\sigma = \sqrt{\sigma^2} = \$219$$

Thus, the coefficient of variation for the project is 0.438 ($219 ÷ $500).

The computer simulation has provided us with an estimate of the expected NPV and an estimate of its relative risk. Although the results provide valuable information for effective capital budgeting decisions, they do not indicate whether the project should be accepted or rejected. To answer this question, the risk-return information estimated by the computer simulation model should be combined with the utility theory.

SENSITIVITY ANALYSIS

A logical extension of simulation analysis enables us to perform a sensitivity analysis. We have seen that the net present value of a project depends on many factors, such as sales volume, sales price, etc. Once we calculate the net present values of the project under alternative assumptions, we can measure the sensitivity of project return to individual variables. In this way, it is possible to identify variables that are most criti-

145

cal to project return so that management can direct its efforts to these variables for further investigation. But it should be noted that unlike the simulation model, this method does not depend on probability theory.

Example 8-10 To perform a sensitivity analysis with Example 8-9, recall that the net present value of the project for a particular combination of values was $516. Determine the effects of errors of 2 per cent in all estimates on this estimated net present value.

Suppose that the financial manager wants to know the effect of a 2 per cent decrease in sales price on this estimated net present value ($516). The budgeted sales price per unit was $50 and thus the new sales price per unit becomes $49 ($50 - $50 x 0.02). If the values of all the other variables remain unchanged, the net present value is

$$R_1 = \left[(\$350(1 + 0.00)^1 (0.20) (\$49 - \$30) - \$800 - \$200)\right]$$

$$(1 - 0.50) + \$200$$

$$= \$365$$

$$NPV = \sum_{t=1}^{5} \frac{\$365}{(1.10)^t} - \$1,000 = \$384$$

Because the estimated net present value for the project is $516, the 2 per cent decrease in sales price will cause the net present value to decline by $132 ($516 - $384) or 25.6 per cent ($132 ÷ $516). If plus and minus signs are ignored, the 2 per cent decrease and increase in sales price produce an identical change of $132 or 25.6 per cent in the estimated net present value.

To isolate those variables that are more crucial and more risky, the effects of errors of 2 per cent in all estimates should be computed by the same procedure. Table 8-4 shows these calculation results for most of the variables. It is important to remember that the effect of an error of 2 per cent in each estimate of the selected

146

variables is computed by changing one of the
variables at a time.

Table 8-4   Changes in Net Present Value Caused by
             2 Per Cent Errors in Estimates

Variable	$ Changes in NPV	% Change in NPV
Sales Volume (S)	$ 53	10.3
Market Share (M)	53	10.3
Sales Price (P)	132	25.6
Variable Cost (V)	80	15.5
Fixed Costs (F)	31	6.0
Tax Rate (T)	15	2.9
Depreciation (D)	7	1.4
Project Cost (C_O)	20	3.9

The estimated net present value for the project is most sensitive to variations in sales price
per unit. An error of 2 per cent in sales price
causes the estimated net present value to change
by $132 or 25.6 per cent. This means that, if the
firm can increase its sales price by 2 per cent
while all the other estimates remain constant, the
expected net present value will be $648 ($516 + $132)
instead of $516.   Errors of 2 per cent in estimates
of the remaining variables cause the estimated net
present value to change by much less than this amount.

The second most critical variable is variable
cost. Sales volume and market share are in a third-
place tie. Errors of 2 per cent in estimates of
fixed costs, tax, depreciation, and project cost
change the estimated net present value by less than
6 per cent. Thus, the financial manager must make
every effort to refine and improve the estimates of
the first four variables before the project is accepted. It is equally important to pay close attention to these same variables even after the project is undertaken.

METHODS TO ADJUST FOR RISK

The utility curve shows the risk-return tradeoff in terms of preference. Once the risk-return
preferences are given, we are now in the position

147

to discuss the methods used to adjust project estimates for risk. The certainty equivalent approach,
the risk-adjusted discount rate method, and the
capital asset pricing model are three formal approaches which are commonly used to incorporate
risk into the analysis. The first two methods are
discussed in the remainder of this chapter and the
third is considered in Chapter 9.

Risk-Adjusted Discount Rate

The risk-adjusted discount rate (RADR) method
adjusts for risk by varying the discount rate--increas-
ing it for more risky projects and reducing it for
less risky projects. Projects with average riskiness should be discounted at the firm's cost of
capital because it reflects the normal risk faced
by the firm. Those projects with greater-than-
normal risk should be discounted at a rate in excess of the cost of capital. In contrast, those
projects with less-than-normal risk should be discounted at a rate between the risk-free rate and
the cost of capital. The RADR (k') is computed
as follows:

$$k' = R_f + R_p + R_a \qquad (8\text{-}11)$$

where R_f = risk-free rate

R_p = premium for the firm's normal risk

R_a = adjustment for above or below the
firm's normal risk

It is important to note that the sum of R_f and
R_p is the firm's cost of capital.

The amount of risk adjustment (R_a) reflects
an investor's perception of the risk associated
with the project because this adjustment is based
on the investor's preference for risk aversion.
It is possible to assign the amount of risk adjustment according to the categories of investments. Of course, these risk adjustments reflect
the utility preferences for the firm at a particular time.

148

The risk-adjusted NPV is computed by the following formula:

$$NPV_r = \sum_{t=1}^{n} \frac{\bar{R}_t}{(1 + k')^t} - C_o \qquad (8\text{-}12)$$

where NPV_r = risk-adjusted NPV

$\bar{R}_t$ = expected value of possible net cash flows in period t

C_o = expected value of possible costs

Example 8-11 Assume that the RADR for a project under consideration is 30 per cent and the project has the following cash flows:

Original Cost		Cash Flow in Year 1		Cash Flow in Year 2	
Proba-bility	Amount	Proba-bility	Amount	Proba-bility	Amount
0.3	$ 7,000	0.2	$7,000	0.2	$ 8,000
0.4	9,000	0.4	7,500	0.6	9,000
0.3	11,000	0.3	8,000	0.1	10,000
		0.1	9,000	0.1	11,000

To determine the net present value of this project, we must first compute the expected value for each cash flow. The expected cost is $9,000, the expected value of cash flows for the first year is $7,700, and the expected value of cash flows for the second year is $9,100. Thus, the risk-adjusted NPV of the project is computed as follows:

$$NPV_r = \frac{\$7,700}{(1.30)^1} + \frac{\$9,100}{(1.30)^2} - \$9,000 = \$2,308$$

The decision rule is to accept the project if the risk-adjusted NPV is positive and to reject the project if the risk-adjusted NPV is negative. Because the project in Example 8-11 has a positive risk-adjusted NPV, it represents a candidate for acceptance.

149

While the concept of RADR is appealing for its simplicity, it has a number of practical problems. First, it is extremely difficult to determine the appropriate discount rate for each project or each project class. Second, it does not adjust for the variability of the cash flow which is subject to risk. Third, it applies the same discount-rate risk premium to the project throughout its useful life.

Certainty Equivalent Approach

The certainty equivalent (CE) approach incorporates the manager's utility preference for risk versus return directly into the capital budgeting decision. While the RADR method adjusts for risk in the denominator of the NPV formula, the CE approach adjusts for risk in the numerator of the same equation.

When the CE method is used, the annual cash flows are multiplied by a CE coefficient, which is a certain cash flow divided by an uncertain cash flow. If management is indifferent between a certain $140 and an uncertain $200, its CE coefficient is 0.70 ($140 ÷ $200). The CE coefficient assumes a value of between 0 and 1. It varies inversely with risk. If the firm perceived greater risk, it would use a lower CE coefficient which would deflate the dollar return value. Once all the risky cash flows are adjusted downward to reflect uncertainty through the use of the CE coefficient, these certain cash flows are then discounted at the risk-free rate to determine the certain NPV:

$$NPV_c = \sum_{t=1}^{n} \frac{\partial_t \bar{R}_t}{(1 + R_f)^t} - C_o \qquad (8\text{-}13)$$

where NPV_c = certain net present value

∂_t = CE coefficient in period t

$\bar{R}_t$ = expected value of possible cash flows in period t

C_o = expected cost of the project

150

Example 8-12 Assume that a project has the following characteristics:

Year	Expected Cash Flow	CE Coefficient
0	-$10,000	0.0
1	5,000	0.8
2	6,000	0.7
3	8,000	0.6

With a 5 per cent risk-free discount rate, the certain NPV of the project is

$$NPV_c = \frac{\$5,000(0.8)}{(1.05)^1} + \frac{\$6,000(0.7)}{(1.05)^2} + \frac{\$8,000(0.6)}{(1.05)^3} - \$10,000$$

$$= \$1,764$$

The decision rule is to accept the project if the certain NPV is positive and to reject the project if the certain NPV is negative. Because the certain NPV is positive, we would accept this project.

The CE approach may be able to more accurately adjust for risk than the RADR method. First, the CE approach adjusts for risk in the expected cash flows which are subject to risk. Second, the CE coefficient represents a probability factor reflecting the degree of confidence that the decision maker has in obtaining a particular cash flow. Third, the CE approach requires us to use a different CE coefficient for each year.

Risk-Adjusted Discount Rate Versus Certainty Equivalent

If the RADR (k') and the risk-free rate (R_f) are constant for all future periods, these two methods should yield the same results. Expressing this equality, we have:[4]

$$\frac{\partial_t \bar{R}_t}{(1 + R_f)^t} = \frac{\bar{R}_t}{(1 + k')^t} \qquad (8\text{-}14)$$

Solving Equation (8-13) for ∂_t, we obtain:

$$\partial_t = \frac{(1 + R_f)^t}{(1 + k')^t} \qquad (8-15)$$

For period $t + 1$ the CE coefficient would be expressed as follows:

$$(8-16)$$

$$\partial_{t+1} = \frac{(1 + R_f)^{t+1}}{(1 + k')^{t+1}}$$

Equations (8-14) and (8-15) indicate that k' must be greater than R_f if k' and R_f are constant over time. This is because ∂_t assumes a value of between 0 and 1. If k' is always greater than R_f, it follows that ∂_1 must be larger than ∂_2, ∂_2 must be larger than ∂_3, and so on. To illustrate, assume $k' = 20$ per cent and $R_f = 10$ per cent. The CE coefficient in period 1 is

$$\partial_1 = \frac{(1.10)^1}{(1.20)^1} = 0.917$$

The CE coefficient in period 2 is

$$\partial_t = \frac{(1.10)^2}{(1.20)^2} = 0.840$$

Thus, the application of a constant k' assumes that ∂_t tends to decrease with time. That is, the CE coefficient is an increasing function of time.

FOOTNOTES

1. See James C.T. Mao, "Survey of Capital Budgeting: Theory and Practice," Journal of Finance (May 1970), pp. 349-360.

2. Here we express a decision maker's attitude toward risk in terms of monetary units. We may also express it in terms of nonmonetary units called utiles. If this concept is

152

used for capital expenditure analysis, we should calculate the expected utility of an investment project rather than its expected value. For details, see John Von Neumann and Oskar Morgenstern, Theory of Games and Economic Behavior (Princeton, N.J.: Princeton University Press, 1955).

3. David H. Hertz, "Risk Analysis in Capital Investment," Harvard Business Review (January/February 1964), pp. 95-106.

4. For details, see Alexander A. Robichek and Stewart C. Myers, Optimal Financing Decisions (Englewood Cliffs, N.J.: Prentice-Hall, 1965), pp. 82-86.

CHAPTER 9

PORTFOLIO THEORY AND THE CAPITAL ASSET PRICING MODEL

Chapter 8 focused on risk analysis of individual projects. In the real world, however, practically no company or individual invests everything in a single project. Thus, it is useful to consider the risk and return of a particular project in conjunction with its counterparts in existing assets or new investment opportunities. This chapter shifts the focus of evaluation from individual projects to combinations of projects. First, we analyze the basic elements of portfolio theory. Second, we attempt to show how portfolio theory can be extended to relate securities' risks to their rates of return through the capital asset pricing model.[1]

PORTFOLIO RETURN AND RISK: MARKOWITZ PORTFOLIO SELECTION

Portfolio return is the expected return of a portfolio of securities. The expected return is simply a weighted average of the expected returns of the securities which make up the portfolio. The portfolio return may be computed as follows:

$$\bar{R}_p = \sum_{j=1}^{n} x_j \bar{R}_j \qquad (9\text{-}1)$$

where $\bar{R}_p$ = portfolio return

x_j = percentage of funds invested in Security j

$\bar{R}_j$ = expected return of Security j

n = total number of securities

The expected return of Security j is

$$\bar{R}_j = \sum_{i=1}^{m} R_i P_i \qquad (9\text{-}2)$$

where R_i = return associated with the ith state of nature

155

P_i = probability associated with the ith state of nature

m = number of the states of nature

The standard deviation of a portfolio measures the riskiness of the portfolio and can be computed as follows:

$$\sigma_p = \sqrt{\sum_{j=1}^{n} x_j^2 \sigma_j^2 + 2 \sum_{j=1}^{n} \sum_{k=j+1}^{n} x_j x_k Cov_{jk}} \qquad (9\text{-}3)$$

where σ_p = standard deviation of the portfolio

σ_j^2 = variance of Security j

x_k = percentage of funds invested in Security k

Cov_{jk} = covariance between Securities j and k

If there are only two securities, e.g., 1 and 2, Equation (9-3) may be reduced to the following:

$$\sigma_p = \sqrt{x_1^2 \sigma_1^2 + x_2^2 \sigma_2^2 + 2 x_1 x_2 Cov_{12}} \qquad (9\text{-}4)$$

If there are three securities, Equation (9-3) can be reduced to the following:

$$\sigma_p = \sqrt{x_1^2 \sigma_1^2 + x_2^2 \sigma_2^2 + x_3^2 \sigma_3^2 + 2 x_1 x_2 Cov_{12} + 2 x_1 x_3 Cov_{13}}$$

$$+ 2 x_2 x_3 Cov_{23} \qquad (9\text{-}5)$$

The actual number of variances in Equation (9-3) is equal to the number of securities and the number of covariances is equal to $\frac{n(n-1)}{2}$. For example, a portfolio of 100 securities would have 100 variances and 4,950 covariances $(\frac{100(100-1)}{2})$.

Covariance

The key point of portfolio risk analysis is the degree of covariance. The covariance of any two random Securities j and k may be defined as follows:

$$Cov_{jk} = \sum_{i=1}^{m} (R_{ij} - \bar{R}_j)(R_{ik} - \bar{R}_k)P_{ijk} \qquad (9-6)$$

where R_{ij} = return associated with the ith state of nature for Security j

R_{ik} = return associated with the ith state of nature for Security k

$\bar{R}_k$ = expected return for Security k

P_{ijk} = joint probability that Returns R_{ij} and R_{ik} will occur simultaneously.

The covariance is a useful device to understand how the possible returns of two random securities react to the states of nature. There are three possibilities in the covariance between any two securities: positive covariance, negative covariance, and zero covariance. The positive covariance occurs when the variation in Security j and the variation in Security k move in the same direction. The negative covariance exists when these two variations move in the opposite direction with each other. The zero covariance arises when the variation in one of these two securities or both securities equals zero.

The covariance may also be calculated by the correlation coefficient between two securities and their standard deviations:

$$Cov_{jk} = r_{jk}\sigma_j\sigma_k, \quad \text{or} \quad r_{jk} = \frac{Cov_{jk}}{\sigma_j\sigma_k} \qquad (9-7)$$

where r_{jk} = correlation coefficient between Securities j and k

σ_j = standard deviation of Security j's returns

157

σ_k = standard deviation of Security k's returns

The correlation coefficient is a relative measure of correlation between two variables. Its values range from zero (no correlation or independence) to ± (perfect correlation).

Substituting Equation (9-6) for Cov_{jk} in Equation (9-7), we can rewrite Equation (9-6) as

$$r_{jk} = \sum_{i=1}^{m} \left(\frac{R_{ij} - \bar{R}_j}{\sigma_j} \right) \left(\frac{R_{ik} - \bar{R}_k}{\sigma_k} \right) P_{ijk} \qquad (9-8)$$

Substituting Equation (9-7) for Cov_{jk} in Equation (9-3), we can rewrite Equation (9-3) as

$$\sigma_p = \sqrt{\sum_{j=1}^{n} x_j^2 \sigma_j^2 + 2 \sum_{j=1}^{n-1} \sum_{k=j+1}^{n} x_j x_k r_{jk} \sigma_j \sigma_k} \qquad (9-9)$$

Joint Probability

Another important concept necessary to carry out the overall risk of a portfolio is joint probability. This was briefly described in Chapter 8. The joint probability may be defined as the probability that two or more events will occur simultaneously or successively. If Events e_1 and e_2 are statistically independent, the joint probability of these two events is

$$P(e_1 e_2) = P(e_1) P(e_2) \qquad (9-10)$$

Events e_1 and e_2 are statistically independent if the probability for Event e_1 to occur is the same regardless of what the outcome is for Event e_2. Thus, the probability of obtaining both of the tails in the two successive tosses of one coin is

$$P(e_1 e_2) = P(e_1) P(e_2) = (1/2)(1/2) = 1/4$$

where e_1 = probability of obtaining a tail in the first toss

158

e_2 = probability of obtaining a tail in the second toss.

However, the concept of conditional probability must be introduced in considering joint probabilities. Suppose that we obtained a tail in the first toss. Given this information, what is the probability that we will also obtain a tail in the second toss? This is the conditional probability, which may be computed as follows:

$$P(e_2/e_1) = \frac{P(e_2e_1)}{P(e_1)} \qquad (9\text{-}11)$$

where $P(e_2/e_1)$ = conditional probability of Event e_2 given Event e_1

   $P(e_1)$ = simple probability

If the conditional probability is equal to the simple probability, i.e., $P(e_2/e_1) = P(e_2)$, Events e1 and e2 are statistically independent. The conditional probability of a tail in the second toss (e2) given a tail in the first toss (e1) is

$$P(e_2/e_1) = \frac{P(e_2e_1)}{P(e_1)} = \frac{1/4}{1/2} = 1/2$$

It should be noted that the conditional probability of 1/2 is equal to the simple probability of obtaining a tail in the second toss, $P(e_2) = 1/2$. Thus, Events e_2 and e_1 are statistically independent. If $P(e_2/e_1)$ does not equal $P(e_2)$, these two events are dependent. Alternatively, they are correlated with each other.

Sample Problem 9-1

Assume that a two-security portfolio calls for a total investment of $1,000. Security A requires an investment of $400 and Security B requires an investment of $600. The expected returns of these two securities under different states of economy are as follows:

Economic Condition	Associated Probability	Returns at End of Year 1 Sec. A	Sec. B
Recession	0.20	0.05	0.20
Normal	0.60	0.10	0.15
Boom	0.20	0.15	0.10

Both securities have one-year life spans.

To compute the expected return of the two-security portfolio, we must first calculate the expected returns of Securities A and B:

$$\bar{R}_A = \sum_{i=1}^{3} R_i P_i = (0.05)0.20 + (0.10)0.60 + (0.15)0.20$$

$$= 10\%$$

$$\bar{R}_B = \sum_{i=1}^{3} R_i P_i = (0.20)0.20 + (0.15)0.60 + (0.10)0.20$$

$$= 15\%$$

Because the percentage of the portfolio invested in Security A is 40 per cent and that of Security B is 60 per cent, the portfolio return is[2]

$$\bar{R}_P = \sum_{j=1}^{2} x_j \bar{R}_j = (0.40)0.10 + (0.60)0.15$$

$$= 13\%$$

To compute the standard deviation of the portfolio, we should know the standard deviations of these two securities, their joint probabilities, and the covariance between the two securities. The standard deviations of Securities A and B are computed by Equation (8-2):

$$\sigma_A = \sqrt{(0.05 - 0.10)^2 0.20 + (0.10 - 0.10)^2 0.60 + (0.15 - 0.10)^2 0.20}$$

$$= \sqrt{0.0010} = 0.0317$$

160

$$\sigma_B = \sqrt{\begin{aligned}&(0.20 - 0.15)^2 0.20 + (0.15 - 0.15)^2 0.60 + \\ &(0.10 - 0.15)^2 0.20\end{aligned}}$$

$$= \sqrt{0.0010} = 0.0317$$

To determine the joint probabilities of these two securities under different economic conditions, assume that (1) Events recession, normal, and boom for Security A are denoted by e_1, e_2, and e_3 and (2) Events recession, normal, and boom for Security B are denoted by e_4, e_5, and e_6. Then we may construct a contingency table to derive the joint probabilities of these six events for the two securities. This is given in Table 9-1.

Table 9-1   Joint Probabilities of Two Independent Securities

Returns of Security B		Returns of Security A			
		5%	10%	15%	
	e_i / e_{i+3}	e_1	e_2	e_3	Column Totals
20%	e_4	0.04	0.12	0.04	0.20
15%	e_5	0.12	0.36	0.12	0.60
10%	e_6	0.04	0.12	0.04	0.20
Row Totals		0.20	0.60	0.20	1.00

The values in the cells of Table 9-1 are the joint probabilities of the respective outcomes denoted by the column e_i (i = 1, 2, and 3) and the row e_{i+3}. It is important to note that this table was constructed on the basis of the assumption that paired events are independent. If any two events are statistically independent, the joint probability is the product of the two simple probabilities. For example, the joint probability $P(e_1 e_4)$ is determined as follows:

$$P(e_1 e_4) = P(e_1) P(e_4) = (0.20(0.20) = 4\%$$

The values in other cells are obtained by the same procedure. Note that there are nine joint probabilities in the table.

The statistical independence of Events e_1 and e_4 can be easily verified by the conditional probability. Recall that the two events are statistically independent if their conditional probability is equal to the simple probability. For instance, the conditional probability of e_4 given e_1 is

$$P(e_4/e_1) = \frac{P(e_4 e_1)}{P(e_1)} = \frac{0.04}{0.20} = 20\%$$

Because the conditional probability $P(e_4/e_1) = 0.20$ equals the simple probability $P(e_4) = 0.20$, Events c_1 and e_4 are statistically independent. The column totals and the row totals are the simple probabilities, but they are frequently called the marginal probabilities. These marginal probabilities are simply the sums of the respective joint probabilities. For example, the marginal probability $P(e_4)$ of 20 per cent is obtained by adding the joint probabilities $P(e_4 e_1) = 0.04$, $P(e_4 e_2) = 0.12$, and $P(e_4 e_3) = 0.04$.

Next, we compute the covariance between Securities A and B. We have to use the joint probabilities in the cells of Table 9-1 and restate the table in a form consistent with Equation (9-6). To do this, recall that the expected return was 10 per cent for Security A and 15 per cent for Security B. This computation is given in Table 9-2.

Table 9-2 shows that the covariance between these two securities equals zero. This is because two statistically independent variables tend to have a zero covariance. Thus, we do not need to calculate the actual value of covariance if two securities are statistically independent. The statistical independence between any two random variables may be determined by inspecting the joint probability table such as Table 9-2. If they are not statistically independent, we must compute the covariance using Equation (9-6).

Table 9-2 Computation of Covariance Between Securities A and B

State of Nature	$R_{iA} - \bar{R}_A$	$R_{iB} - \bar{R}_B$	$(R_{iA} - \bar{R}_A)(R_{iB} - \bar{R}_B)$	$P(e_i, e_{i+3})$
$e_1 e_4$	$0.05-0.10 = -0.05$	$0.20-0.15 = +0.05$	-0.0025	0.04
$e_1 e_5$	$0.05-0.10 = -0.05$	$0.15-0.15 = 0.00$	0.0000	0.12
$e_1 e_6$	$0.05-0.10 = -0.05$	$0.10-0.15 = -0.05$	$+0.0025$	0.04
$e_2 e_4$	$0.10-0.10 = 0.00$	$0.20-0.15 = +0.05$	0.0000	0.12
$e_2 e_5$	$0.10-0.10 = 0.00$	$0.15-0.15 = 0.00$	0.0000	0.36
$e_2 e_6$	$0.10-0.10 = 0.00$	$0.10-0.15 = -0.05$	0.0000	0.12
$e_3 e_4$	$0.15-0.10 = +0.05$	$0.20-0.15 = +0.05$	$+0.0025$	0.04
$e_3 e_5$	$0.15-0.10 = +0.05$	$0.15-0.15 = 0.00$	0.0000	0.12
$e_3 e_6$	$0.15-0.10 = +0.05$	$0.10-0.15 = -0.05$	-0.0025	0.04

Table 9-2   Computation of Covariance Between Securities A and B

State of Nature	$(R_{iA} - \bar{R}_A)(R_{iB} - \bar{R}_B)P(e_i e_{i+3})$
$e_1 e_4$	-0.0001
$e_1 e_5$	0.0000
$e_1 e_6$	+0.0001
$e_2 e_4$	0.0000
$e_2 e_5$	0.0000
$e_2 e_6$	0.0000
$e_3 e_4$	+0.0001
$e_3 e_5$	0.0000
$e_3 e_6$	-0.0001
	$\text{Cov}_{AB} = 0.0000$

To examine some variations of our two-security portfolio, let us reproduce some results of the computation we have just completed: the percentage of funds invested in Security A (x_A) = 40%; the percentage of funds invested in Security B (x_B) = 60%; the portfolio return ($\bar{R}_p$) = 13%; the variance of Security A (σ_A^2) = 0.1%; the standard deviation of Security A (σ_A) = 3.17%; the variance of Security B (σ_B^2) = 0.1%; and the standard deviation of Security B (σ_B) = 3.17%.

It is important to recognize that the portfolio return is the same regardless of correlation of returns for Securities A and B. However, the degree of portfolio risk varies according to intersecurity-return behavior. Intersecurity returns can be statistically independent, perfectly positively correlated, and perfectly negatively correlated.

Case 1: Statistical Independence

If Securities A and B are statistically independent, the correlation coefficient between the two securities is 0 and thus their covariance is 0. The portfolio return and the standard deviation of the portfolio are

$$\bar{R}_p = 13\%$$

$$\sigma_p = [(0.4)^2(0.001) + (0.6)^2(0.001)$$
$$+ 2(0.4)(0.6)(0)(0.0317)(0.0317]^{1/2} = 0.0228$$

Because the standard deviations of Securities A and B are 0.0317 each, their weighted average is 0.0317 (0.0317 x 0.40 + 0.0317 x 0.60). Thus, the standard deviation of the portfolio is 72 per cent of this weighted average (0.0228/0.0317). This means that diversification can reduce risk significantly if a considerable number of statistically independent securities are available.

Case 2: Perfectly Positive Correlation

If Securities A and B are perfectly positively correlated with each other, their correlation co-

efficient becomes 1. The expected return of the
portfolio and its standard deviation are

$$\bar{R}_p = 13\%$$

$$\sigma_p = \sqrt{\frac{(0.4)2(0.001) + (0.6)^2(0.001) + 2(0.4)(0.6)(1)}{(0.0317)(0.0317)}}$$

$$= 0.0317$$

The standard deviation of the portfolio equals the
weighted average of the two individual standard deviations. Thus, if all alternative investments are
perfectly positively correlated, diversification
would not reduce risk at all.

Case 3: Perfectly Negative Correlation

     If these two securities are perfectly nega-
tively correlated, their correlation coefficient
becomes -1. This portfolio return and its standard deviation are

$$\bar{R}_p = 13\%$$

$$\sigma_p = \sqrt{\frac{(0.4)^2(0.001) + (0.6)^2(0.001) + 2(0.4)(0.6)(-1)}{(0.0317)(0.0317)}}$$

$$= 0.0063$$

Thus, the portfolio standard deviation is only 20
per cent of the weighted average of the two individual standard deviations (0.0063/0.0317). If a
considerable number of perfectly negatively correlated projects are available, risk can be entirely diversified away. However, perfect negative correlation is seldom found in the real world.

The Efficient Frontier

     Assume that Cases 1, 2, and 3 are three dif-
ferent portfolios which require the same amount of
investment ($1,000). If we plot these three risk-
return possibilities in Figure 9-1, we can quickly

166

notice that Case 3 incurs the smallest risk for a
given level of return (13%). Case 3 is called an
efficient portfolio. The efficient portfolio also
exists when a portfolio provides the highest expected return for a given level of risk. If we
compute more points such as Case 3, we may obtain
Line EF by connecting such points. This line is
called the efficient frontier, which is the locus
of all efficient portfolios. Cases 1 and 2 are in
the right of the efficient frontier. They are in-
efficient because some other portfolio could give
either a lower risk for the same rate of return or
a higher return for the same degree of risk. Portfolios to the left of the efficient portfolio are
unobtainable with the funds available for investment. It should be noted that all attainable risk-
return combinations with a given amount of investment are surrounded by Points EFBA.

Figure 9-1   Efficient Frontier

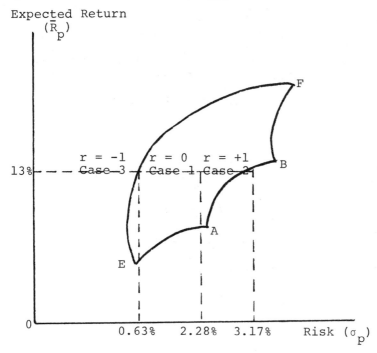

Risk-Return Indifference Curve

There are numerous efficient portfolios along
the efficient frontier. The efficient frontier
does not tell us which portfolio to select, but
rather shows a collection of portfolios that minimize the risk for any expected return or that maximize the expected return for any degree of risk.
The objective of the investor is to choose the optimal (best) portfolio among those on the efficient
frontier. Thus, the efficient frontier is necessary but not sufficient for selecting the optimal
portfolio. Given an efficient frontier, the choice
of the optimal portfolio depends on the risk-return
indifference curve of the investor.

An indifference curve is the locus of risk-return combinations that result in a fixed level of
expected utility. Thus, the investor is indifferent
between any combination of expected return and standard deviation on a particular curve. Figure 9-2 illustrates a set of indifference curves. The indifference curve is convex toward the horizontal axis
due to the law of diminishing marginal utility.
That is, larger increases in return are required
to compensate for small increases in risk. Each

Figure 9-2 A Set of Indifference Curves

Expected Return ($\bar{R}_p$)

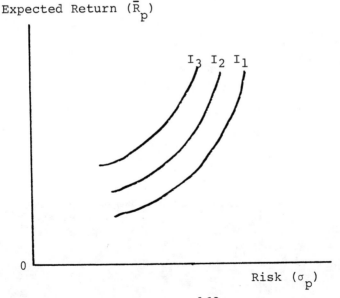

Risk (σ_p)

successive curve to the left in Figure 9-2 represents a higher level of expected utility. Thus,
I_3 represents the best risk-return combinations
among three indifference curves in Figure 9-2.
The slope of the indifference curve indicates the
investor's attitude toward the risk for each additional unit of return. Then it should be obvious that the larger the slope is, the more the
investor is averse to risk.

Selection of the Optimal Portfolio

If an investor wants to select the optimal
portfolio from those portfolios on a particular
efficient frontier, he should land on the highest
indifference curve. This optimal portfolio is
found at the tangency point between the efficient
frontier and the indifference curve. The tangency
condition requires that the slope of the efficient
frontier and that of the indifference curve are the
same. Tangency Point T in Figure 9-3 marks the
highest level of utility that the investor can obtain with the funds available for investment.

Figure 9-3 Selection of Optimal Portfolio

Expected Return ($\bar{R}_p$)

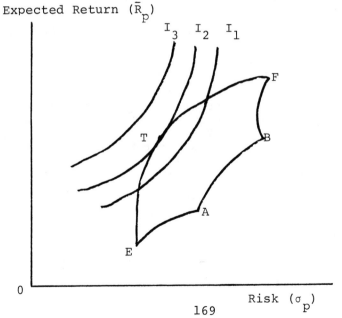

Risk (σ_p)

THE CAPITAL ASSET PRICING MODEL

The first half of this chapter has shown us
that the standard deviation of a portfolio is
generally less than the weighted average of the
standard deviations for those individual securities that make up the portfolio. Hence, it is
desirable to consider the riskiness of a security
in terms of its contribution to the riskiness of
the portfolio rather than in terms of its separate
riskiness. The capital asset pricing model is designed to measure the return and standard deviation
of a security to a broad-based economic indicator
such as Standard & Poor's 500 Stock Index.

The portfolio selection process using Equation
(9-3) requires us to compute an unmanageably large
number of covariances or correlation coefficients.
But the capital asset pricing model simplifies the
selection process by estimating the covariance or
correlation between the return of a specific security and that of some market index.[3] In the remaining portion of this chapter, we consider two
things: (1) the implications of the capital asset
pricing model for the expected return of a particular security and (2) how portfolio theory can
be simplified.

Efficient Markets

Companies and investors make risk-return decisions in the framework of available capital markets. Our discussion on the capital asset pricing
model is based on the concept of efficient capital
markets. Efficient markets exist when security
prices reflect all available information and market
prices adjust quickly to new information. Because
capital markets are highly competitive in such a
situation, the market participants buy and sell
securities in a way that eliminates all profits
in excess of the minimum required to sustain their
continued participation.

There are many strong indications that capital
markets are efficient. Securities are traded by
many companies and individuals who have broad market contacts, sophisticated analytical capabilities,
and modern communications. Because new information

170

is widely, quickly, and cheaply disseminated to investors, market prices are rapidly adjusted to reflect significant developments. Various government agencies such as the Securities and Exchange Commission and various laws such as the Securities Act of 1933 provide the pressure toward efficiency.

Just like all other financial theories, the capital asset pricing model depends on a number of assumptions. These assumptions, as summarized by Michael C. Jensen,[4] are as follows:

1. All investors are single-period expected utility of internal wealth maximizers who choose among alternative portfolios on the basis of the mean and standard deviation of portfolio returns.

2. All investors can borrow and lend an unlimited amount at an exogenously given risk-free rate of interest.

3. All investors have identical subjective estimates of the means, variances, and covariances of returns among assets; that is, investors have homogeneous expectations.

4. All assets are perfectly divisible and perfectly liquid with no restrictions on short sales of any asset.

5. There are no transaction costs.

6. There are no taxes.

7. All investors are price takers. (Investors assume that their own purchases and sales will not affect stock prices.)

8. The quantities of all assets are given.

171

The Capital Market Line

The capital market line is the locus of the risk-return tradeoffs for portfolios which comprise risky and riskless securities. The expected return of a portfolio and its standard deviation are computed in the same manner as before:

$$\bar{R}_p = x_f R_f + (1 - x_f)\bar{R}_m \qquad (9\text{-}12)$$

where x_f = percentage of funds invested in the riskless security

R_f = riskless rate of interest

$\bar{R}_m$ = expected return of the market portfolio, which is a group of risky securities such as Standard & Poor's 500 Stocks.

$$\sigma_p = \sqrt{x_f^2 \sigma_f^2 + (1 - x_f)^2 \sigma_m^2 + 2x_f(1 - x_f)r_{fm}\sigma_f\sigma_m} \qquad (9\text{-}13)$$

where σ_f^2 = variance of the riskless security

σ_m^2 = variance of the market portfolio

r_{fm} = correlation coefficient between the riskless security and the market portfolio

σ_f = standard deviation of the riskless security

σ_m = standard deviation of the market portfolio

Because the riskless security has no variance and standard deviation, the standard deviation of the portfolio depends entirely on the standard deviation of Portfolio m:

$$\sigma_p = \sqrt{(1 - x_f)^2 \sigma_m^2} = (1 - x_f)\sigma_m \qquad (9\text{-}14)$$

Figure 9-4 shows a graphic representation of this risk-return relationship.

Figure 9-4   Capital Market Line

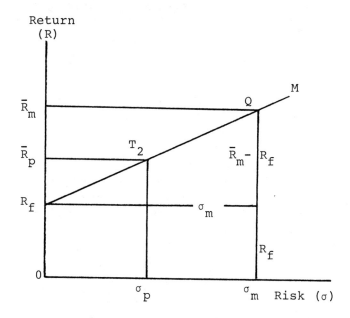

Line R_fM is known as the capital market line. It has an intercept of R_f and a slope of $(\bar{R}_m - R_f)/\sigma_m$:

$$\bar{R}_p = R_f + \left(\frac{\bar{R}_m - R_f}{\sigma_m}\right)\sigma_p \qquad (9\text{-}15)$$

The term in brackets represents the market price of risk, which reflects the attitudes of individuals in the aggregate toward risk. The investor would be fully committed to reckless securities if $(1 - x_f) = 0$. Because σ_p equals $(1 - x_f)\sigma_m$, the investor's expected return becomes $\bar{R}_p = R_f$ with $\sigma_p = 0$. This risk-return relationship is given at point R_f in Figure 9-4. On the other hand, the investor would be fully committed to risky securities if $(1 - x_f) = 1$. This corresponds to Point Q and thus $\bar{R}_p = \bar{R}_m$ with $\sigma_p = \sigma_m$. If the investor picked

173

any random Point T_2 between Points R_f and Q, his
portfolio represents a combination of risky and
riskless securities. Inclusion of riskless securities such as U.S. government securities in
portfolios makes it possible for the investor to
preserve returns at less risk and to move a higher
indifference curve.

Portfolio Selection and Riskless Security

        Under the capital asset pricing model, a new
portfolio combines a riskless security and a portfolio of risky securities. Thus, the portfolio
selection process described in the first half of
this chapter should be modified. Because the investor is free to divide his funds between risky
and riskless securities, his choices are not
limited to points along Efficient Frontier EF in
Figure 9-5. If the investor's choices are limited
to portfolios on Curve EF, his optimal portfolio
is found at Point T_1 where Indifference Curve I_1
is tangent to Curve EF. However, the investor can
move from Point T_1 to Point T_3 if his new portfolio
combines a riskless security with the portfolio of
risky securities. Because Point T_3 is on a higher
indifference curve than Point T_1, the portfolios
on Line R_fT_2 dominate all portfolios on Curve EF.
Thus, Line R_fT_2M becomes the investor's new efficient frontier.

        The optimal investment policy is determined at
Point T_3, which is the point of tangency between
the highest indifference curve (I_2) and the new
efficient frontier (R_fT_2M). Point T_3 consists of
an investment in both the riskless security and the
portfolio of risky securities. It is the point
where the investor attains the highest return for
a given level of risk (σ_p) or the smallest risk for
a given level of return ($\bar{R}_p$). Hence, the application of the capital market line is limited to a
special category of portfolios, which combine the
market portfolio and riskless securities.

Security Market Line

        The capital market line deals with the rela-
tionship between the risk and expected return for

174

Figure 9-5   Investor Equilibrium: Riskless and
             Risky Securities

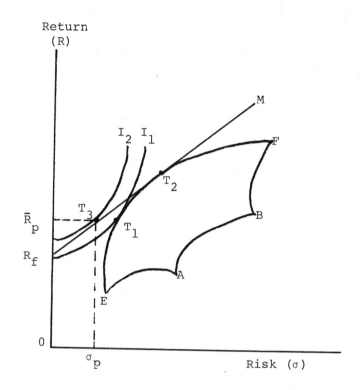

portfolios comprising the riskless security and
the market portfolio.   Its basic assumption is
that the investor can attain a better risk-return
combination by varying the proportion of the riskless security and the market portfolio.   Because
the riskless security and the market portfolio
constitute a new portfolio, the capital market
line relates the market model to portfolios.   In
contrast, the security market line relates the
model to individual securities.

    If the market is in equilibrium, the expected
return of an individual security (j) is stated as
follows:

175

$$\bar{R}_j = R_f + \left(\frac{\bar{R}_m - R_f}{\sigma_m^2}\right) r_{jm}\sigma_j\sigma_m \qquad (9\text{-}16)$$

The term $(\bar{R}_m - R_f)/\sigma_m^2$ is the price of risk; and the term $r_{jm}\sigma_j\sigma_m$ is the covariance between Security j and Portfolio m. This covariance measures the risk of Security j.

Another important concept in the development of the capital asset pricing model is to express the risk of a particular risky security in terms of its beta coefficient. The beta coefficient of Security j may be defined as

$$\beta_j = \frac{r_{jm}\sigma_j\sigma_m}{\sigma_m^2} \qquad (9\text{-}17)$$

where β_j is the systematic risk of Security j. The beta coefficient is simply the covariance divided by the variance of the market portfolio.

The capital asset pricing model implies that the total risk of a security consists of systematic risk (undiversifiable risk) and unsystematic risk (diversifiable risk). When an individual security is added to the investor's existing portfolio, the relevant measure of risk for the security is not its total risk as given by its standard deviation. However, the relevant measure of risk is that portion of the total risk remaining after diversification.[5] Unsystematic risk is totally eliminated by diversification, while systematic risk cannot be eliminated by diversification. Thus, systematic risk should be measured to determine an optimal investment policy. The size of beta coefficient indicates the level of undiversifiable risk. The larger the beta coefficient, the greater the security's systematic risk.

Equation (9-16) may be changed to reflect the beta coefficient as follows:

176

$$\bar{R}_j = R_f + \left(\frac{\bar{R}_m - R_f}{\sigma_m^2}\right) r_{jm}\sigma_j\sigma_m$$

$$= R_f + (\bar{R}_m - R_f)\frac{r_{jm}\sigma_j\sigma_m}{\sigma_m^2}$$

$$= R_f + (\bar{R}_m - R_f)\beta_j \qquad\qquad (9-18)$$

Equation (9-18) is known as the security market line, which consists of the riskless rate of interest (R_f) and a risk premium (($R_m - R_f)\beta_j$).

Sample Problem 9-2

What is the minimum required rate of return on Security j if this security and Market Portfolio m have the following characteristics:

Riskless rate of interest (R_f)	= 0.05
Standard deviation of Security j (σ_j)	= 0.15
Standard deviation of Market Portfolio m (σ_m)	= 0.10
Expected return of Market Portfolio m ($\bar{R}_m$)	= 0.08
Correlation coefficient between Security j and Portfolio m (r_{jm})	= 0.90

The beta coefficient of Security j is

$$\beta_j = \frac{r_{jm}\sigma_j\sigma_m}{\sigma_m^2} = \frac{(0.90)(0.15)(0.10)}{(0.10)^2} = 1.35$$

and thus, the required rate of return on Security j is

$$\bar{R}_j = R_f + (\bar{R}_m - R_f)\beta_j = 0.05 + (0.08 - 0.05)(1.35) = 9.05\%$$

If the expected rate of return for Security j is greater than its 9.05 per cent required rate of return, the security can be accepted.

The general decision rule for accepting a risky Security j can be stated as follows:

$$\bar{R}_j > R_f + (\bar{R}_m - R_f)\beta_j \qquad\qquad (9\text{-}19)$$

This decision rule implies that to accept Security j, its expected return must exceed the investor's hurdle rate, which is the sum of the riskless rate of interest plus a risk premium for the riskiness of the security. Figure 9-6 shows the decision criterion in general terms: accept all securities that plot above the security market line and reject all securities that plot below the security market line.

Figure 9-6 The Security Market Line

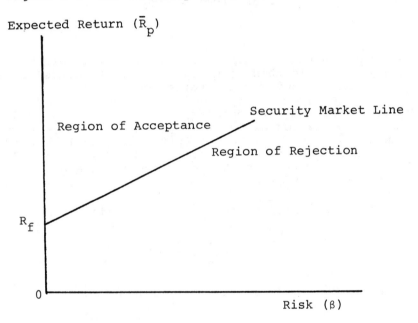

Calculating Beta in Practice

Beta may be estimated solely on the basis of subjective probability distributions. However, it is the common practice to use past data to estimate future betas. Beta may be estimated on the basis of the historical data using the following simple linear regression equation:

$$R_{jt} = \partial_j + \beta_j R_{mt} \qquad\qquad (9\text{-}20)$$

where R_{jt} = rate of return on Security j in year t

R_{mt} = rate of return on Market Portfolio m in year t

∂_j and β_j = parameters for Security j

This regression equation determines the parameters ∂j and βj so that returns on individual securities can be estimated using the equation and an estimate for the value of the market portfolio. Given many pairs of items in a sample, the parameters ∂j and βj are determined by the method of least squares:

$$\beta_j = \frac{n \sum\limits_{t=1}^{n} R_{mt} R_{jt} - \left(\sum\limits_{t=1}^{n} R_{mt}\right)\left(\sum\limits_{t=1}^{n} R_{jt}\right)}{n \sum\limits_{t=1}^{n} R_{mt}^2 - \left(\sum\limits_{t=1}^{n} R_{mt}\right)^2}$$

$(9\text{-}21)$

$$\partial_j = \frac{\sum\limits_{t=1}^{n} R_{jt}}{n} - \beta_j \frac{\sum\limits_{t=1}^{n} R_{mt}}{n} = \bar{R}_j - \beta_j \bar{R}_m \qquad (9\text{-}22)$$

Sample Problem 9-3

Assume that a security under consideration is similar to the security whose percentage returns over a 10-year period are shown below. The percentage returns on a market portfolio are also shown.

Because the linear regression model relies on the assumption of a linear relationship between the two variables, a significant caveat in its interpretations relates to the existence of curvilinearity or nonlinearity. Thus, these two groups of returns should be examined for nonlinearity so that the validity of the model could be established. This test may be conducted by plotting the relationships between these two variables on a dot chart called a scatter

179

Year	Similar Security R_{jt}	Market Portfolio R_{mt}
19-0	23	10
19-1	7	2
19-2	15	4
19-3	17	6
19-4	23	8
19-5	22	7
19-6	10	4
19-7	14	6
19-8	20	7
19-9	19	6

diagram. Figure 9-7 shows the scatter diagram. The plotted dots generally follow a straight line, thus suggesting a linear relationship between the two variables.

Figure 9-7   Scatter Diagram for Security j and Market Portfolio m

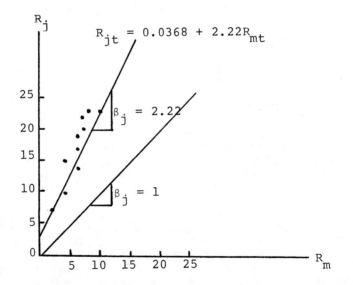

The parameters ∂_j and β_j are computed as follows:[6]

Year	R_{jt}	R_{mt}	$R_{mt}R_{jt}$	R_{mt}^2	R_{jt}^2
19-0	0.23	0.10	0.0230	0.0100	0.0529
19-1	0.07	0.02	0.0014	0.0004	0.0049
19-2	0.15	0.04	0.0060	0.0016	0.0225
19-3	0.17	0.06	0.0102	0.0036	0.0289
19-4	0.23	0.08	0.0184	0.0064	0.0529
19-5	0.22	0.07	0.0154	0.0049	0.0484
19-6	0.10	0.04	0.0040	0.0016	0.0100
19-7	0.14	0.06	0.0084	0.0036	0.0196
19-8	0.20	0.07	0.0140	0.0049	0.0400
19-9	0.19	0.06	0.0114	0.0036	0.0361
Totals	1.70	0.60	0.1122	0.0406	0.3162

$$\beta_j = \frac{10(0.1122) - 0.60(1.70)}{10(0.0406) - (0.60)^2} = 2.22$$

$$\partial_j = \frac{1.70}{10} - 2.22\left(\frac{0.60}{10}\right) = 0.0368$$

We can now substitute the values of β_j = 2.22 and ∂_j = 3.68 per cent into Equation (9-20) to obtain the following regression equation:

$$R_{jt} = 0.0368 + 2.22R_{mt} \qquad (9\text{-}23)$$

Equation (9-23) is plotted in Figure 9-7. This regression equation indicates that Security j earns 3.68 per cent due to its own merits and it will also earn 222 per cent of the expected return on the market portfolio. Equation (9-23) is usually called the characteristic line. The second characteristic line has a slope of 45° and is appropriate for any security with the same risk as the market portfolio. This is because a stock's beta is a measure of its volatility relative to a market index and the market index is assigned a beta of 1.

The concept of a characteristic line may be

181

used to classify stocks into two broad categories: aggressive stocks and defensive stocks. Aggressive stocks are those stocks which have betas greater than 1. Their returns rise (fall) more than the market index rises (falls). Defensive stocks are those stocks which have betas less than 1. Their returns fluctuate less than the market index. Finally, those stocks with betas equal to 1 are frequently called neutral stocks.

Current estimates of beta for actively traded stocks are available on a commercial basis. These betas are estimated on the basis of weekly, monthly, or quarterly data for several months or several years in the past. The better-known services include those of Merrill Lynch Pierce Fenner & Smith Inc., Wells Fargo Bank, and the Value Line Investment Survey. Table 9-3 illustrates betas for five aggressive stocks and five defensive stocks.

Table 9-3   Estimates of Beta for Ten Selected Stocks

Aggressive Stocks ($\beta > 1$)		Defensive Stocks ($\beta < 1$)	
Boeing	1.43	Consolidated Foods	0.53
McDonnell Douglass	1.63	General Mills	0.64
Northrop	1.72	Gerber Products	0.67
Cessna	1.83	CPC International	0.83
Lockheed	2.77	General Foods	0.87

Source: Merrill Lynch Pierce Fenner & Smith Inc., Monthly Research Review (June 1980).

Coefficient of Determination

Betas for various stocks are computed and published by several organizations, but some very important factors are generally omitted. One is the coefficient of determination, which is the strength of the relationship between the returns on a stock and those of the market index. It may be defined as a measure of the extent to which the market index accounts for the variability in the returns on the stock.

The coefficient of determination varies from zero (no correlation) to one (perfect correlation). If the regression line were to pass through every point, the coefficient of determination is at a maximum of 1. If the points were scattered more like a shotgun pattern, the coefficient of determination tends toward 0. The low coefficient of determination indicates a weak relationship between the market index and the stock price. This weak relationship in turn suggests that the historically computed beta is a poor predictor of its future beta. On the other hand, the high coefficient of determination indicates that the beta computed from historical data is a good surrogate for the true beta reflecting investors' estimates of the stock's future volatility.

The coefficient of determination (r^2) can be computed as follows:

$$r^2 = \frac{\left(\sum_{t=1}^{n} R_{mt}R_{jt} - \bar{R}_m \sum_{t=1}^{n} R_{jt} \right)^2}{\left(\sum_{t=1}^{n} R_{mt}^2 - \bar{R}_m \sum_{t=1}^{n} R_{mt} \right)\left(\sum_{t=1}^{n} R_{jt}^2 - \bar{R}_j \sum_{t=1}^{n} R_{jt} \right)} \quad (9\text{-}24)$$

Let us return to Sample Problem 9-3 involving the relationship between the returns on Security j and those on the market index. Because Equation (9-23) only involves quantities already calculated, we obtain

$$r^2 = \frac{(0.1122 - 0.06 \times 1.70)^2}{(0.0406 - 0.06 \times 0.6)(0.3162 - 0.17 \times 1.7)}$$

$$= \frac{0.0001040}{0.0001251}$$

$$= 0.83$$

Thus, about 83 per cent of the variance in the returns on Security j was explained by the variance in the returns on the market portfolio.

183

FOOTNOTES

1. This chapter discusses both the Markowitz portfolio theory and the capital asset pricing model in the context of security analysis. However, they may be also used to evaluate capital expenditures for plant and equipment. For details, see John J. Clark, Thomas J. Hindelang, and Robert E. Pritchard, <u>Capital Budgeting: Planning and Control of Capital Expenditures</u> (Englewood Cliffs, N.J.: Prentice-Hall, Inc., 1979), Chapters 9 and 10; and Harold Bierman, Jr. and Seymour Smidt, <u>The Capital Budgeting Decision</u> (New York: Macmillan Publishing Company, 1980), Chapter 14.

2. If the $\bar{R}_p$ represents a dollar value and projects are indivisible, $x_j = (0,1)$ where 0 = rejection of a project as a whole and 1 = acceptance of a project as a whole. Hence, the expected return of a portfolio is obtained by adding the net present values of all projects accepted. For example, assume that a portfolio consists of a project with a net present value of \$100 and another with a net present value of \$200. The expected return of this two-project portfolio is \$300 (\$100 + \$200).

3. For details, see William F. Sharp, "A Simplified Model for Portfolio Analysis," <u>Management Science</u> (January 1963), pp. 277-293.

4. Michael C. Jensen, "Capital Markets: Theory and Evidence," <u>Bell Journal of Economics and Management Science</u> (Autumn 1972), pp. 258-359. Certainly, these conditions are not completely met in practice. Thus, capital markets are assumed to be efficient if the conditions are only reasonably met. Evidence indicates that such capital markets as the New York Stock Exchange are efficient. See Eugene F. Farma, "Efficient Capital Markets: A Review of Theory and Empirical Work," <u>Journal of Finance</u> (May 1970), pp. 383-417; and James H. Lorie and Mary T. Hamilton, <u>The Stock Market</u> (Homewood, Ill.: Richard D. Irwin, 1973), Chapter 4.

5. The capital asset pricing model assumes that individual investors can eliminate all risk other than systematic risk by diversification in their portfolios of securities. Thus, when this model is applied to the firm's portfolios of capital assets, diversification in the firm is not beneficial for its stockholders. This is because the firm cannot reduce its overall risk for investors that they cannot reduce for themselves. See Steward C. Myers, "Procedures for Capital Budgeting Under Uncertainty," Industrial Management Review (Spring 1968), pp. 1-15; and Haim Levy and Marshall Sarnat, "Diversification, Portfolio Analysis, and the Uneasy Case for Conglomerate Mergers," Journal of Finance (September 1970), pp. 795-802.

CHAPTER 10

THE COST OF CAPITAL

The three discounted cash-flow approaches described in Chapter 4 all measure cash flows of a project in terms of a required rate of return to determine its acceptability. The required rate of return was defined as the firm's cost of capital. As noted in our discussion of risk analysis in Chapters 8 and 9, the actual required rate of return applied may be the cost of capital adjusted to compensate for project risk, which could differ from that of the normal risk complexion of the firm.

Our concern in this chapter is the effect of variations in the firm's capital structure (debt, preferred stock, and equity) on the cost of capital. First, we discuss the necessity of using a weighted average cost of capital. Second, we compute the cost of the individual components of the capital structure. Third, the individual component costs are brought together to determine the weighted average cost of capital. Fourth, we examine the relationship between the capital structure and the cost of capital. Fifth, we use the capital asset pricing model to determine the cost of capital and the value of a project. Finally, we consider the relationship between the weighted average cost of capital and the required rate of return computed by the capital asset pricing model.

RATIONALE FOR THE USE OF A WEIGHTED AVERAGE COST OF CAPITAL

The weighted average cost of capital should be used as the firm's cost of capital (the acceptance criterion) for a number of reasons. First, if a single component cost is used as the acceptance criterion, it is possible to accept projects with a low rate of return while rejecting projects with a high rate of return. Some low-return projects would be accepted because they can be financed with a cheaper source of capital such as debt. Some high-return projects would be rejected because they have to be financed with an expensive source of capital such as equity capital. If the firm uses up some of its potential for obtaining new low-cost debt, subsequent expansions will require it to use additional equity financing or the debt ratio will become too large.

To illustrate, let us assume that the firm has a 10 per cent cost of debt and a 16 per cent cost of equity capital. In the first year it may use up its debt capacity to finance projects yielding 11 per cent. In the second year it may have projects that yield 15 per cent, well above the return on the first-year projects. However, it cannot accept them because they would have to be financed with 16 per cent equity money. To avoid this problem, the firm should use the weighted average cost of capital.

Second, if the firm accepts those projects that yield more than its weighted average cost of capital, it is able to increase the market value of its common stock. This increase occurs because these projects are expected to earn more on their equity-financed portion than the cost of equity.

Because the investment analyst is concerned with the cost of obtaining new funds, this chapter concentrates on incremental funds and their associated costs. The weighted average cost of incremental capital refers to the cost incurred by the firm in acquiring an additional amount of capital for investment purposes. This and some other similar terms, such as the incremental cost of capital and the marginal cost of capital, can be interchangeably used.

CALCULATING THE COST OF CAPITAL

Cost of Debt

The explicit cost of debt can be defined as the discount rate that equates the net proceeds of the debt issue with the present value of interest plus principal payments. If we want to express all cost-of-capital rates on an after-tax basis, we must adjust this explicit cost of debt for taxes, because interest charges are tax deductible. If we denote the after-tax cost of new debt by k_i, it can be approximated by

$$k_i = \frac{I(1 - t)}{P(1 - F)}$$

$$= k_d(1 - t) \qquad\qquad (10\text{-}1)$$

where I = annual dollar amount of interest

t = firm's marginal tax rate

P = sales price

F = flotation cost as a per cent of the sales price

k_d = before-tax cost of new debt

Cost of Preferred Stock

Preferred stock is treated as a middle ground between debt and equity in a firm's capital structure. On the one hand, it represents an ownership interest to the extent that preferred dividends are not a tax-deductible expense. On the other hand, it is considered debt in the sense that preferred dividends are fixed. Failure of the firm to pay interest on debt results in bankruptcy, but its failure to pay preferred dividends does not necessarily result in bankruptcy. In liquidation, the claims of the various creditors take precedence over those of the preferred stockholders, and the claims of the preferred stockholders take precedence over those of the common stockholders. Thus, from the firm's point of view preferred stock is less risky than debt, but it is more risky than common stock.

Because most preferred stocks are perpetual in nature, their explicit cost is viewed in the same terms as a perpetuity. If preferred stock has no maturity, its cost is

$$k_p = \frac{D_p}{P(1 - F)} \qquad\qquad (10\text{-}2)$$

where k_p = cost of new preferred stock

189

D_p = stated dividend per year on new pre-ferred stock

Cost of Common Stock

Interest and dividends are directly measurable component costs of debt and preferred stock, but we do not have such a measurable element for the cost of common stock. This is because dividend declarations on common stock are made at the discretion of the firm's board of directors. Thus, the cost of common stock is the most difficult concept to measure.

The dividend valuation model for common stock states that the price of common stock is a function of the expected future dividends. That is, the cost of common stock is the discount rate that equates the present value of all expected future dividends per share with the current market price per share:

$$P = \frac{D_1}{(1 + k_c)^1} + \frac{D_2}{(1 + k_c)^2} + \dots + \frac{D_\infty}{(1 + k_c)^\infty} \quad (10\text{-}3)$$

where P = current market price per share

D_t = dividends to be paid at the end of year t

k_c = cost of common stock

If dividends per share are expected to grow at a constant growth rate g indefinitely, Equation (10-3) can be modified to consider this growth:

$$P = \frac{D_o(1 + g)^1}{(1 + k_c)^1} + \frac{D_o(1 + g)^2}{(1 + k_c)^2} + \dots + \frac{D_o(1 + g)^\infty}{(1 + k_c)^\infty} \quad (10\text{-}4)$$

where D_o = dividend per share paid in year 0.

Multiplying Equation (10-4) by $(1 + k_c)/(1 + g)$ and subtracting Equation (10-4) from this product, we obtain:

190

$$\frac{P(1 + k_c)}{(1 + g)} - P = D_o - \frac{D_o(1 + g)^\infty}{(1 + k_c)^\infty}$$ (10-5)

If k_c is greater than g, the second term on the right-hand side of Equation (10-5) is equal to zero for all practical purposes. Hence, we obtain

$$P\left(\frac{1 + k_c}{1 + g} - 1\right) = D_o$$

$$P\left(\frac{(1 + k_c) - (1 + g)}{1 + g}\right) = D_o$$

$$P(k_c - g) = D_o(1 + g)$$

$$P = \frac{D_1}{k_c - g}$$ (10-6)

Rearranging Equation (10-6) results in Equation (10-7):

$$k_c = \frac{D_1}{P} + g$$ (10-7)

As was the case for debt and preferred stock, we must consider flotation costs for new issues of common stock. Thus, Equation (10-7) is modified as

$$_n k_c = \frac{D_1}{P(1 - F)} + g$$ (10-8)

where $_n k_c$ = cost of new common stock

Cost of Retained Earnings

Equation (10-7) is used to determine the cost of retained earnings under the following assumptions: (1) the stockholders pay no income taxes on additional dividends and (2) they incur no transaction costs on investments. However, dividends are subject to double taxation, and reinvestment of addi-

191

tional dividends involves transaction costs such as brokerage fees. Thus, the opportunity cost of retained earnings is slightly less than k_c. If alternative investments of additional dividends earn k_c, the cost of retained earnings is

$$k_r = k_c (1 - t_p)(1 - B) \qquad (10\text{-}9)$$

where k_r = cost of retained earnings

t_p = average of all the stockholders' marginal tax rate

B = average percentage transaction cost

Marginal Cost of Capital

To compute the marginal cost of capital: (1) calculate the cost of each component, (2) determine the weight of each component, and (3) multiply each weight by its corresponding cost and sum these products.

Example 10-1 Given the following data, compute the marginal cost of capital.

Debt: $20,000 at 10% with a flotation cost of 0.5% and a tax rate of 50%

Preferred stock: $90,000 with a flotation cost of 2%; sold at $40 per share with a stated dividend of $3 per share

Common stock: $70,000 with a flotation cost of 10% and an expected dividend of $1 a share in year 1; dividend expected to grow at 10% a year indefinitely; sold at $50 a share

Retained earnings: $28,000 with k_c = 11%; stockholders' average tax rate of 30%; average transaction cost of 5%

The cost of each component is computed below.

$$k_i = \frac{\$2{,}000(1 - 0.50)}{\$20{,}000(1 - 0.005)} = \frac{\$1{,}000}{\$19{,}900} = 0.0503$$

$$k_p = \frac{\$3}{\$40(1 - 0.02)} = \frac{\$3}{\$39.2} = 0.0765$$

$$_n k_c = \frac{\$1}{\$50(1 - 0.10)} + 0.10 = 0.0222 + 0.10 = 0.1222$$

$$k_r = 0.11(1 - 0.30)(1 - 0.05) = 0.0732$$

The marginal cost of capital is computed as follows:

Capital	Net Proceeds	Weight	After-Tax Cost	Marginal Cost
Debt	20,000(.995) = 19,900	.0995	.0503	.00500
Preferred	90,000(.980) = 88,200	.4410	.0765	.03374
Common	70,000(.900) = 63,000	.3150	.1222	.03849
R/E	28,900 = 28,900	.1445	.0732	.01058
Total	200,000	1.0000		.08781

Thus, the marginal cost of capital is approximately 8.781 per cent.

OPTIMUM CAPITAL STRUCTURE

The optimum capital structure is defined as the combination of debt and equity that yields the lowest overall cost of capital. The optimum mix of debt and equity leads the firm to attain the maximization of its market value.

Some individuals argue that the weighted average cost of capital remains constant throughout all degrees of financing leverage and thus, there is no such thing as an optimum capital structure. For example, David Durand contends that an optimum capital structure does not exist because an increase in the use of low-cost debt offsets exactly the risk in the cost of equity.[1] Franco Modigliani and Merton H. Miller

argue that the market value of the firm is independent of its capital structure due to the existence of arbitrage in the capital markets.[2]   Assume that Firm A has a market value greater than
Firm B only because the former uses low-cost debt
and the latter does not.   Then it is possible to
earn more on the same investment if investors in
Firm A sell their holdings and invest these funds
in Firm B.   These arbitrage transactions cause the
price of Firm A's stock to fall and the price of
Firm B's stock to rise until the value of these two
firms becomes identical.

In contrast, the traditional approach to valuation and leverage assumes that an optimum capital
structure exists.   This model implies that the varying effects on the market capitalization rates for
debt and equity allow the firm to lower its cost of
capital by the intelligent use of leverage.   Debt
has two types of cost: explicit cost and implicit
cost.   The explicit cost is the interest rate, whereas
the implicit cost refers to the fact that added debt
causes both the cost of equity and the cost of debt
to rise.

If we start with an all-equity capital structure,
the introduction of debt enables the firm to lower
its cost of capital and to increase its market value.
At first, the interest rate either remains constant
or increases slowly with leverage, and the cost of
equity also rises.   But the weighted average cost
of capital falls with leverage, because the increase
in the cost of equity does not offset completely
the use of low-cost debt.

The traditional approach implies that beyond
some point both the cost of equity and the cost of
debt increase at an increasing rate.   With the heavy
use of leverage, the increase in the cost of equity
more than offsets the use of low-cost debt.   Thus,
at a critical turning point the subsequent introduction of additional leverage causes the overall
cost of capital to rise and the firm's market value
to fall.   The optimum capital structure is the point
at which the weighted average cost of capital bottoms out or the market value of the firm tops out.

Example 10-2 The Western Clothing Company has an all-equity capital structure of $50,000 and wants to maintain this book value indefinitely. The firm now earns $10,000 before taxes of 50 per cent, all of which are paid in dividends. To retire a part of its common stock, the firm wants to issue some debt. The financial manager estimates that debt and equity would have the following costs at various levels of debt:

Debt	Before-Tax Cost of Debt	Cost of Equity
$ 0	8.0%	10.0%
5,000	8.0	10.1
10,000	9.0	10.5
15,000	10.4	11.5
20,000	13.0	13.5

To determine its optimum capital structure, the Western Clothing Company must first compute the weighted average cost of capital under different debt ratios. This computation is given in Table 10-1. The table shows that the firm minimizes its overall cost of capital at the point at which its capital structure consists of 20 per cent debt and 80 per cent equity. Below a debt ratio of 20 per cent, the weighted average cost of capital declines with leverage. Above that point, the weighted average cost of capital increases with leverage. Thus, the average cost-of-capital curve bottoms out at a capital structure of 20 per cent debt and 80 per cent equity.

The total market value of the firm at the optimum capital structure can be computed as follows:

Earnings before taxes and interest		$10,000
Less: interest (9% of $10,000)		900
Earnings before taxes		$ 9,100
Less: taxes at 50%		4,550
Earnings after taxes		$ 4,550
Market value of stock	$4,550/0.105	$43,333
Market value of debt		10,000
Total value of firm		$53,333

Table 10-1 The Weighted Average Cost of Capital
           Under Different Debt Ratios

Capital Structure (1)	% of Total Capital (2)	After-Tax Cost of Component (3)	Weighted Average Cost of Capital (2) x (3) ÷ 100
Debt	0%	4.0%	0.00%
Equity	100	10.0	10.00
Total	100		10.00
Debt	10	4.0	0.40
Equity	90	10.1	9.09
Total	100		9.49
Debt	20	4.5	0.90
Equity	80	10.5	8.40
Total	100		9.30
Debt	30	5.2	1.56
Equity	70	11.5	8.05
Total	100		9.61
Debt	40	6.5	2.60
Equity	60	13.5	8.10
Total	100		10.70

By the same method, we can compute the total market
value of the firm under different debt ratios, and
these computation results are given in Table 10-2.

Table 10-2 Value of the Firm Under Different
            Debt Ratios

Debt Ratio	EBIT	EAT	Value of Debt	Value of Stock	Value of the Firm
0%	$10,000	$5,000	$ 0	$50,000	$50,000
10	10,000	4,800	5,000	47,525	52,525
20	10,000	4,550	10,000	43,333	53,333
30	10,000	4,220	15,000	36,696	51,696
40	10,000	3,700	20,000	27,407	47,407

As can be seen in the table, a capital structure of 20
per cent debt and 80 per cent equity yields a total

196

market value of $53,333, and no other combination attains more than this market value.

ALTERNATIVE APPROACH: THE CAPITAL ASSET PRICING MODEL

Because the marginal cost of capital represents the overall risk position of the company, it does not reflect the risk of a particular project under consideration. Therefore, in Chapter 8 we noted the necessity to adjust project estimates for risk. We indicated three methods were available: the certainty equivalent approach, the risk-adjusted discount rate, and the capital asset pricing model. Chapter 8 discussed the first two methods, and the remainder of this chapter demonstrates how the capital asset pricing model (CAPM) can be employed in project evaluation. It is important to remember that beta can be estimated on the basis of subjective probability distributions as well as on the basis of past data. We consider both cases but take up the former case first.

CAPM Based on Subjective Probability Distributions

Table 10-3 shows the returns from Market Portfolio m and Security A for four possible states of economy. Probabilities in the table represent estimates for single periods for the market index and the security. Determine whether or not Security A would be accepted.

Table 10-3   Possible Returns for Market Portfolio
                     m and Security A

State of the Economy	Associated Probability	Returns	
		Market Portfolio m	Security A
Deep Recession	0.10	0.00	-0.30
Mild Recession	0.20	0.06	0.00
Normal	0.50	0.30	0.30
Prosperity	0.20	0.20	0.40

To determine beta for Security A, we should know two things: σ_m^2 = variance for Market Portfolio m and Cov_{Am} = covariance between the returns on Security

197

A and the returns on Portfolio m. Because the expected return is 20.2 per cent for the market portfolio and 20 per cent for Security A, we obtain:

$$\sigma_m^2 = \sum_{i=1}^{n} (R_{im} - \bar{R}_m)^2 P_i$$

$$= (0.00 - 0.202)^2 0.10 + (0.06 - 0.202)^2 0.20 +$$

$$(0.30 - 0.202)^2 0.50 + (0.20 - 0.202)^2 0.20$$

$$= 0.012916$$

$$\text{Cov}_{Am} = \sum_{i=1}^{n} (R_{iA} - \bar{R}_A)(R_{im} - \bar{R}_m) P_{iAm}$$

$$= (-0.30 - 0.20)(0.00 - 0.202) \, 0.10 + (0.00 - 0.20)$$

$$(0.06 - 0.202) \, 0.20 + (0.30 - 0.20)(0.30 - 0.202)$$

$$0.50 + (0.40 - 0.20)(0.20 - 0.202) \, 0.20$$

$$= 0.02062$$

Thus, beta for Security A is computed as follows:

$$\beta_A = \frac{\text{Cov}_{Am}}{\sigma_m^2} = \frac{0.020620}{0.012916} = 1.596$$

If the riskless rate of return is 7 per cent, the required rate of return for Security A (R_A) is

$$R_A = R_f + (\bar{R}_m - R_f)\beta_A = 0.07 + (0.202 - 0.07)1.596 = 28.$$

Security A would be rejected because its expected rate of return (20%) is less than its required rate of return (28.1%).

CAPM Based on Past Data

It is the common practice to estimate betas on the basis of the historical data rather than on the basis of subjective probability distributions. If the beta computed from historical data is a reliable surrogate for the future beta, the financial manager has an important new tool to assist him in the formulation of profitable capital budgeting decisions. Some empirical surveys on the stability of historical beta information over time indicate that past betas are useful in predicting future betas.[3] It is important to note that betas tend to have greater stability when the number of securities in a portfolio is larger and when the time intervals being studied are longer.

Example 10-3 Suppose that during the last five years, the one-year returns for Security j, returns for Standard & Poor's 500 Stock Index, and the riskless rates of return as depicted by the yield on short-term government securities were those shown in the following table:

Year	Security j R_{jt}	Market Portfolio R_{mt}	Government Security R_{ft}
19-0	0.10	0.10	0.04
19-1	0.13	0.11	0.05
19-2	0.12	0.12	0.05
19-3	0.12	0.11	0.05
19-4	0.11	0.10	0.06

Several computations necessary to determine β_j and R_j are given below:

Year	R_{ft}	R_{jt}	R_{mt}	$R_{mt}R_{jt}$	R_{mt}^2
19-0	0.04	0.10	0.10	0.0100	0.0100
19-1	0.05	0.13	0.11	0.0143	0.0121
19-2	0.05	0.12	0.12	0.0144	0.0144
19-3	0.05	0.12	0.11	0.0132	0.0121
19-4	0.06	0.11	0.10	0.0110	0.0100
Totals		0.58	0.54	0.0629	0.0586
Average	0.05	0.116	0.108		

Using Equation (9-21), the beta is

$$\beta_j = \frac{n \sum_{t=1}^{n} R_{mt}R_{jt} - \left(\sum_{t=1}^{n} R_{mt}\right)\left(\sum_{t=1}^{n} R_{jt}\right)}{n \sum_{t=1}^{n} R_{mt}^2 - \left(\sum_{t=1}^{n} R_{mt}\right)^2}$$

$$= \frac{5(0.0629) - (0.54)(0.58)}{5(0.0586) - (0.54)^2}$$

$$= 0.93$$

Because β_j is 0.93 and R_f is 0.05, the required rate of return for Security j is

$$R_j = R_f + (\bar{R}_m - R_f)\beta_j = 0.05 + (0.108 - 0.05)0.93 = 10.394\%$$

Security j would be accepted because its expected rate of return (11.6%) exceeds its required rate of return (10.394%).

Example 10-4 Consider the five "aggressive" stocks and five "defensive" stocks whose betas were shown in Table 9-3. These betas measure the average response of the stock price to moves in the aggregate market over the past six months from December 1979 to May 1980. Estimate the cost of equity, based on the CAPM, for these ten stocks with the assumption that during the same period, the average rate of return on the market portfolio was 16.4 per cent and the average riskless interest rate was 8.7 per cent.

Substituting the observed values for R_f and $\bar{R}_m$ in the required-rate-of-return formula, we obtain the following equation:

$$R_j = 0.087 + (0.164 - 0.087)\beta_j = 0.087 + 0.077\beta_j \qquad (10\text{-}10)$$

Equation (10-10) is applied to each of the ten stocks in Table 10-4. Column 1 shows the systematic risk for each firm; column 2 sets out the risk premium for each firm; and column 3 gives the specific cost of equity. The cost of equity for aggressive stocks ranged from 19.71 per cent for Boeing to 30.03 per cent for Lockheed. The minimum required rates of

Table 10-4 The Cost of Equity for Ten Stocks

Companies	(1) Systematic Risk β_j	(2) Risk Premium $(0.077) \times (1)$	(3) Cost of Equity $R_j = 0.087 + (2)$
Boeing	1.43	0.11011	0.1971
McDonnell Douglas	1.63	0.12551	0.2125
Northrop	1.72	0.13244	0.2194
Cessna	1.83	0.14091	0.2279
Lockheed	2.77	0.21329	0.3003
Consolidated Foods	0.53	0.04081	0.1278
General Mills	0.64	0.04928	0.1363
Gerber Products	0.67	0.05159	0.1386
CPC International	0.83	0.06391	0.1509
General Foods	0.87	0.06699	0.1540

return for defensive stocks were all less than 16 per cent.

Required Rate of Return for an Investment Project

To estimate the required rate of return for a project on the basis of the CAPM, we need to determine the relationship between its cash flows and the returns available on the market portfolio. Using the CAPM described in Chapter 9 as well as in this chapter, the required rate of return on Project k is

$$R_k = R_f + (\bar{R}_m - R_f)\beta_k \qquad (10\text{-}11)$$

where β_k is the average response of project return to the return on the market portfolio. This expression of a project's required rate of return appears straightforward in concept. However, it is difficult to measure a project's required rate of return using Equation (10-11), because the usual measures of return for a security and for a project are not directly comparable.

The return on a security or on a market portfolio depends on the time interval used. The typical analysis involves monthly returns on the security and the market portfolio. In certain cases, quarterly or annual returns instead of monthly returns are employed. In other words, this return is expressed as the return on investment for a month, a quarter, or a year. Hence, the return on investment is

$$R = \frac{P_t - P_{t-1} + D_t}{P_{t-1}}$$

(10-12)

where P_t = stock price or market index at period t

D_t = dividend paid during period t

Because one-period returns are estimated in the same way for both the stock and the market portfolio, the procedure is appropriate.

In contrast, the return on an investment project is usually expressed in terms of the internal rate of return or the net present value. Because the return for the market portfolio is a single-period measure and the return on a project is a multiperiod measure, these two returns are not directly comparable. In addition, the two measures are not computed in the same way. The return on the market portfolio takes account of changes in capitalized value from period to period, whereas the cash-flow measures of profitability for a project do not.

One way to overcome this problem is to express the profitability of a project in terms of its cash flow during the period and its change in value from one period to another. The one-period return for a project is

$$R_t = \frac{A_t + V_t - V_{t-1}}{V_{t-1}}$$

(10-13)

where A_t = net cash flow at the end of period t.

V_t = market value of the project at the end of period t

202

It is certainly difficult to determine the value of
the project at the end of a period. However, certain assets such as machine tools have a good sec-
ondary market where prices are established for used
assets of various ages.[4]

Example 10-5 Consider an all-equity company. The
company is considering the purchase of a new machine
for $15,000. It has bought similar machines in the
past and feels that it is appropriate to use past
behavior as a proxy for the future. Assume that a
comparable machine produced annual net cash flows
of $2,100, $3,300, $2,960, $1,720, and $1,550 for
its five-year life. Its market value was $11,000
in year 0, $10,000 in year 1, $8,000 in year 2,
$6,000 in year 3, $5,000 in year 4, and $4,000 in
year 5. Let us further assume that the one-year
returns on the market portfolio and short-term
government securities were the same as those used
in Example 10-3.

   To determine the required rate of return for
the new machine, we need to compute the annual percentage returns of the comparable new machine.
Column 4 in Table 10-5 shows these returns, which
are computed by Equation (10-13). Remember that

Table 10-5 History of a Comparable Machine

Year	(1) Pur- chase Price	(2) External Market Value	(3) Actual Net Cash Flow	Annual [4] Return $\frac{(3)_t + (2)_t - (2)_{t-1}}{(2)_{t-1}}$
0	$11,000			
1		$10,000	$2,100	0.10
2		8,000	3,300	0.13
3		6,000	2,960	0.12
4		5,000	1,720	0.12
5		4,000	1,550	0.11

the annual percentage returns of the comparable
machine are identical with the one-year returns
on Security j in Example 10-3. Because we assumed that the returns for the market portfolio
and for short-term government securities in this
example are identical with those used in Example

203

10-3, the required rate of return or the cost of
capital for the new machine is 10.394 per cent.
To determine the net present value of the new machine, its expected cash flows would be discounted
at this rate. If the internal-rate-of-return method
is used to evaluate the project, the cost of capital
(10.394) could be used as a cutoff point.

REQUIRED RATE OF RETURN VERSUS COST OF CAPITAL

It is the common capital budgeting practice to
use the weighted average cost of capital (WACC) as
a cutoff point for making accept or reject decisions.
The WACC represents the required rate of return for
the firm as a whole. If the WACC is used as a single
cutoff point for project selection, no project will
be undertaken unless it earns at least as much as
this cutoff rate. The required rate of return based
on the CAPM also provides a consistent framework for
allocating capital resources among projects with
different risks. The higher the risk of a project,
the higher the required rate of return.

Figure 10-1 illustrates both the required-rate-
of-return and the WACC lines. The two lines imply
different investment criteria, but each line is the

Figure 10-1   Required Rate of Return and WACC

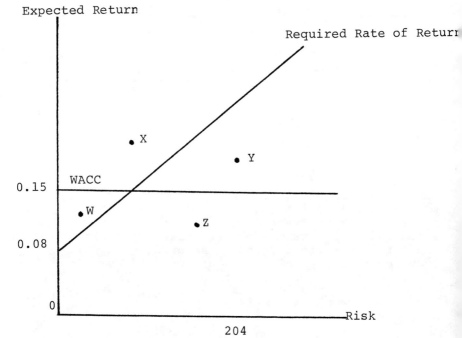

boundary between the accept region (above the line) and the reject region (below the line). For Projects X and Z both criteria lead to the same decision. For Projects W and Y, however, these two decision rules lead to different decisions. If we use the WACC as the accept criterion, we should accept Project Y and reject Project W. On the other hand, the CAPM approach suggests that we should accept Project W and reject Project Y.

Such conflicting results occur because the required rate of return reflects the relative risk of individual projects whereas the WACC does not. When the two decision criteria lead to the same decision, there is no problem. When they produce conflicting decisions, however, the final decision depends on the perceived importance of risk. On the basis of this perception, each decision maker would prefer one over the other and make a decision.

One important limitation of the WACC approach is that it does not consider variations in the riskiness of different projects. The WACC approach tends to reject low-risk projects such as Project W, despite the fact that their rates of return are more than enough to compensate for their risk. The WACC approach tends to accept high-risk projects such as Project Y, despite the fact that their rates of return are not great enough to compensate for their risk.

FOOTNOTES

1. David Durand, "The Cost of Debt and Equity Funds for Business," in The Management of Corporate Capital, ed., Ezra Solomon (New York: Free Press, 1959), pp. 91-116.

2. Franco Modigliani and Merton H. Miller, "The Cost of Capital, Corporation Finance and the Theory of Investment," American Economic Review (June 1958), pp. 261-297.

3. Marshall E. Blume, "On the Assessment of Risk," Journal of Finance (March 1971), pp. 1-10; Robert A. Levy, "On the Short-Term Stationarity of Beta Coefficients," Financial Analysts Journal (November-December 1971), pp. 55-62;

and Frank J. Fabozzi and Jack Clark Francis, "Stability Tests for Alphas and Betas over Bull and Bear Market Conditions," _Journal of Finance_ (September 1977), pp. 1093-1099.

4.   If a project is sufficiently similar to a company whose stock is publicly held, we can use the company's beta in estimating the required rate of return for the project. Assume that an oil company was considering the establishment of a real estate subsidiary. If we can identify publicly traded stocks that are engaged entirely in real estate business, we could use the beta for one of these companies or a group of them as the required rate of return for the project. For details, see James C. Van Horne, _Financial Management and Policy_ (Englewood Cliffs, N.J.: Prentice-Hall, Inc., 1980), pp. 196-203.

PART FOUR   SPECIAL TOPICS IN CAPITAL BUDGETING

CHAPTER 11

LEASING

A lease is a contractual arrangement by which the owner of an asset (lessor) allows another party (lessee) to use the services of the asset for a stated period of time. The lessee agrees to pay a periodic rent and live up to other conditions of the lease contract in exchange for the right to use the asset of the lessor for a specified period of time. After the initial period of the lease, the lessee may continue to utilize the asset at a reduced rent or may be given an option to buy it. This financing method has become increasingly popular in the last two decades, and today it is possible to lease almost any kind of fixed asset. This chapter covers such topics as lease versus purchase, types of leases, the lease-purchase decision, and FASB No. 13.

LEASE VERSUS PURCHASE

Many considerations become important in deciding whether to lease or purchase. They are described below.

Tax Considerations

Because lease payments are deductible as expenses for income-tax purposes, leases are competitive alternatives to loans that can be used to buy an asset. The tax law had permitted a faster tax write-off of leases than that of purchased assets until the passage of the 1954 tax code which introduced accelerated depreciation for assets. This provision wiped out the tax advantage associated with leases.

However, leases still have one tax advantage over loans. Many financial leases involve the lease of land. When the land is purchased, the firm cannot depreciate it for income-tax purposes. In contrast, when the land is leased, the firm can deduct it for income-tax purposes, thus allowing it to write off the cost of the land.

In Chapter 2, we saw that the investment tax credit is available to those who invest in certain types of assets. The tax law permits the lessor and the lessee to divide up the investment credit. It also allows either the lessor or lessee to take the entire credit. If the lessor takes the entire tax credit and does not pass it to the lessee, the credit may make it more advantageous to buy the asset than to lease it.

Effects on Future Financing

Leasing may conserve existing sources of credit for other uses. By surrendering the benefits of holding title to a fixed asset, the lessee may avoid the need to buy it. Because leasing frees funds from financing fixed assets, it permits the firm to have more cash available for alternative uses.

Some argue that leasing increases a firm's borrowing capacity, because it does not necessarily increase the assets or liabilities on the firm's balance sheet. If the lease obligation does not appear as debt on the firm's balance sheet, it does not adversely affect the firm's debt capacity. Although many creditors take the lease obligations fully into account, research indicates that they are more conscious of debt obligations than leasing commitments.

Most loan agreements for the purchase of fixed assets require the borrower to make a certain amount of down payment. Thus, the borrower receives less than the purchase price of the asset. On the other hand, leasing provides 100 per cent financing, because a down payment is not required. But there is no guarantee that leasing provides more financing. Lease payments are usually made in advance and these advance payments may be viewed as a type of down payment.

There are some other effects of leasing on future financing. (1) Many loan indentures contain various protective covenants, but lease contracts avoid most of these covenants. (2) Lease payments are fixed, thus avoiding the risks associated with short and/or intermediate financing and refinancing.

Risk of Obsolescence

Another advantage of leasing is that the lease arrangement shifts the risk of obsolescence from the user (lessee) to the owner (lessor). High rates of obsolescence for such capital assets as computers and calculating equipment increase the risk of ownership. The firm may avoid the risk of obsolescence if the lease term is quite short or if the lessor fails to accurately anticipate the obsolescence of assets in setting the lease payments.

Salvage Value

Salvage value is the value of the leased property at the end of the lease and it belongs to the lessor. Hence, high salvage values reduce the cost of ownership. It may be wise to buy assets if they are expected to appreciate over the life of a lease agreement. Although the salvage values of many assets are highly uncertain, appreciation in the value is highly likely when land and/or buildings are involved.

Maintenance

The lease contract usually specifies the responsibility of maintenance, insurance, and taxes, on the leased property. Although these charges are reduced by tax shields, they represent an expense of ownership. If the leasing arrangement requires the lessor to assume these expenses, the lessor usually passes them to the lessee in the form of increased lease payments. This makes leasing a more attractive alternative if the lessor can maintain and operate more cheaply due to the economies of scale.

Discount Rate

Although the after-tax borrowing rate is used most widely as the discount rate, it is perhaps one of the most controversial features in the lease-purchase decision. Both leasing and buying involve cash outflows over an extended period of time. Therefore, these cash outflows must be discounted for the time value of money and for risk. The problem arises because lease payments are normally fixed and certain, whereas salvage values, operating expenses, and interest charges are highly uncertain. Although we will not discuss this problem further, it can swing the decision one way or the other.

TYPES OF LEASES

There are three types of leases: (1) sales and leaseback arrangements, (2) operating leases, and (3) financial or capital leases. Nearly all lease arrangements fall into one of these three categories.[1]

Sales and Leaseback Arrangements

Under a sales and leaseback arrangement, the owner of the property sells his property to another party and simultaneously enters an agreement to lease the property back under specific terms. Retail stores, office buildings, and multiple-purpose industrial structures are usually financed through this arrangement. The seller-lessee obtains the sales price in cash and retains the economic use of the property. On the other hand, the buyer-lessor obtains the title to the property and periodic rental payments. These rental payments are made to amortize the loan and to provide the buyer-lessor with a specified rate of return on his investment.

Operating Leases

This leasing arrangement allows a firm to acquire the use of an asset it did not own previously. Operating leases cover such types of equipment as computers, trucks, automobiles, and furniture.

Operating leases have a number of important characteristics. (1) The lessor maintains and services the leased property. Thus, the lease payments include the costs of these services and maintenance. (2) The lessee frequently retains the right to cancel the agreement before the expiration of the basic lease period. (3) The lease contract usually covers a period of time that is less than the economic life of the leased property.

Hence, the original lessee does not return the full value of the leased asset to the lessor.

Financial or Capital Leases

Financial leases generally require that: (1) the lessee maintains and services the leased property, (2) the lessee cannot cancel the lease contract before its maturity, and (3) the lessee fully amortizes the leased property.

Ordinarily, the lessee selects the equipment, negotiates its price, and other terms with the manufacturer, arranges with a bank to buy it, and immediately leases it from the bank. A sales and leaseback arrangement is treated as a special type of financial lease.

THE LEASE-PURCHASE DECISION

The lease-purchase decision is a decision that companies must make in acquiring new fixed assets. There are two types of the analytical framework for comparing leasing and purchasing alternatives: present-value approach and internal-rate-of-return approach.

Present-Value Approach

Under this approach, we compute the present value of after-tax cash outflows for both alternatives and choose the alternative whose present value is smaller.

Example 11-1 The Long Beach Company has decided to acquire a machine with a cost of $10,000 and an expected useful life of five years. The machine is expected to have no salvage value on retirement. If the machine is purchased, the company can finance it with a loan at 10 per cent; the principal and the interest are to be paid in five equal annual installments. The machine is to be depreciated on a straight-line basis and the applicable investment tax credit of 7 per cent is available in year 0. The company's marginal tax rate is 50 per cent. If the machine is leased, the lessor requires that the lessee amortize the

entire cost of the machine and that it provide a
10 per cent return. As usual, annual lease payments are to be made in advance; the rent for the
use of the machine during year 1 would be paid at
the end of year 0. Because leases are analogous
to loans, the after-tax cost of borrowing is to be
used as an appropriate discount rate to determine
the present value of the after-tax cash outflows.

If the machine is purchased, the 7 per cent investment credit reduces the purchase price by $700
to $9,300. It is important to remember that the
credit does not affect the basis for depreciation.
The amount of the annual loan payment may be calculated by solving the formula for the present
value of an annuity:

$$PA = A \times ADF_{n,i} \quad \text{or} \quad A = PA \div ADF_{n,i} \qquad (11\text{-}1)$$

where PA = net cost of the asset to be acquired

$$A = \text{annual loan payment}$$

$$ADF_{ni} = \text{annuity discount factor}$$

Therefore, the amount of annual loan payment is

$$A = \$9,300 \div ADF_{5,10\%} = \$9,300 \div 3.791 = \$2,453$$

The five annual installments of $2,453 would retire
the $9,300 loan and provide the lender with a 10
per cent return. We can break down the annual payments into interest and principal repayments and
Table 11-1 shows this.

Table 11-2 shows the schedule of cash outflows
and the present value of these cash outflows. The
tax shield is the interest expense plus the depreciation charge multiplied by the marginal tax rate.
The after-tax cash outflow for each year is the
annual loan payment minus the tax shield. The
after-tax cash outflow in the first year is $988:

Annual Payment		$2,453
Less: Interest	$ 930	
Depreciation	2,000	
Total Expense	$2,930	

212

$2,453

	Total Expense	$2,930	
	x Tax Rate	x .50	
	Tax Shield		1,465
After-Tax Cash Outflow			$ 988

Table 11-1 Term Loan Amortization Schedule

End of Year	Annual Payment	Interest* at 10%	Principal Repayment	Remaining Balance
0				$9,300
1	$2,453	$930	$1,523	7,777
2	2,453	778	1,675	6,102
3	2,453	610	1,843	4,259
4	2,453	426	2,027	2,232
5	2,453	223	2,230	0

*Interest Rate x the Remaining Balance at the End of the Previous Year. For example, $930 = $9,300 x .10.

Table 11-2 The Present Value of Cash Outflows: Buying Alternative

Year	Annual Pay.	Interest	Dep.	Tax Shield	After-Tax Outflow	PV at 5%
1	$2,453	$930	$2,000	$1,465	$ 988	$ 941
2	2,453	778	2,000	1,389	1,064	965
3	2,453	610	2,000	1,305	1,148	992
4	2,453	426	2,000	1,213	1,240	1,021
5	2,453	223	2,000	1,115	1,341	1,051
					Present Value =	$4,970

The present value of $4,970 for the buying alternative is obtained by discounting these after-tax cash outflows at 5 per cent. There is some disagreement about the discount rate to be used in computing the present value of the after-tax cash outflows for both the buying alternative and the leasing alternative. However, the after-tax cost of borrowing is most widely used as a discount rate in present-value analysis of these two financing alternatives.[3] The use of this rate is based on two assumptions: (1) the company's marginal tax rate will

213

stay the same and (2) its future taxable income will exceed the tax shield associated with lease payments.

Since the lease payments are made in advance, the first lease payment is made at the end of year 0. Therefore, we must solve for the annual lease payment that equates the cost of the machine with the first lease payment plus the present value of the remaining four lease payments. This is given as follows:

$$\$10,000 = A + A \times ADF_{4,10\%}$$

$$= A (1 + 3.170)$$

$$A = \$10,000 \div 4.170$$

$$= \$2,398$$

Thus, the five equal lease payments of $2,398 are necessary to amortize the cost of the machine and to return 10 per cent to the lessor.

Lease payments are treated as tax deductible expenses for federal income tax purposes, but they are deductible only in the year in which the payments apply. Hence, each lease payment is deductible for tax purposes in the following year. Table 11-3 shows the schedule of cash outflows and the present value of these cash outflows. We see from the table that the present value of the total cash outflows for the leasing alternative is $5,710.

Table 11-3   The Present Value of Cash Outflows: Leasing Alternative

End of Year	Lease Payment	Tax Shield	After-Tax Cash Outflows	Present Value at 5%
0	$2,398	$ 0	$2,398	$2,398
1-4	2,398	1,199	1,199	4,252
5			-1,199	-940
			Present Value =	$5,710

The present value of the after-tax cash outflows for the leasing alternative is $4,970.
Thus, the firm should acquire the machine through
the debt alternative. It is important to recognize that this conclusion occurs despite the fact
that both alternatives have an equal investment
rate of 10 per cent and an equal discount rate of
5 per cent. The advantage of the debt alternative
is due to the realization of the investment credit
at the outset and the one-year time lag between
the loan repayment and the lease payment. If the
lessor passes all or a part of the investment credit
to the lessee, the leasing alternative could be
more attractive than this analysis indicates. Because lease payments are made in advance while
loan repayments are not, the lease payments are
multiplied by the lower discount factors and consequently the present value of the lease payments
becomes greater.

Internal-Rate-of-Return Approach

The internal rate of return method is an alternative to the present value method.[4]   Under this
method, we compute the internal rate of return for
the leasing alternative and compare it with the
after-tax cost of debt. We saw in Chapter 8 that
the internal rate of return approach avoids the
problem of selecting the discount rate in advance.

The internal rate of return for the total cash
outflows of the leasing alternative is:

$$C_o - IC = \sum_{t=0}^{n-1} \frac{L_t}{(1+r)^t} - \sum_{t=1}^{n} \frac{(L_{t-1} - D_t)T}{(1+r)^t} \qquad (11\text{-}2)$$

where C_o = cost of the asset to be leased

$\quad$ IC = investment tax credit

$\quad L_t$ = lease payment at the end of year t

$\quad D_t$ = depreciation in year t that would
$\qquad$ occur if the asset were purchased

$\quad$ T = tax rate

215

n = maturity of the lease

r = internal rate of return

The cost of the leasing alternative is the rate of discount that equates the cost of the asset minus the investment credit with the present value of the lease payments and the loan payments. In other words, the cost of the leasing alternative depends upon not only the lease payments but also the depreciation tax deduction and the amount of investment credit. If the asset is leased, the depreciation tax deduction and the investment credit would be foregone and thus these two tax benefits represent opportunity costs for the leasing alternative.

Let's solve our earlier example with this technique. Since the machine has a cost of $10,000 and an investment credit of $700, the left-hand side value of Equation (11-2) is $9,300. The numerator of its right-hand side expression of Equation (11-2) represents the cash-flow stream and Table 11-4 shows this stream. The last column of the table represents the cash flow data and we have to find the discount rate that will equate the $9,300 with the present value of these cash flows. Thus, we can establish the following relationship:

$$\$9,300 = \$2,398 + \frac{\$2,199}{(1 + r)^1} + \frac{\$2,199}{(1 + r)^2} + \frac{\$2,199}{(1 + r)^3} +$$

$$\frac{\$2,199}{(1 + r)^4} - \frac{\$199}{(1 + r)^5}$$

If we solve for r, we find it to be about 9 per cent. The 9 per cent is the cost of the leasing alternative. The after-tax cost of the buying alternative is simply the before-tax cost of debt times one minus the tax rate or the before-tax cost of debt $(1 - T)$. Recall that Example 11-1 has a before-tax cost of 10 per cent and a tax rate of 50 per cent. Hence, the after-tax cost of the buying alternative is 5 per cent. Because the buying alternative is cheaper than the leasing alternative, the firm will have to purchase the machine.

216

Table 11-4 Schedule of Cash Outflows: Leasing
         Alternative

(1) End of Year	(2) L_t	(3) D_t	(4) $L_{t-1} - D_t$	(5) $(L_{t-1} - D_t)T$	(6) (2)-(5)
0	$2,398	–	–	–	$2,398
1	2,398	$2,000	$399	$199	2,199
2	2,398	2,000	399	199	2,199
3	2,398	2,000	399	199	2,199
4	2,398	2,000	399	199	2,199
5		2,000	399	199	(199)

FASB NO. 13

Traditionally, perhaps the most important feature
of lease contracts from the standpoint of lessees has
been that leases were "off-balance-sheet" financing
arrangements. The Financial Accounting Standards
Board issued No. 13 (FASB No. 13), Accounting for
Leases, in November 1976. FASB No. 13 fundamentally
changed this feature. It requires that the leased
property appear on the asset side of the balance
sheet and the related lease obligation appear on
the liability side. Thus, the attraction of leases
as off-balance-sheet obligations ceased to exist.

Background

The traditional position concerning executory
contracts such as leases is that neither asset nor
associated liability should be recorded. Assets
are recorded only when prepayments are made. Liabilities are recorded only when services are received. This traditional position justified the
omission of the rights and obligations under long-
term lease contracts from the main body of the
balance sheet. The lessee did not have to show
the leased property among his assets and the
periodic lease payments as his liabilities until
they came due. Although sophisticated lenders
were not fooled by this method, it has been one
of the most important advantages claimed for
leases over purchases.

217

The question of how leases should be treated in financial statements was neglected until the American Institute of Certified Public Accountants issued Accounting Research Bulletin No. 38, Disclosure of Long-Term Leases in Financial Statements of Lessees, in 1948. The growing importance of leasing as a financial device was recognized by the accounting profession in 1965, when the Accounting Principles Board (APB) issued Opinion No. 5, Reporting of Leases in Financial Statements of Lessees. This opinion suggested that financial statements of the lessee should disclose a sufficient amount of information about noncancellable leases. The basic objective of the opinion was to enable the user of financial statements to assess the effect of the lease on the lessee's financial condition. Subsequent APB Opinions (Nos. 7, 27, and 31) reaffirmed the general principle made in Opinion No. 5 with respect to disclosures of long-term lease commitments by the lessee.

FASB No. 13 culminated a three-decade-long concern of the accounting profession with the treatment of leases. A lease is classified as a capital lease if it satisfies one or more of the following four criteria. Otherwise, it is classified as an operating lease.

1. The lease transfers ownership of the property to the lessee by the end of the lease term.

2. The lease contains a bargain purchase option.

3. The lease term is equal to 75 per cent or more of the estimated economic life of the leased property.

4. The present value of the minimum lease payments, less executory costs to be paid by the lessor, exceeds 90 per cent of the fair value of the leased property, less any related investment credit to be retained by the lessor. However, if the beginning of the lease term falls within the last 25 per cent of the total estimated economic life of the leased property, Criteria 3 and 4 shall not be used for purposes of classifying the lease.

FASB No. 13 has a number of other major elements: (1) The lessee must record a capital lease as an asset and an obligation equal to the present value of minimum lease payments or the fair value of the leased property, whichever is lower. (2) The discount rate to be used in computing the present value of the minimum lease payments should be the lessee's incremental borrowing rate or the lessor's implicit rate of interest, whichever is less. It is important to recognize that the use of the lower discount rate tends to increase the present value of the minimum lease payments. Hence, it raises the possibility that the 90 per cent test under Criterion 4 will be met and that the lessee will have to classify the lease as a capital lease. (3) If the lease transfers ownership of the property to the lessee by the end of the lease term, the asset recorded as a capital lease should be amortized over its estimated useful life in a manner consistent with the lessee's normal depreciation policy for its own assets. Otherwise, the asset classified as a capital lease should be amortized over the lease term. (4) During the lease term, each periodic lease payment should be allocated between a reduction of the obligation and interest, in order to produce a constant periodic rate of interest on the remaining balance of the obligation.

In addition to these stipulations for capital leases, FASB No. 13 requires the lessee to disclose more detailed information for both capital and operating leases in footnotes. The balance sheet capitalization of capital leases and standard disclosure requirements for operating leases should make it easier for creditors and other users of financial reports to secure additional information on the lease obligations of companies.

Accounting for Capital Leases

FASB No. 13 requires the lessee to estimate the values of at least three variables to account for a capital lease. They are (1) the discount rate to be used in calculating the present value of minimum lease payments, (2) the amount to be capitalized as an asset, and (3) the constant periodic rate of interest.

The discount rate is the lessee's incremental borrowing rate or the lessor's implicit rate of interest, whichever is lower. The incremental borrowing rate is the rate incurred to borrow the funds necessary to buy the leased property.

The lessor's implicit rate of interest is the rate that equates the fair value of the leased property minus the investment credit with the present value of minimum lease payments plus the unguaranteed residual value that will accrue to the lessor. The minimum lease payments include the minimum rental payments called for by the lease plus any guaranteed residual value by the lessee. However, they exclude executory costs such as insurance, taxes, and maintenance to be paid by the lessor. Thus, one can establish the following relationship to compute the lessor's implicit rate of interest:

$$FV - IC = \sum_{t=0}^{n-1} \frac{(R - E)}{(1 + s)^t} + \frac{GR}{(1 + s)^n} + \frac{UR}{(1 + s)^n} \qquad (11\text{-}3)$$

where FV = fair value of the leased property at the beginning of the lease term

    IC = investment credit retained by the lessor

    R = periodic lease payments

    E = executory costs paid by the lessor

    GR = residual value guaranteed by the lessee

    UR = unguaranteed residual value, or the estimated residual value of the leased property at the end of the lease term minus the guaranteed residual value

    s = lessor's implicit rate of interest

    n = term of the lease

    t = time period of the lease payment

If the lease contains a purchase option, GR and UR are replaced by the option price/$(1 + s)^n$. In either case, the lessor's implicit rate of interest is obtained by trial and error.

The amount capitalized as an asset and obligation is the present value of the minimum lease payments at the inception of the lease term or the fair value of the leased property, whichever is less. The fair value of the leased property is the price for which the property could be sold in an arm-length transaction between unrelated parties. One can obtain the present value of the minimum lease payments as follows:

$$PV = \sum_{t=0}^{n-1} \frac{(R - E)}{(1 + d)^t} + \frac{GR}{(1 + d)^n} \qquad (11\text{-}4)$$

where PV = present value of the minimum lease payments

d = discount rate

The constant periodic rate of interest on the capitalized obligation is the interest rate that equates the amount capitalized as an asset with the present value of the minimum lease payments. Therefore, one can obtain the amount capitalized as follows:

$$AC = \sum_{t=0}^{n-1} \frac{(R - E)}{(1 + c)^t} + \frac{GR}{(1 + c)^n} \qquad (11\text{-}5)$$

where AC = amount capitalized

c = constant periodic rate of interest on the capitalized lease

If the present value of the minimum lease payments is capitalized, the constant periodic rate of interest is identical with the discount rate (d). However, if the fair value of the leased property is capitalized, the constant periodic rate of interest must be calculated by trial and error using Equation (11-5). It is important to recognize that four interest rates may be needed in accounting for a capital lease if the fair value of the leased asset is

221

capitalized: (1) the incremental borrowing rate
(b); (2) the lessor's implicit rate of interest
(s); (3) the discount rate (d); and (4) the
constant periodic rate of interest (c).

Example 11-2 The Utica Plastic Company desires to
acquire a machine. The machine has a cost of
$80,300, an estimated economic life of eight years,
and no expected salvage value on retirement. The
company depreciates its assets on a straight-line
basis. Its tax rate of 50 per cent is expected to
stay the same for the next eight years. If the
company decides to purchase the machine, it can
finance the project with a loan at 9 per cent.
The lender requires the company to repay its loan
in eight equal annual installments. The Utica
Plastic Company has also found that it could lease
the same machine under the following terms: (1)
The fair value of the machine at the inception of
the lease term is $80,300. (2) The lease has a
noncancelable term of seven years with an annual
lease payment of $15,000. (3) Annual lease pay-
ments are made at the beginning of each year. (4)
The lessee pays executory costs. (5) Although
the lease does not contain a renewal option, the
lessee has the option to buy the machine at the
end of seven years for $8,000; this $8,000 is
the estimated fair market value of the machine
at the end of the lease term. (6) The lessor does
not retain the investment tax credit.

A number of computations are necessary to classify this lease as a capital lease or an operating
lease. Equation (11-3) is used to compute the
lessor's implicit rate of interest:

$$\$80,300 - 0 = \sum_{t=0}^{6} \frac{(\$15,000 - 0)}{(1 + s)^t} + \frac{\$8,000}{(1 + s)^7}$$

$$s = 12\%$$

Because the lessee's incremental borrowing of
9 per cent (given) is less than the lessor's implicit interest rate of 12 per cent, the lessee
must use the 9 per cent as a discount rate to
determine the present value of his minimum lease
payments. The present value is obtained by Equa-

tion (11-4):

$$PV = \sum_{t=0}^{6} \frac{(\$15,000 - 0)}{(1 + .09)^t} + 0$$

$$= \$82,290$$

The present value of the minimum lease payments ($82,290) is greater than the fair value of the leased machine ($80,300). Thus, the amount capitalized as an asset is $80,300. This requires the lessee to compute the constant periodic rate of interest using Equation (11-5):

$$\$80,300 = \sum_{t=0}^{6} \frac{(\$15,000 - 0)}{(1 + c)^t} + 0$$

$$c = 10\%$$

Thus, the constant periodic rate of interest is 10 per cent, and this 10 per cent is used to allocate each periodic lease payment between a reduction of the obligation and interest. Table 11-5 shows the breakdown of the interest and principal for annual lease payments of $15,000.

Table 11-5 Allocation of Lease Payment between a Reduction of the Obligation and Interest Expense

End of Year	Lease Payment	Imputed Interest at 10%	Reduction of Obligation	Remaining Balance
0	$15,000	$ 0	$15,000	$65,300
1	15,000	6,530	8,470	56,830
2	15,000	5,683	9,317	47,513
3	15,000	4,751	10,249	37,264
4	15,000	3,726	11,274	25,990
5	15,000	2,599	12,401	13,589
6	15,000	1,359	13,641	-

Classification of Lease and Its Disclosure

Criterion 1. Not Met. The lease does not transfer ownership of the machine to the lessee by the end of the lease term.

223

Criterion 2.   Not Met. The lease does not contain a bargain purchase option.

Criterion 3.   Met. The lease term (seven years) exceeds 75 per cent of the estimated economic life of the machine (eight years). In this case, the lease term is 87.5 per cent of the estimated economic life of the machine (7 years ÷ 8 years).

Criterion 4.   Met. The present value of the minimum lease payments ($82,290) exceeds 90 per cent of the machine's fair value ($80,300). In this case, the present value of the minimum lease payments is 102.5 per cent of the machine's fair value ($82,290 ÷ $80,300).

Since the lease meets two of the four criteria, it is a capital lease. Therefore, the lease must be disclosed in the main body of the balance sheet.

The amount capitalized as an asset is $80,300 and the Utica Plastic Company depreciates its assets on a straight-line basis. Hence, the annual depreciation charges for the capitalized obligation of $80,300 are $10,037.50($80,300 ÷ 8). It is important to recognize that the leased machine with a term of seven years is amortized over its economic life of eight years, because the lease has a purchase option. If the lease does not have a purchase option, this lease obligation is amortized over only seven years.

Assuming that the inception of the lease term is January 1, 1980, the book value of the leased machine will appear on the asset side of the lessee's balance sheet with the following schedule: 1/1/80 = $80,300; 1/1/81 = $70,262.5; 1/1/82 = $60,225; 1/1/83 = $50,187.5; 1/1/84 = $40,150; 1/1/85 = $30,112.5; 1/1/86 = $20,075; and 1/1/87 = $10,037.5. The entries on the liability side of the balance sheet can be obtained from Table 11-5. Table 11-6 illustrates one way of meeting the disclosure requirements of FASB No. 13.

Table 11-6   Utica Plastic Company, Balance Sheet, January 1,

	1980	1981	1982	1983	1984	1985	1986	1987
ASSETS								
Leased property under capital leases less accumulated depreciation	$80,300	$70,262.5	$60,225	$50,187.5	$40,150	$30,112.5	$20,075	$10,037.5
LIABILITIES								
Current obligation under capital leases	$15,000	$ 8,470	$ 9,317	$10,249	$11,274	$12,401	$13,641	$ 0
Noncurrent obligations under capital leases	$65,300	$56,830	$47,513	$37,264	$25,990	$13,589	$ 0	$ 0

FOOTNOTES

1. There is a special form of leasing developed
   in recent years. This leasing is known as
   leveraged leasing. It involves at least
   three parties: a lessee, a lessor, and a
   long-term creditor. From the standpoint of
   the lessee, leveraged leases are identical
   with any other types of leases. But the
   role of the lessor is changed. The lessor
   finances a part of the asset and the balance
   is provided by a long-term creditor. The
   lessor is owner of the asset as well as the
   borrower. The Internal Revenue Service
   permits the lessor to deduct all depreciation charges associated with the asset and
   to take the entire investment credit. See
   Robert J. Ryan, Jr., "Leveraged Leasing,"
   Management Accounting (April 1977), pp. 45,
   46, and 50; and E. Richard Packham, "An
   Analysis of the Risks of Leveraged Leasing,"
   Journal of Commercial Banking Lending (March
   1975), pp. 2-29.

2. Those who are not familiar with Equation
   (11-1) should refer back to Chapter 3.

3. See Richard D. Bower, "Issues in Lease
   Financing," Financial Management (Winter
   1973), pp. 25-34; and Myron J. Gordon,
   "A General Solution to the Buy or Lease
   Decision: A Pedagogical Note," Journal
   of Finance (March 1974).

4. For details, see Chapman Findlay, III, "A
   Sensitivity Analysis of IRR Leasing Models,"
   Engineering Economist (Summer 1975), pp.
   231-241; and Ivar W. Sorensen and Ramon
   E. Johnson, "Equipment Financial Leasing
   Practices and Costs: An Empirical Study,"
   Financial Management (Spring 1977), pp.
   33-40.

CHAPTER 12

CAPITAL BUDGETING FOR THE MULTINATIONAL CORPORATION

The basic principles of analysis are the same for foreign and domestic investment projects. However, the foreign investment decision results from a complex process which differs in some key respects from the domestic investment decision. (1) The cash flow analysis for foreign investment projects is much more complex than that for domestic investment projects. (2) The cost of capital for foreign investment projects is typically higher than that for domestic investment projects.

The relevant net cash flows are the dividends and royalties that would be repatriated by each subsidiary to the parent company. Since these net cash flows must be converted into currency of the parent company, they are subject to future exchange rate changes. Normally, foreign projects are more risky than domestic projects. Hence, the cost of capital for a foreign project is higher than that for a similar domestic project. This higher risk comes from two major sources: exchange risk and political risk. In Chapter 12 we examine use of capital budgeting analysis for direct foreign investment projects.

DIRECT FOREIGN INVESTMENT AND HOST COUNTRIES

Host countries can benefit from direct foreign investment in many ways. Foreign investment helps transfer technology and skills which are frequently in short supply. It provides local workers with an opportunity to learn managerial skills. It increases both employment and domestic wages. It also contributes to tax revenues and helps fill foreign exchange gaps.

Although foreign investment tends to contribute much-needed resources to host countries (developing countries in particular), it is viewed by many with misgivings.[1] Arguments against foreign investment range from excessive cost of resources transferred, a loss of political and economic sovereignty, decreases in competitiveness of domestic markets, and increases in exploitations. Some charge that foreign

investment undermines indigenous cultures and so-
cieties by imposing Western values and lifestyles
on developing countries.

It would thus seem apparent that while direct
foreign investment has the potential to contribute
positively to development, there is no guarantee
that it would have no harmful impact on host countries. But the question of foreign investment need
not be a zero sum game. What is needed is to set
up a feasible framework for investment to define the
rights and responsibilities of both parties. This
framework should allow both a reasonable return to
the investor and a positive contribution to development goals of the host country.

DIRECT FOREIGN INVESTMENT POSITION

Table 12-1 shows U.S. direct investment position
abroad and direct foreign investment position in the
United States for a number of selected years. U.S.
direct investment abroad increased from $31.9 billion

Table 12-1 United States: Direct Foreign Invest-
            ment Position (in billions of dollars)

Year	U.S. Investment Abroad	Investment in U.S.
1960	31.9	6.9
1965	49.5	8.8
1970	78.2	13.2
1975	124.1	27.7
1976	136.4	30.8
1977	148.8	34.1

Source: U.S. Department of Commerce, Survey of Current
         Business, various issues.

in 1960 to $124.1 billion in 1975, almost a four-fold
increase. This means that it has increased at almost
10 per cent per year. Although direct foreign investment in the United States has been under 25 per cent
of the U.S. foreign investment for the 15-year period,
it has a similar increase pattern. In other words,
foreign investment in the United States increased
four times during this period with an annual growth
rate of about 10 per cent.

228

THE INVESTMENT DECISION MAKING PROCESS

The foreign investment decision involves the allocation and commitment of funds to foreign investment projects.[2] The rational use of capital resources is critical for the future well-being of the multinational company. This is because such an investment usually requires a very large sum of money and is made in expectation of benefits to be realized over a number of years.

The foreign investment decision process involves the entire process of planning expenditures in foreign countries whose returns are expected to extend beyond one year. The choice of one year is arbitrary, but the one-year boundary is rather widely accepted. There are many steps and elements in the entire process of planning capital expenditures in foreign countries. Each element is a sub-system of the capital budgeting system. Thus, the foreign investment decision process may be viewed as an integral unit of many elements which are directly or indirectly interrelated. Here we assume that the entire foreign investment decision process consists of six phases: (1) the decision to search for foreign investment, (2) an assessment of the political climate in the host country, (3) an examination of the company's overall strategy, (4) cash flow analysis, (5) the required rate of return, and (6) economic evaluation.

Search for Foreign Investment

A system should be established to stimulate ideas for capital expenditures abroad and to identify good investment opportunities. This is because the availability of good investment opportunities provides the foundation for a successful investment program. Moreover, good investment opportunities do not just appear. A continuous stream of attractive investment opportunities comes from hard thinking, careful planning, and frequently large outlays for research and development.

The first phase in the foreign investment decision process is an analysis of the forces that lead some company officials to focus attention on the possibilities of foreign investment. If the company recognizes foreign investment as a legitimate program, its search for foreign investment opportunities will start. The economic and political forces in the host countries are largely responsible for the expansion of foreign investment. Many companies also desire foreign investment to seek new markets, raw materials, and production efficiency.

In any particular case it is not easy to pinpoint one motive for a decision to invest abroad or to find out exactly who was the originator of a foreign project. The decision to search for foreign investment results from a series of events, a combination of several motivating forces, and activities of different persons. Typically, the decision to look abroad depends upon the interaction of many forces. Considerations such as profit opportunities, tax policy, and diversification strategies are economic variables which may affect a decision to look overseas. In addition, environmental forces, organizational factors, and a drive by some high-ranking officials inside the company could be the major forces which lead a company to look abroad.

Essentially, advantages of superior knowledge and economies of scale determine direct foreign investment.[3] These two types of advantages permit a multinational company to operate its subsidiary more profitably than local competitors. The term "knowledge" is used here to mean production technologies, managerial skills, industrial organization, knowledges of product, and factor markets.

In addition to superior knowledge, direct foreign investment allows the multinational company to obtain economies of scale. Vertical foreign investment reduces the costs and uncertainties that exist when subsequent stages of production are handled by different producers. Horizontal foreign investment provides the multinational company with opportunities to eliminate duplicate facilities as well as to consolidate the functions of production, marketing, and purchasing.

Political Climate

One major concern of multinational companies is the possibility that the political climate of the host country may deteriorate. The multinational financial manager must analyze the political environ-

230

ment of the proposed host country and determine whether or not the economic environment would be receptive to the proposed project. In general, those projects designed to reduce the country's need for imports and thus save foreign exchange are given the highest priority by the host government.

Political actions such as government takeovers and operational restrictions adversely affect company operations. Thus, the emphasis of the analysis must center on such factors as the host government's attitudes toward foreign investment, the desire of the host government for national rather than foreign control, and its political stability. It is also important to determine that adequate and prompt compensation is guaranteed if nationalization becomes desirable in the public interest.

Company's Overall Strategy

If the initial screening of the political climate is favorable, the multinational company can move on to the next stage of the decision process. An assessment of the company's overall strategy is useful to determine whether and which foreign operations would allow the company to use its strength or to strengthen its weakness. This approach allows the company to reduce the number of alternatives to a manageable number. At this stage, the company must check whether the suggested project conflicts with company policies and resources. The emphasis of analysis must also center on such factors as whether the company has the experience to handle the project and how the project could be integrated into existing projects.

Cash Flow Analysis

The fourth stage of the screening process involves a standard cash flow analysis. The after-tax cash outflows and inflows directly associated with each project must be estimated to evaluate capital investment alternatives. The multinational company must forecast its expected expenditures for the proposed project. Ordinarily, these forecasts can be obtained from the historical data of similar ventures. They may be also estimated by such forecasting techniques as the per cent of sale method or a

231

linear regression analysis. An important difference
in the application of cash flow analysis for foreign
investment is that there are two sets of cash flow
analyses: cash flows for the project itself and
cash flows available to the parent company.

Demand Forecast   The first step in the analysis of
cash flows for any investment proposal is a forecast
of demand. Such usage estimates are highly correlated with such factors as historical demands, popu-
lation, income, alternative sources of products,
competition, the feasibility of serving nearby markets, and general economic conditions.

There are a number of obvious reasons for the
strong emphasis on the market size in the investment
decision process. First, the expected market size
can be used as an indication of profit possibility
for the proposed investment project. Second, small
markets tend to have high uncertainty. If the market is small, the multinational company has little
or no leeway left in case of error of estimate.
Third, small markets are not worth the effort. Because one of the scarce resources in the company is
management, the proposed project should be large
enough to support the management time that would
have to be spent on project analysis.

Duties and Taxes   Because foreign investment cuts
across national boundaries, a unique set of tax laws
and import duties may be applicable. The multinational company must review the tax structure of
the host country. Analysis would include the definition of a taxable entity, statutory tax rates,
tax treaties, the treatment of dual taxation, and
tax incentive programs. It is also important for
the multinational company to know whether the host
government would impose any customs duties on im-
ported production equipment and materials that could
not be obtained from local sources.

Exchange Rate   Another important feature of foreign
investment analysis is that project inflows available to the investor are subject to foreign exchange
rates and restrictions. When the host country has
a stable exchange rate, no problems are presented.
However, if the exchange rate is expected to change
or allowed to float, cash flow analysis becomes more
complicated. This is because it is necessary to fore-

cast the exchange rate which may be applicable to convert cash flows into hard currencies.

It is equally important to recognize that many host governments have various exchange control regulations. Under these regulations, permission may be required to buy foreign exchange with local currency for payment of loan interest, management fees, royalties, and most other billings for services provided by foreign suppliers. Applications for permission to purchase foreign exchange may be subject to considerable delay. The granting of permission to buy foreign exchange does not guarantee the availability of the related exchange in time. This is because commercial banks can allocate to their customers only such amounts as are made available by the central bank.

There are many factors that affect the blockage of funds to nonresidents. They include an unexpected shortage of foreign exchange, a long-run deficiency of the foreign exchange, and certain types of domestic political pressures. If all funds are blocked in perpetuity, the value of the project to the parent is zero. However, in actuality funds are likely to be only partially blocked because multinational companies have many ways to remove blocked funds. These methods include transfer price adjustments, loan repayments, royalty adjustments, and fee adjustments. Furthermore, most host countries limit the amount of fund transfer to nonresidents or block the transfer of funds only on a temporary basis. Nevertheless, multinational companies must analyze the impact of blocked funds on project return. It is critical to determine the amount of blocked funds, their reinvestment return, and ways in which funds can be transferred under the host country's law.

Project vs. Parent Cash Flows   To yield the after-tax profits from the proposed project, the multinational company must develop a demand forecast, forecast its expected expenditures, and review the tax structure of the host country. The estimated sales less the estimated expenses plus non-cash outlays such as depreciation give the cash inflows from operations.

Typically, the multinational company desires to maximize the utility of project cash flows on a worldwide basis. The parent multinational company must value only those cash flows which can be repatriated because only these funds can be used to reinvest in other subsidiaries, pay dividends, pay debt obligations, or invest in new ventures. Project cash flows would have little value if they could not be used for these alternatives.

Project cash flows and parent cash flows can have substantial differences mainly due to tax regulations and exchange controls. Moreover, some project expenses such as management fees and royalties are returns to the parent. In general, incremental cash flows to the parent are worldwide parent cash flows after investment minus worldwide parent cash flows before investment. The existence of such differences raises the question of which cash flows should be used as the relevant cash flows in project evaluation. Because the value of a project is determined by the net present value of future cash flows to the investor, cash flows available for repatriation should be used as the relevant cash flows in foreign investment analysis. Hence, the multinational company must analyze the impact of taxation, expropriation, and exchange controls on cash flows to the parent.

The Required Rate of Return

The required rate of return is the minimum rate of return that a project must yield in order to be accepted by a company. This minimum rate of return is sometimes called the discount rate, the hurdle rate, or the cutoff rate. The most widely accepted required rate of return has been their cost of capital.

The cost of capital provides the conceptual background necessary to properly evaluate capital structure decisions. Our concern is the effect of variations in the capital structure on the cost of capital. We should not consider the cost of capital as one particular cutoff point for a number of reasons. (1) The cost of capital varies with the amount of funds actually raised. (2) The cost of capital is a field still in the process of further refinement. (3) The cost of capital is measured on the basis of forecasts. Thus, it is a value within a broad range.

234

Optimum Capital Structure   The optimum capital
structure is defined as the combination of debt and
equity that yields the lowest cost of capital or
maximizes the overall value of the company. Evidence
suggests that companies seek the optimum capital
structure. For instance, financial ratios published
by Dun and Bradstreet, Robert Morris Associates, and
other organizations indicate rather considerable
similarities in the capital structure among companies
in the same industry.

These considerations may not be equally applicable
to the multinational case because we cannot ignore the
modifying effects of environmental variables peculiar
to international operations. Table 12-2 shows that
the capital structure of companies in the same industry
varies widely from country to country. For example,
the debt ratio for most Japanese companies is much
higher than the comparable debt ratio for American
companies in the same industry. This additional debt
is partly because: (1) the Bank of Japan provides
major industries with loans through commercial banks
and (2) lenders know that the government protects
their business. It is also important to note that
debt ratios for Germany, Italy, Japan, and Sweden are
considerably higher than those for the United States
or the United Kingdom. This may be due to the fact
that the former group of countries has thinner equity
markets than the latter group of countries.

The Appropriate Cost of Capital   To accept or reject
investment projects, companies must have an appropriate
cost of capital which is used as a discount rate or a
cutoff rate. Multinational companies have three
choices in deciding their appropriate cost of capital:
(1) the parent cost of capital, (2) the subsidiary
cost of capital, and (3) some weighted average of
the two.

If the parent company should finance the entire
cost of its foreign project by itself, the parent
cost of capital should be used as the appropriate
cost of capital for the project. If the company obtains all of the capital for the project overseas,
the foreign cost of capital should be used as the
appropriate cost of capital. In most cases, however,
the multinational company uses the whole world as a
combined source of funds. Thus, the appropriate

235

Table 12-2 Debt Ratios in Selected Industries and Countries*

	Alcoholic beverages	Automobiles	Chemicals	Electrical	Foods	Iron and Steel	Non-ferrous metals	Paper	Textiles	Total
Benelux	45.7	–	44.6	37.5	56.2	50.0	59.2	35.9	54.2	47.9
France	35.8	36.0	34.3	59.1	24.7	33.7	55.0	35.5	20.9	37.2
Germany	59.2	55.1	54.8	67.5	42.5	63.8	68.1	71.8	44.9	58.6
Italy	64.9	77.3	68.2	73.6	66.4	77.9	67.5	–	66.6	70.3
Japan	60.9	70.3	73.2	71.1	78.3	74.5	74.5	77.7	72.2	72.5
Sweden	–	76.4	45.6	60.1	46.8	70.0	68.7	60.7	–	61.2
Switzerland	–	–	59.7	50.8	29.2	–	26.3	–	–	41.5
United Kingdom	43.8	56.5	38.7	46.9	47.6	44.9	41.7	46.6	42.4	45.5
United States	31.1	39.2	43.3	50.3	34.2	35.8	36.7	33.9	44.2	38.7
Total	48.8	58.7	51.4	57.4	47.3	56.3	55.3	51.7	49.4	–

*The number in the matrix represents average total debt as a per cent of total assets based on book value. Each company is weighted equally, i.e., the individual company debt ratios are summed and divided by the number of companies in each sample.

Source: Arthur Stonehill and Thomas Stitzel, "Financial Structure and Multinational Corporations," California Management Review (Fall 1969), pp. 91-96.

cost of capital is an overall weighted average of
the two.

The Risk Adjusted Discount Rate   The risk adjusted
discount rate consists of the rate of return on a
default free asset such as a government security plus
a risk premium. The risk premium is the additional
return necessary to compensate the investor for each
additional unit of risk. The multinational company
may increase the discount rate applicable to foreign
projects relative to the rate used by domestic projects. In other words, the foreign project's risk-
adjusted cost of capital is increased to reflect such
risks as political risks, foreign exchange risks, and
other risks perceived in foreign operations.

Measuring the Profitability of the Investment

        The net present value and internal rate of re-
turn methods are often called discounted cash flow
approaches. The net present value of a project is
the present value of its expected cash inflows minus
the present value of its expected cash outflows.
The decision rule tells us to accept a project if
its net present value is positive.

Example 12-1 In August 1981, the International TV
Corporation was approached by the government of Samson in West Africa with a request that the company
establish a plant in Samson to assemble television
sets for sale in Samson and other West African countries. In return for an increase in tariffs against
other companies in the industry, the International
TV Corporation wishes to invest a total of 1,500 Samson liras in the proposed plant. This SL1,500 will
be financed with only common stock, all of which
will be owned by the parent company. The plant is
to be depreciated over a five-year period on a
straight-line basis for tax purposes. It is expected
to have a salvage value of SL750 at the end of five
years. The company will pay income taxes at 20 per
cent on net income earned in Samson and no withhold-
ing taxes on dividend repatriated. The United States
also has a 50 per cent tax rate with direct credit
for Samson's taxes. This means that net income
earned in Samson by U.S. companies will be subject
to a total tax of 50 per cent. Expected revenues,
operating costs, and applicable exchange rates are

237

given in Table 12-3 and 12-4. There is no restriction on dividend repatriation, but depreciation cash flows may not be repatriated until the company is liquidated. These cash flows can be reinvested in Samson's government bonds to earn tax-exempt interest at the rate of 8 per cent. The company's cost of capital is 15 per cent.

Table 12-3 shows the projected cash flows for the proposed plant. It is important to recognize that for the first year a total tax of 50 per cent (SL225) will be levied: 20 per cent of the Samson tax (SL90) and 30 per cent of the U.S. tax (SL135).

Table 12-3 Projected Earnings After Taxes for the Proposed Plant

	Year 1	Year 2	Year 3	Year 4	Year 5
Revenues	1,500	1,650	1,800	1,950	2,100
Operating Costs	900	900	1,050	1,050	1,200
Depreciation	150	150	150	150	150
Taxable income	450	600	600	750	750
Total tax at 50%	225	300	300	375	375
Earnings after tax	225	300	300	375	375

Table 12-4 shows the depreciation cash flows and interest-compounded depreciation cash flows at the termination of the project at the end of five years. Thus, a total of SL880 will be repatriated to the United States along with the plant's fifth year earnings of SL375 at the end of five years.

Table 12-4 Depreciation Cash Flows

Year	Depreciation	Factor at 8%	Terminal Value
1	SL150	1.360	SL204
2	150	1.260	189
3	150	1.166	175
4	150	1.080	162
5	150	1.000	150
			SL880

238

The last two steps in the analysis are: (1) to convert the cash flows from liras to dollars and (2) to determine the net present value of the plant. Table 12-5 shows these two computation steps. It should be noted that the fifth year cash flow of SL2,005 consists of dividends (SL375), the estimated salvage value of the plant (SL750), and the interest-accumulated depreciation cash flows (SL880).

Table 12-5   The Parent's Net Present Value

Year	Cash Flows	Exchange Rate	Cash Flows	Pres. Val. at 15%	Cum. Net Pres. Val.
0	-SL1,500	5.00	-$300	-$300	-$300
1	225	5.00	45	39	- 261
2	300	5.25	57	43	- 218
3	300	5.51	54	36	- 182
4	375	5.79	65	37	- 145
5	2,005	6.08	330	164	19

The current exchange rate of five liras to the dollar is expected to hold during the first year. But the lira is expected to depreciate at a rate of 5 per cent per year after the first year. The expected cash flows in dollars are obtained by dividing the cash flows in liras by the exchange rates. The dollar cash flows are then discounted at the firm's cost of capital (15%) to arrive at a present value figure for each year. Cumulative net present values are the final amounts given in Table 12-5. We see that from the parent's point of view, the plant would break even on a discounted cash flow basis during the fifth year. Because the net present value of the project is positive ($19), the International TV Corporation should accept the proposed plant in order to maximize the market value of the company. The project's internal rate of return is approximately 17 per cent. Because the internal rate of return (17%) is greater than the cost of capital (15%), the internal rate of return criterion also indicates acceptance.

FOOTNOTES

1. Dirk W. Stikker, The Role of Private Enterprise in Investment and Promotion of Exports in De-

veloping Countries, United Nations Conference
on Trade and Development (New York: 1968),
p. 14.

2.   For an extensive discussion of motives for
      foreign investment, see Suk H. Kim, An Intro-
      duction to International Financial Management
      (Washington, D.C.:   University Press of America,
      1980), Chapter 2.

3.   Charles P. Kindleberger, American Business
      Abroad: Six Lectures on Direct Investment
      (Yale University Press, 1969).

CHAPTER 13

REFUNDING OPERATION AND RETIREMENT DECISION

This chapter deals with two special topics of capital investment analysis: refunding operation and retirement decision. A refunding operation is the sale of low-yielding securities to retire the high-rate issue when interest rates drop. Of course, this refunding operation is based on the assumption that the existing issue is callable. Because long-term asset management is a dynamic process, capital investments cannot be viewed as a commitment to the end. If the retirement value of a project is greater than the present value of its subsequent net cash flows, the project should be retired.

REFUNDING OPERATION

Most corporate bond and preferred stock issues have a call provision. If interest rates or preferred dividends should decline significantly, the company can call these issues and refinance them at a lower cost. This is called a refunding operation. The refunding operation of bonds is identical with that of preferred stock except for the fact that interest payments are a tax deductible expense while preferred dividends are not.

The decision to refund a bond or a preferred stock is analyzed in much the same way as an investment project.[1] To analyze a project, we should know the initial cash outflow of the project and its future cash benefits. By the same token, the refunding decision involves an initial cash outflow in the form of the call premium and future cash benefits in the form of interest savings. Because the interest savings occur over the life of the original security, we have to determine the present value of these future interest savings and then compare it with the initial cash outflow of the refunding operation. The interest savings of the new bonds are usually known with relative certainty and consequently we have to use the after-tax cost of the new debt as a discount rate.

Example 13-1 The Colby Plastic Company issued $100 million of 30-year bonds with a coupon rate of 8 per cent ten years ago. Within the ten years interest

rates dropped to 7 per cent. Rather than continue to
pay higher rates of interest, the company plans to
call in its bonds and to sell a $100 million new is-
sue of 20-year bonds with a coupon rate of 7 per cent.
It sold its old bonds at par and can also sell its
new bonds at par; the new bonds are sold one month
before the old bonds are called. The old bonds have
an unamortized flotation cost of $1.5 million and a
call premium of 5 per cent. The new bonds have an
underwriting spread of 2.75 per cent. With a tax
rate of 50 per cent, should the company refund its
$100 million worth of bonds?

The refunding decision process requires the following computation steps.

Step 1. Determine the initial net cash outflow of
the refunding decision: the gross cash
outlay of the refunding decision minus
its tax savings.

(a) Gross Cash Outlay

Call premium ($100,000,000 x 5.00%)	$5,000,000
Underwriting cost of new bonds ($100,000,000 x 2.75%)	2,750,000
Overlapping interest on old bonds[2] ($100,000,000 x 8.00%/12)	666,667
Gross cash outlay	$8,416,667

(b) Tax Savings

Overlapping interest on old bonds	$ 666,667
Call premium	5,000,000
Unamortized flotation cost of old bonds	1,500,000
Total tax deductible expense	$7,166,667
x Tax rate (50%)	x 50%
Tax savings	$3,583,333

(c) Net Cash Outflow

Net cash outflow = gross cash outlay - tax savings
= $8,416,667 - $3,583,333
= $4,833,334

242

Step 2. Determine the annual interest savings of
        the refunding decision: the annual net
        cash outflow on the old bonds minus the
        annual net cash outflow on the new bonds.

(a) Annual Net Cash Outflow on Old Bonds

        (1) Interest expense ($100,000,000 x 8%) $8,000,000
        Less: Tax savings
               Interest expense   8,000,000
               Amortization of flotation cost
               ($1,500,000 ÷ 20)   75,000
               Total tax deductible expense $8,075,000
               x Tax rate (50%)   x 50%
        (2) Tax savings $4,037,500
        Annual net cash outflow = (1) - (2) $3,962,500

(b) Annual Net Cash Outflow on New Bonds

        (3) Interest expense ($100,000,000 x 7%) $7,000,000
        Less: Tax savings
               Interest expense   7,000,000
               Amortization of underwriting
               cost ($2,750,000 ÷ 20)   137,500
               Total tax deductible expense $7,137,500
               x Tax rate (50%)   x 50%
        (4) Tax savings $3,568,750
        Annual net cash outflow = (3) - (4) $3,431,250

(c) Annual Interest Savings = (a) - (b)
                             = $3,962,500 - $3,431,250
                             = $531,250

Step 3. Determine the present value of annual in-
        terest savings for the next 20 years.
        Since the after-tax cost of the new debt
        is 3.5 per cent, the present value is
        $7,550,125 = $531,250 x $ADF_{20,3.5\%}$ (14.212).

Step 4. The net present value of the refunding
        decision = Step 3 - Step 1
                  = $7,550,125 - $4,833,334
                  = $2,716,731

Since the net present value of the refunding decision is positive ($2,716,731), the issue should
be refunded.

Also, we can solve this example by the internal rate of return method. Because the internal rate of return for the example is approximately 9 per cent, it exceeds the required return of 3.5 per cent; the issue should be refunded.

RETIREMENT DECISION

In capital investment analysis, insufficient attention in the literature is paid to the possibility of future retirement. Ordinarily, projects are evaluated as though the company were committed to the project over its entire economic life. However, it may become more profitable to retire a project before the end of its estimated useful life rather than to continue its operation. If this factor is taken into consideration in the capital budgeting process, the project's expected net present value may increase and the standard deviation of returns may fall. Hence, the possibility of future retirement must be considered in the capital budgeting process if capital is to be allocated optimally. This section will discuss retirement decisions under conditions of certainty.

Introduction

Retirement decisions are terminal decisions to the extent that an asset withdrawn from its original service will not be replaced by another asset which will perform the same service. When investment proposals are originally considered, key financial variables are identified and assumptions are made to make some choice. As time passes, some unforeseen problems can occur that could affect these key variables. Initial assumptions may turn out to be incorrect, or perhaps some additional investment opportunities may arise. If projects are no longer desirable, they should be retired. By the same token, if funds released from existing projects could be used for substantially better investment opportunities, these projects must be retired.

Major causes of asset retirement include: (1) improved alternatives, (2) changes in service requirements, (3) changes in the old assets themselves, (4) changes in public requirements, and (5) casualties.[3]

244

It is important to recognize that these causes are not mutually exclusive. For example, a growing company may decide to retire its computer partly because of obsolescence (cause 1), partly because of inadequacy (cause 2), and partly because of increasing annual expenditures for repairs and maintenance (cause 3).

Evaluation Method

If the duration of the investment and production processes are well defined in the appraisal of an investment proposal, it is not difficult to determine the optimal length of the project. The economic rationale behind the investment decision rule can be applied directly to the retirement decision. If a firm uses the net present value method in its capital expenditure analysis, the firm should retire its project at that point in time that the retirement value of the project exceeds the present value of the project's subsequent net cash flows discounted at the company's cost of capital. If the company uses the internal rate of return in its capital budgeting analysis, it should retire a project when the rate of return on retirement value is less than the company's cost of capital. If there are diminishing returns to the investment of additional time in the production process, there should be a point where further waiting brings a return no greater than the company's cost of capital. We employ the net-present-value method to determine the optimal length of a project because it is better than the internal-rate-of-return method.

Retirement Decisions Under Conditions of Certainty

Let us assume that the company has the option to retire an asset at various points throughout its useful life. If the asset has a useful life of n years, there are n opportunities for retirement, i.e., one at the end of each year. We may estimate the cash-flow series associated with the asset on the assumption that it will be retired at the end of each year. If we compute the net present value of the asset at the end of each year, we then have n net present values to compare. Thus, this methodology basically finds the maximum net present value of the project's net cash flows by considering all possible periods when the project can be retired.

245

The net present value of a project can be expressed as a function of its retirement period:

$$NPV(n) = \sum_{t=1}^{n} \frac{A_t}{(1 + k)^t} + \frac{S_n}{(1 + k)^t} - C \qquad (13\text{-}1)$$

where $NPV(n)$ is the net present value of the project if it is retired at the end of year n; A_t is the net cash flow in year t; S_n is the salvage value of the project in year n; k is the firm's cost of capital used as a discount rate; and C is the cost of the project. In this case, the optimal length of the project is the time period that maximizes $NPV(n)$.

We may approach the same problem by asking whether it is better to retire the project at the end of year n or at the end of year n + 1. It is important to recognize that if $NPV(n)$ is a maximum, then $NPV(n)$ - $NPV(n-1) > 0$ and $NPV(n)$ - $NPV(n + 1) > 0$. If we solve these algebraic equations, we find that the optimal life of the project is the time period at which the following inequality first holds:

$$S_n(1 + k) - S_{n + 1} > R_{n + 1} \qquad (13\text{-}2)$$

where k is the reinvestment rate. This inequality states that the decline in the salvage value of the project in any given year ($S_n(1 + k) - S_{n + 1}$) is greater than the net cash benefits from holding the asset another year ($R_{n + 1}$). In other words, this formula permits us to determine whether it is best to retire at the end of year 1 vs. 2, 3, ..., n; at the end of year 2 vs. 3, 4, ..., n; etc.

Example 13-2 The Quick Transport Company provides scenic bus tours, cruises in Great Lakes, and limousine shuttle service between Renaissance Center in downtown Detroit and the Detroit Metropolitan Airport. Quick Transport has one limousine which has a cost of $3,000, an expected useful life of five years, and an estimated salvage value of $500 at the end of five years. The limousine is expected to be depreciated on a straight-line basis. The company has a contract with a group of Renaissance Area companies to shuttle business executives between Renaissance Center and the airport for the next five years. However, it may terminate the service at any time on a one-year

246

notice. The contract assures stable revenues of
$4,000 per year, but operating costs are expected
to increase by $265 per year. Thus, the cash flows
from operation are expected to fall rather rapidly.
The first-year operating costs for the limousine
are $2,296. Quick Transport's marginal tax rate
is 46 per cent and its cost of capital is 12 per
cent. The salvage values of the limousine at the
end of each year are estimated to be equal to its
book value.

First, we must determine the net present value
of the investment. To determine the net present
value of the investment, the expected net cash flows
from the limousine service must be computed, as
shown in Table 13-1. Thus, for an investment of
$3,000, Quick Transport expects to result in an-
nual net cash flows of $1,150, $1,007, $864, and
$1,078 over the next five years. The net present
value of the investment is:

$$\text{NPV} = \frac{\$1,150}{(1+.12)^1} + \frac{\$1,007}{(1+.12)^2} + \frac{\$864}{(1+.12)^3} + \frac{\$721}{(1+.12)^4} +$$

$$\frac{\$1,078}{(1+.12)^5} - \$3,000$$

$$= \$3,515 - \$3,000$$

$$= \$515$$

This indicates that the investment would be profitable.

When should Quick Transport retire the limousine?
We begin by calculating the cash-flow series associated with retirement at the end of each year. If
the company retires the limousine at the end of one
year, it would receive $1,150 from operation and
$2,500 from salvage; at the end of two years, the
company would receive $1,007 from operation and
$2,000 from salvage, in addition to $1,150 from
the first-year operation, etc. We then compute
the net present value of each cash-flow series by
discounting the individual cash flows at the firm's
cost of capital, 12 per cent. For example, the net

Table 13-1 The Computation of Expected Net Cash Flows for Limousine

Item	Year 1	Year 2	Year 3	Year 4	Year 5
Revenues	$4,000	$4,000	$4,000	$4,000	$4,000
Less: Operating Expenses	2,296	2,561	2,826	3,091	3,356
Depreciation	500	500	500	500	500
Taxable Income	$1,204	$ 939	$ 674	$ 409	$ 144
Less: Taxes at 46%	554	432	310	188	66
Earnings After Taxes	$ 650	$ 507	$ 364	$ 221	$ 78
Add: Depreciation	500	500	500	500	500
Salvage Value					500
Annual Net Cash Flow	$1,150	$1,007	$ 864	$ 721	$1,078

Table 13-2 Net Present Values of the Investment at the End of Each Year

Holding Period	Cash Outlay	Annual Net Cash Flows					Salvage Value	Pres. Val. at 12%	NPV
		1	2	3	4	5			
1	$3,000	$1,150					$2,500	$3,259	$259
2	3,000	1,150	$1,007				2,000	3,424	424
3	3,000	1,150	1,007	$864			1,500	3,513	513
4	3,000	1,150	1,007	864	$721		1,000	3,539	539
5	3,000	1,150	1,007	864	721	$578	500	3,515	515

present value of the series associated with retirement at the end of two years is computed as follows:

$$NPV(2) = \frac{\$1,150}{(1+.12)^1} + \frac{\$1,007}{(1+.12)^2} + \frac{\$2,000}{(1.12)^2} - \$3,000$$

$$= \$3,424 - \$3,000$$

$$= \$424$$

The net present values of the investment at the end of each year are given in Table 13-2. The table shows that the company can maximize net present value by retiring the limousine at the end of four years.

FOOTNOTES

1. For details, see Harold Bierman, Jr., "The Bond Refunding Decision," <u>Financial Management</u> (Summer 1972), pp. 27-29; Aharon R. Ofer and Robert A. Taggart, Jr., "Bond Refunding: A Clarifying Analysis," <u>Journal of Finance</u> (March 1977), pp. 21-30; and Gene Laber, "Repurchases of Bonds Through Tender Offers: Implications for Shareholder Wealth," <u>Financial Management</u> (Summer 1978), pp. 7-13.

2. Most college texts in finance acknowledge that a bond refunding operation involves duplicate interest payments for a thirty-day overlap period between the time the new bonds are sold and the time the old bonds are called. But they do not agree upon which interest companies should use as the overlapping interest cost: the interest on the old bonds or the interest on the new bonds. We use the interest on the old bonds as the overlapping interest cost. For a detailed discussion of this topic, see James S. Ang, "The Two Faces of Bond Refunding," <u>Journal of Finance</u> (June 1975), pp. 869-874; and Douglas R. Emery, "Overlapping Interest in Bond Refunding: A Reconsideration," <u>Financial Management</u> (Summer 1978), pp. 19-20.

3. Eugene L. Grant and W. Grant Ireson, <u>Principles of Engineering Economy</u> (New York: The Ronald Press, 1960), p. 183.

CHAPTER 14

CORPORATE GROWTH THROUGH MERGERS

Growth is essential to the future well-being of
a business enterprise. It provides management with
opportunities for promotion and creative activity.
The possible opportunities for promotion and chal-
lenging activity are vital to attract and retain
able executives. Much of the material presented
in the previous chapters relates to the principles
by which the financial manager can maximize the market value of the owners' equity. Although this
chapter deals with somewhat specialized topics,
they draw upon these principles.

INTERNAL GROWTH VERSUS EXTERNAL GROWTH

Funds for growth can come from the retention of
earnings, the accumulation of depreciation and de-
pletion allowances, and the sale of new securities
such as bonds, preferred stock, and common stock.
The company grows when these funds are used to provide new capacity and new products and to serve new
markets. Internal growth occurs when this all takes
place within the same company, through the same organization, and under the same management. In contrast, external growth exists when the funds are
used to acquire the ownership interests of various
other companies.

Although internal growth is usually natural and
economical, the process of growth may be very slow.
In recent years, growth through merger with the
existing business activities of another firm has
received substantial publicity as an alternative to
internal growth. For a variety of reasons such as
antitrust prosecution,[1] the external growth of business has become more visible to investors and financial analysts than year-to-year internal expansion.

Traditionally, company growth through mergers
has been treated as a special topic outside the main-
stream of financial management. It is true to the
extent that the management rarely faces the need to
familiarize itself with the details involved in mergers. However, mergers should be treated as the main-
stream of financial management for a number of reasons.

Much of the material in the previous chapters has a direct bearing upon the financial manager's potential contribution to the company's external growth. Management may decide to acquire the facilities of another firm rather than to build its own. By the same token, it may enter the market for a product through acquisition rather than through the development of a substitute. All these decisions are long-term investment problems and thus they should be evaluated on the basis of discounted cash flows.

TYPES OF BUSINESS COMBINATION

The term merger refers to a combination of two or more formerly independent firms into one organization with a common management and ownership. Although in business practice other terms such as acquisition or consolidation are used in a similar context, the lines of distinction are frequently unclear. Thus, it may be helpful to begin with the clear definition of these terms. There are three basic forms of business combinations: consolidations, mergers, and holding companies.

Consolidations

The corporation laws of the various states contain formal statutory provision for business combinations. A statutory consolidation takes place when two or more companies are combined to form a completely new corporation. The new company absorbs the assets and liabilities of the old companies and consequently the old companies cease to exist. Consolidations are ordinarily used when companies of approximately the same size combine. When companies consolidate, shares of their common stock are exchanged for shares in the new company.

Mergers

A statutory merger refers to a combination of two corporations by which one loses its identity. The surviving corporation acquires the assets and liabilities of the acquired corporation and it pays for its acquisition in either cash or common stock. Typically, this form of business combination is used when the two companies differ significantly in size. For instance, a larger company may use the merger to

252

obtain the assets or the common stock of a smaller
company.

Holding Companies

A holding company is a company that has a controlling interest in one or more other companies.
The holding company is called the parent company
and the controlled companies are called subsidiaries.
The effective working control of a subsidiary by the
parent company does not require a majority of the subsidiary's voting stock. The ownership of between 10
and 20 per cent of the voting stock is frequently
sufficient to control a company.

There are a number of significant differences
between the holding company and the merger. The
merger involves the acquisition of the entire company, while the holding company does not acquire the
entire company. Hence, the holding company arrangement makes it possible for a company to enjoy greater
asset control per dollar than a merger. The second
difference is the fact that a holding company consists
of a number of separate corporations called subsidiaries, whereas a mergered company is a single
organization.

ECONOMIC MOTIVES FOR COMBINATION

Although there are some important differences
between the words merger and consolidation, their
similarity should be clear at this point. In practice they tend to be used interchangeably in order
to describe the combination of two or more companies.
Thus, the remainder of this chapter ignores the difference between these two forms of combination.

The combination of two or more companies is eco-
nomically justified only if it increases the total
value of a firm. We observed in the Optimum Capital
Structure of Chapter 10 that the total value of the
firm consists of the market value of its common stock
and the market value of its debt. The traditional
capitalization approach to the valuation of the firm
rests upon four basic steps:[2] (1) Determine the
earnings after taxes the company expects to produce
over the years or earnings before taxes (1 - tax
rate). (2) Determine the capitalization rate (dis-

count rate) for these earnings. (3) Determine the extent to which the company may be levered or the appropriate amount of debt. (4) Compute the total value of the firm from the following valuation formula:

$$\text{Value of Firm} = \frac{\text{Earnings Before Taxes (1 - Tax Rate)}}{\text{Capitalization Rate}} +$$

Amount of Debt

One can examine the effect of a merger on each of the factors that affect the total value of the firm.

Earnings Before Taxes

It should be clear from the valuation model that an increase in the expected earnings before taxes would increase the total value of the firm. A merger itself creates a larger physical size and opportunities for synergistic effects. The synergistic effects of business combinations are certain economies of scale from the firms' lower overhead. A synergistic effect is said to exist when the combined companies are worth more than the sum of their parts. This effect has been frequently defined as "2 + 2 = 5." That is, the two companies when combined together produce a greater net operating income than if they had remained separate.

The merger allows the firm to acquire necessary management skills and to spread existing management skills over a larger operation. There are opportunities to eliminate duplicate facilities as well as to consolidate the functions of production, marketing, and purchasing. These types of operating economies and better management can increase the profit margin and reduce risks as well.

Operating economies may best be described in combination with three forms of growth: a horizontal merger, a vertical merger, and a conglomerate merger. A horizontal merger occurs when firms in the same type of production or in marketing the same product are combined. Certain operating economies result from this form of combination for three major reasons. (1) It reduces the number of competitors. (2) It eliminates duplicate facilities. (3) It provides the

254

firm with an opportunity to expand its operation in an existing product line. A vertical merger occurs when a company acquires its suppliers or its retail outlets. The economies achieved by this combination stem primarily from the firm's greater control over the purchase of raw materials or the distribution of finished goods.[3] A conglomerate merger occurs when two or more companies in unrelated lines of businesses are combined. For example, the combination of a food processing company and an aircraft manufacturing company is a conglomerate merger. One cannot expect real operating economies from this type of combination because a conglomerate merger involves the combination of firms in unrelated businesses. The key benefit of this combination is diversification which reduces risk, broadens the product base, and balances cyclical fluctuations.

Tax Considerations

Some have argued that a key motive for some mergers is to take advantage of a tax loss. The tax benefit comes from the fact that one of the firms has a tax loss carryforward.[4] The tax loss carryforward expires at the end of seven years unless the firm makes sufficient profits to offset it completely. There are two situations where mergers could actually avoid corporate income taxes. First, when a profitable company acquires companies with a large tax loss carryforward, it can reduce its effective tax rate and consequently the merger increases its net operating income after taxes. Second, a company with a tax loss carryforward may acquire profitable companies in order to use its carryforward. Otherwise, a portion of the tax loss carryforward might have been lost forever for the lack of sufficient profits to utilize it completely.

Capitalization Rates

An important advantage of mergers, especially conglomerate mergers, is the fact that the earnings of larger companies are capitalized at lower rates. Through conglomerate mergers companies become larger and they are more able to diversify. The securities of larger companies have better marketability than those of smaller companies. Larger companies are also better known among investors. A conglomerate

merger can make all these factors happen and they
lead to lower required rates of return and higher
price-earning ratios. Since conglomerate diversification reduces the overall risk of the merged
firm and thereby its capitalization rate, its value
exceeds the values of the companies operating
separately.

The argument for the reduction in the firm's
overall risk through conglomerate diversification
is exactly the same as that advanced in our discussion of capital budgeting. Most conglomerate mergers involve companies whose product lines and geo-
graphic markets are different. Therefore, their
returns are not perfectly positively correlated with
each other. If returns are not perfectly positively
correlated, the merger of two or more companies can
reduce the risk of the residual owners. Investors
are basically risk averters and thus they view such
a risk reduction favorably. However, it is important
to recognize that they can achieve the same objective
by diversifying their own investment portfolios.
Thus, it is unlikely that they will pay positive
utility to have their company do this for them.

Debt Capacity

The appropriate mix of debt and equity reduces the
overall cost of capital and thus it raises the market
value of the firm. The varying effects of financial
leverage on the capitalization rates for debt and
equity permit the company to reduce its overall cost
of capital and thereby to increase its market value
by the intelligent use of leverage. There are two
situations where a merger can raise the debt capacity
for the mergered firm above the sum of debt capacities
for the individual firms prior to merger.

First, there are companies that fail to make optimum use of debt. We observed in Chapter 10 that the
company may enhance its market value by raising its
utilization of debt up to its debt capacity. There
are a number of ways which the company can judge its
debt limit. (1) The financial manager may examine
the relationship between the cash flows of similar
firms and their level of debt plus their debt service
charges. (2) He may investigate their ratios of debt
to equity. (3) He can have consultation with invest-

256

ment bankers in order to produce the approximate industry average. The use of leverage enhances the market value of the firm primarily due to the tax deductibility of the interest on debt. Companies with an inadequate use of debt are undervalued in the marketplace. If a company acquires these companies by exchanging debt for its outstanding common stock, the market value of the mergered company would then exceed the values of the companies as separate entities.

Second, sometimes it is possible for the mergered firm to borrow more than the companies were able to borrow individually. If the debt capacity for the mergered company exceeds the sum of debt capacities for the independent companies, a merger would increase its market value above the combined market values of the independent companies. The increased debt capacity of the mergered company stems from two factors: (1) If several different streams of expected cash flows are combined through a merger, the technical insolvency of the mergered firm falls because the merger balances cyclical earnings fluctuations. Certainly, an important condition is that these income streams are not perfectly positively correlated. (2) Lenders are willing to provide more debt to a mergered company than to the independent companies because the mergered company can provide greater protection for its lenders than they can provide for themselves.

It should be noted that the highly levered company may become even more highly levered if it acquires another highly levered company. The merger may then cause the acquiring company's financial risk to rise and consequently the earnings may be discounted by investors at a higher rate. The net result is to reduce the market value of the owners' equity unless tax advantages and additional earnings exceed the financial risk associated with the acquiring company.

TERMS OF COMBINATION

Once management has considered mergers from various aspects, it must then examine the terms of a merger. The key topics in this section are: (1) acquisition of assets versus acquisition of stock, (2) cash payment versus stock payment, and (3) the exchange ratio.

257

Acquisition of Assets Versus Acquisition of Stock

Acquisition of Assets   There are some companies that desire to purchase only a portion of the assets (generally fixed assets) of the selling company. In other instances state laws make it difficult for a company to merge with other companies if the companies involved are chartered in different states. If the selling company obtains the consent of its stockholders for the sale of its assets, its assets are disposed of in exchange for cash, stock, or other securities. The proceeds from the sale are usually distributed to the stockholders of the selling company in the form of a liquidation dividend and the selling company then ceases to exist. If the combination allows the selling company to continue in existence, it should not be treated as a merger.

Acquisition of Stock   If a company wishes to control other going concerns, it must acquire their common stock. This method may be particularly attractive to a company that desires to obtain a controlling interest of another business gradually. There are two acquisition methods of stock: the purchase of stock in the marketplace and a tender offer. If one company seeks controlling interest in another without revealing its intentions, it may buy common shares of another company through a broker on the open market or a block of shares from one large holder on a negotiated basis.

In recent years, some companies have used the tender offer to take over another. With a tender offer, the stockholders of another company are asked to submit (tender) their shares in exchange for a specified price per share. To make its offer more attractive to the stockholders of the company it desires to acquire, the acquiring company sets its tender price significantly above the present market price. The tender offer makes it possible for the acquiring company to bypass the management of the company it intends to acquire and thus the offer serves as some sort of threat to that management. The management may use a number of defensive tactics to resist the tender offer for both business and financial reasons. The management may resort to some legal means as a delaying action or it may attempt to persuade its stockholders that the tender price is too low.

Cash Payment Versus Stock Payment

Mergers involve straight cash purchases, an exchange of stock, or a combination of cash and securities. When a firm desires to acquire the assets of the selling companies or their stock for cash, such acquisitions should be treated as capital budgeting problems.[5] The financial manager can evaluate cash acquisitions of going concerns or another company's assets in the same way as that described in Parts 2 and 3. When a company attempts to acquire another going concern, it must recognize that the estimation of cash flows and certain risk considerations from the changed financial structure make it difficult to apply these capital budgeting techniques.

The acquisition of another company through the exchange of common stock or other securities has certain advantages over the cash acquisition. While the acquiring company could sell its securities on the market to the public for cash, the direct exchange of securities eliminates the underpricing and flotation costs. When companies are combined through the direct exchange of stock, a ratio of exchange occurs. The exchange ratio implies the relative valuation of the companies.

The Exchange Ratio

The exchange ratio is the number of the acquiring firm's shares for each share of the acquired firm. When two companies are combined, the owners of these two companies can consider the ratio of exchange with respect to their book value per share, their earnings per share, and their market price per share.

Book values are generally meaningless as a basis for valuation in merger negotiations because they simply represent the historical investments made in the company. In other words, such investments do not reflect current prices or values which are important in merger negotiations. However, book values have an impact on merger terms under two circumstances: (1) when they significantly exceed market values and (2) when companies are acquired for their liquidity and asset values rather than for their expected earnings.

Mergers have potentially favorable or adverse effects on earnings, on market values of shares, or on both. The effects of a proposed merger on market values are less certain than its effects on earnings per share. There are many variables that affect market prices of shares: future earnings potential, expected dividends, growth, risk class, capital structure, asset values, and managerial talent, and other factors that bear upon valuation. These future events are difficult to predict and consequently stockholders place considerable emphasis on the immediate effects of a proposed merger on earnings per share in the bargaining process.

In addition to earnings, the major emphasis in merger negotiations is on the market-value indicator which portrays the judgment of investors concerning the company. The ratio of market prices per share is the ratio of the market price per share of the acquiring company times the number of shares offered to the market price per share of the acquired company.

Example 14-1: The acquiring company has a market value per share of $100, while the acquired company has a market value per share of $20. What is the ratio of market prices per share if the acquiring company offers .2 shares for each share of the acquired company?

The exchange ratio is computed as follows:

$$\frac{\$100 \times .2}{\$20} = 1.00$$

The exchange ratio of 1 indicates that the stocks of these two companies would be exchanged on a one-to-one market-price basis. In other words, the stockholders of the acquired company are able to buy a share with market value of $20 for each share of their own stock. If the market price per share of the surviving company stays the same, the stockholders of both companies are as well off as before in terms of market value. However, if the acquiring company desperately needs the liquidity of the acquired company, it must offer a price in excess of the current market price per share of the acquired company. Let us assume that the acquiring company offers .6 shares for each share of the acquired company. The market-value exchange ratio would then be 3.00 ($100 x .6/$20). In other words, the stockholders of the acquired company are now able to purchase a share with market value of $60 for each share of their own stock.

SOME ACCOUNTING ASPECTS OF BUSINESS COMBINATIONS

For accounting purposes, business combinations are handled either as purchases or pooling of interests. The distinction between a purchase and a pooling of interests depends upon the nature of the surviving entity. With a purchase, only the acquiring company survives and the others cease to exist. With a pooling of interests, companies combined to carry out their economic activities as a single entity and nearly all of the former ownership interests would continue in the combined company.

The purchase method views a business combination as an investment for the acquiring company. The acquired assets or companies are usually recorded in the accounts of the acquiring company at the market value of the assets given in exchange. The historical cost in the accounts of the acquired company is no longer relevant. This treatment is theoretically valid because the market value of the assets given in exchange represents their current value to the acquiring company. If the acquiring company pays more than the net worth of the acquired company, the excess is treated as goodwill. Goodwill write-offs are not deductible for federal income tax purposes.[6] This accounting treatment results in lower reported earnings for several years and thus this form of business combination is not popular in practice.

If a combination of two companies is treated as a pooling of interests, the assets are carried forward at the book value in the accounts of the acquired company. Thus, the pooling of interests method does not change the underlying asset values of the corporate entities involved and the combination does not result in goodwill. The obvious advantage of this method is that there are no charges against future earnings and thus it would produce higher reported earnings.

Accounting problems in mergers have important implications for the reporting of value and earnings per share after the event of acquisition. There have been some allegations that acquiring companies inflated their performance records and misled the public through the pooling of interests method. However, on August 2, 1970, the Accounting Principles Board of the American Institute of Certified Public Accountants issued its Opinion No. 16 which significantly restricts the conditions under which a pooling of interests could take place. The most important condition is that the surviving company must issue common stock in exchange for at least 90 per cent of the voting common stock of another company.[7] Even before this opinion, the acquisition of a firm's assets or its stock for cash was treated as a clear-cut purchase. However, companies could use securities other than common stock and non-cash assets to acquire another company and treat the transaction as a pooling of interests. There should be no doubt that the opinion will reduce the number of poolings of interests and thereby distortions in reported earnings.

HOLDING COMPANIES

In 1889, New Jersey became the first state which permitted corporations to exist for the sole purpose of owning the stocks of other corporations. A holding company may be a pure holding company which exists only to control other companies; it may be an operating company which exists to carry out some business activities of its own; or it may be an intermediate holding company which controls some subsidiaries but is in turn controlled by the parent company. Sometimes there are several layers of companies within the holding company system and one group of investors or one company can control many firms or a tremendous amount of assets for a relatively small amount of investment.

A holding company has a number of advantages. (1) It allows a company to own or control a large amount of assets with a relatively small investment. (2) The failure of one subsidiary does not cause the failure of the entire holding company because its subsidiaries are separate legal entities. (3) This form of combination does not require a formal approval

262

from the stockholders of the acquired companies.
(4) A holding company with a number of subsidiaries
in different states may have some tax advantages because many state laws favor corporations chartered
by the state over those chartered by other states.
(5) It may achieve some economies of scale through
centralized management.

A holding company also has some disadvantages.
(1) It must pay a tax on 15 per cent of the cash
dividends it receives from its subsidiaries.[8] A
merger allows the acquiring company to avoid this
tax. (2) The holding company system magnifies profits if operations are successful. However, it also
magnifies losses if operations are not profitable.
(3) It is a more expensive form of business organization to administer than a mergered company because
additional costs are necessary to maintain separate
organizations and separate corporate relationships.

FOOTNOTES

1. From a legal standpoint, external expansion is
   more visible than internal expansion for two
   reasons. (1) Enforcement agencies such as the
   Federal Trade Commission and the Justice Department have shown greater interest in external expansion. (2) Legal constraints on external
   growth have become more restrictive.

2. See Robert W. Johnson, Financial Management
   (Boston: Allyn and Bacon, Inc., 1971), pp.
   530-536.

3. Forward integration is said to occur when a
   company expands forward toward the ultimate
   consumer through the acquisition of retail
   outlets. Backward integration is said to
   occur when a company expands backward toward
   the source of raw materials through the acquisition of suppliers.

4. For an extensive discussion of a tax loss
   carryforward, see Chapter 2.

5. Samuel Schwartz, "Merger Analysis as a Capital
   Budgeting Problem," in Albert and Segall, eds.,
   The Corporate Merger (Chicago: University of

Chicago Press, 1966), pp. 139-150.

6. The Accounting Principles Board Opinion No. 17 allows companies to write off their goodwill account over a maximum of 40 years or 2.5 per cent per year.

7. There are some companies that have more than one class of common stock. For example, a company may have two classes of common stock: Class A stock which may have no voting rights but may have prior claims on earnings and Class B stock which may have voting rights but may have lower claims on earnings. At times, some companies such as the Ford Motor Company give some voting power to their Class A stockholders, but this voting power is much smaller than the voting power of their Class B stockholders per dollar of investment.

8. If the parent company owns at least 80 per cent of the voting stock of its subsidiary, its dividend is exempt from taxes.

CHAPTER 15

BUSINESS FAILURES

The preceding 14 chapters have covered issues
associated mainly with the growing, successful firm.
However, it is important for the financial manager
to understand the area of failure because the firm
operates in a world where failure is a fact. Failure
can be defined as either technical insolvency or bankruptcy. Technical insolvency occurs when the firm
cannot meet its current obligations as they come due.
Bankruptcy occurs when the firm's total liabilities
exceed the fair market value of its total assets.
This chapter consists of three major sections. The
first section deals with the nature and causes of
failure. The second section describes the voluntary
actions which may be taken to settle the claims of
creditors. The third section covers legal remedies
for the failed firm.

CAUSES OF FAILURE

There are a wide variety of causes for business
failures, but the underlying cause of most business
failures is management incompetence. A recent Dun
& Bradstreet compilation shows that management incompetence accounts for 93 per cent of all business
failures.[1] Poor planning, overexpansion, faulty
accounting, high production costs, and a poor sales
force are the types of factors that may cause the
ultimate failure of the firm. The firm may also
fail because of neglect, fraud, and natural disaster.
But these factors account for only 7 per cent of all
business failures.

For most companies the signs of potential difficulties are evident prior to actual failure. In recent years researchers have used financial ratios to
predict failure.[2] Among these ratios are cash flow/
total debt, earnings before interest and taxes/total
assets, cash flow/total assets, net income/total
assets, sales/total assets, and total debt/total
assets. These studies have found that these ratios
for healthy firms tend to be significantly different
from those for firms headed toward failure.

VOLUNTARY SETTLEMENTS

When companies find themselves in financial
difficulties, they should take steps to adjust
their cash flows to meet their commitments. They
can increase cash inflow by selling accounts receivable or by reducing inventories through special
sales. They can also increase cash inflow by selling all or a portion of the plant and then leasing
the necessary facilities. On the other hand, some
companies may be able to reduce cash outflows by
reducing salaries and eliminating dividends to stockholders. Expenditures for advertising, new equipment, and so on should frequently be postponed.
Payments to trade creditors may be somewhat delayed.

Because the adjustment of cash flows is often
insufficient to cope with the financial emergency,
a firm may become either technically insolvent or
bankrupt. It then becomes necessary to seek a solution through one of the available remedies. Ini-
tially, the financial manager should consider voluntary settlements because they are typically quicker
and less expensive. If the firm is in temporary insolvency, two voluntary remedies (extension and composition) are available.

Extension

An extension simply postpones the date of required payment of overdue obligations. Extensions
allow creditors to avoid considerable legal expense
and the possible shrinkage of value in liquidation.
They are usually arranged when the creditors feel
confident that the firm can overcome its problems
and resume successful operations. Under this arrangement the creditors will agree not to grant
additional credit to the firm until their claims
have been fully satisfied. They rather require
cash payments for purchases until the claims have
been satisfied.

The major creditors usually form a committee to
work with the firm in formulating a plan mutually
satisfactory for all concerned. However, no creditor
is obligated to go along with the plan. If the
claims of dissenting creditors are relatively small,

they may be paid off to avoid legal proceedings. If a large number of creditors are not willing to go along with the plan, liquidation may be the only alternative. To avoid such problems, the committee is usually composed of both large and small creditors.

In return for their agreement to extend the term of their credit, creditors frequently ask for concessions. For example, the creditors may be allowed to institute controls over the company in order to assure a proper recovery. They may also request that the firm does not increase its officers' salaries and stops dividend payments. In addition, long-term creditors may be offered a higher interest rate, mortgage security, conversion privileges, and other inducements.

Compositions

A composition is an arrangement under which creditors agree to accept a partial payment in discharge of their entire claim, say 70 cents on the dollar. The willingness of the creditors to accept the settlement depends largely on their general evaluation of the effects of liquidation. If they feel that they could obtain more under the composition arrangement than in liquidation after legal expenses, they will probably accept the partial payment to settle their entire claim. Even if the settlement is somewhat less than they could obtain in liquidation, they may still accept it to avoid lengthy legal proceedings.

Other Voluntary Settlements

Creditors may agree to a voluntary settlement only if the firm agrees to having its business operated by the creditor committee. The committee may then take control of the company and operate it until sufficient funds have been generated to repay creditors or until a satisfactory composition can be arranged. One problem with this arrangement is the possibility that stockholders may sue the creditors for mismanagement of the company. Thus, the creditors are frequently reluctant to become active in the management of a failing company.

In certain circumstances, the only acceptable
course of action is the liquidation of the company.
Liquidation can be carried out through either a
private settlement or bankruptcy proceedings. If
the company agrees to accept liquidation, legal
proceedings may not be necessary. An orderly private liquidation enables the creditors to obtain
quicker and higher settlements. A private settlement may also be accomplished through a formal assignment of assets to an appointed trustee. Under
this arrangement, the trustee liquidates the company's assets and distributes the proceeds to the
creditors on a pro rata basis.

LEGAL PROCEDURES

If a voluntary settlement of a failed firm cannot be found, it can be forced into bankruptcy by
its creditors. Most bankruptcy proceedings fall
under the Bankruptcy Act of 1898, as amended by the
Chandler Act of 1938. The Act has two primary objectives. The first objective is to provide for an
equitable distribution of a bankrupt debtor's assets.
The second objective is to discharge the debtor's
debts so that he can rehabilitate himself by making
a fresh start. The Act establishes legal procedures
for both the liquidation of a company and its reorganization. Typically, the court takes over the
operation of the bankrupt company and maintains the
status quo until a decision is made whether to liqui-
date the company or to reorganize it.

Bankruptcy Legislation

The American Bankruptcy Act of 1800 was the first
bankruptcy legislation in the United States. It had
been alternatively repealed and reinstated until the
Bankruptcy Act of 1890 was enacted. This act represents the backbone of the current bankruptcy statute,
the Chandler Act of 1938. The Chandler Act consists
of 15 chapters, but Chapters X and XI are the ones
most commonly cited in cases of corporate bankruptcy.

Chapter XI is considered first because it covers
less serious insolvency situations. It allows a failing company to seek an arrangement, which is basically
a "legal" extension or composition. The arrangement
is instituted by a voluntary petition of the company

and involves only the unsecured creditors. Because
the arrangement does not cover the claims of secured creditors, the company must pay its secured
creditors according to the terms of the obligations.
Once the petition is filed, the unsecured creditors
cannot pursue other legal remedies while an arrangement is being worked out. Once the reorganization
plan is accepted by a Federal Court and the majority
of the unsecured creditors, it becomes binding on all
unsecured creditors. Such settlements are usually
shorter and less costly than other types of formal
settlements.

Chapter X deals with hopeless cases under Chapter
XI. A Chapter XI proceeding allows the management
to remain in control until an arrangement is worked
out. However, a Chapter X proceeding provides that
the court takes away control of the bankrupt company
from its management and turns it over to a trustee.
The trustee manages the company during the proceedings
and formulates a plan of reorganization. The acceptance of a plan requires approval by two-thirds of each
class of creditors and a majority of the stockholders.
If a satisfactory reorganization plan cannot be worked
out under Chapter X, the trustee then liquidates the
company in accordance with procedures discussed later
in this chapter.

Reorganization

The reorganization is a plan of readjusting the
capital structure of a financially troubled firm in
order to reduce its fixed charges and improve its
financial health. For example, the firm's assets
are restated to reflect their current market value,
and its financial structure is restated to reflect
any changes on the asset side of the statement.

If voluntary settlements are not feasible, a reorganization petition may be filed in a federal dis-
trict court either under Chapter X or under Chapter
XI. Once the petition is filed, the court will review it. If the court finds the reorganization
petition in order, it approves the petition. If
the debts of the company exceed $250,000, the court
is required to appoint a trustee. However, if the
company's liabilities are less than $250,000, it
may be left in possession of the assets and may par-

ticipate in the development of the reorganization plan.

The trustee must carry out three steps to formulate a reorganization plan. The first step is to determine the total valuation of the reorganized company. The second step is to formulate a net capital structure of the company. The third step is to determine the valuation of the old securities and their exchange for new securities.

Example 15-1 Assume that the Kinney Company files a petition for a Chapter X reorganization. Its existing capital structure is as follows:

Secured bonds	$ 4,000,000
Debentures	15,000,000
Preferred stock	6,000,000
Common stock (at book value)	12,000,000
	$37,000,000

The trustee estimates that future annual earnings of the company are $3 million and that the overall capitalization rate of similar companies averages 10 per cent. Thus, the firm's potential value is estimated at $30,000,000. Once the potential value of the firm has been determined, the trustee might establish the following capital structure:

Secured bonds	$ 3,000,000
Debentures	2,000,000
Income bonds	5,000,000
Preferred stock	6,000,000
Common stock	14,000,000
	$30,000,000

How should the trustee allocate the new securities?

Under all Chapter X proceedings, the trustee must allocate the new securities according to the absolute priority rule. This rule simply states that all claims on assets must be settled in full before any junior claim can be settled. The trustee may propose the following exchanges:

1. The secured bond holders exchange their $4 million for $3 million in new secured bonds and $1 million in debentures.

270

2. The debenture holders exchange their $15 million for $1 million in new debentures, $5 million in income bonds, $6 million in preferred stock, and $3 million in common stock.

3. The preferred stockholders exchange their $6 million for $6 million in common stock.

4. The remaining $6 million in new common stock goes to the original $12 million common stockholders.

If the court finds that the reorganization plan is fair, equitable, and feasible, it goes to the firm's creditors and stockholders for their acceptance. A plan is considered fair and equitable if it meets the absolute priority rule. To be feasible the plan must offer a reasonable probability that the reorganized firm can operate efficiently, compete with other companies in the industry, and avoid a future reorganization or liquidation.

Liquidation

The liquidation of a bankrupt company typically occurs when the court feels that the reorganization of the company is not feasible. Once the court has determined that there is no hope for the feasible reorganization of the company, it then declares the company bankrupt and proceeds with a plan for an orderly liquidation. There are two types of liquidation: assignment and bankruptcy. Assignment is a liquidation procedure that does not go through the court, but it does not conflict with the Federal Bankruptcy Act. Bankruptcy is a judicial procedure carried out under the supervision of a special court.

Assignment   Because with an assignment there is no need to have the court supervise the liquidation, creditors would receive a larger amount than they would receive in a formal bankruptcy. All creditors must first agree to the settlement. The company then transfers its assets to a third party known as an assignee or a trustee. The assignee then liquidates the assets through a private sale or a public auction. After liquidation, the assignee distributes the proceeds to the creditors on a pro rata basis.

271

Bankruptcy   Bankruptcy proceedings may be voluntary
or involuntary. With a voluntary petition, the company files a petition of bankruptcy in court without
reference to any of the acts of bankruptcy or the
reason for insolvency. A petition for an involuntary
bankruptcy may be filed by three or more creditors
with claims in excess of $500 or by one or more credit-
ors with claims in excess of $500 if the company has
less than 12 creditors in all.

The Six Acts of Bankruptcy   The court will declare
the company involuntarily bankrupt if it has violated
one or more of the six acts of bankruptcy within the
preceding four months:

1. Committing fraud while insolvent. While
    insolvent, the company tries to remove or
    conceal any of the assets with the intent
    to delay or defraud any of the creditors.

2. Preferential transfer of property while
    insolvent. While insolvent, the company
    transfers cash or other assets to one
    creditor in preference to others.

3. Failure to discharge a legal lien while
    insolvent. While insolvent, the company
    permits a creditor to obtain a legal lien
    and fails to remove the lien within 90 days.

4. Assignment for benefit of credit. The
    act involves a general assignment for
    the benefit of creditors. It helps to
    insure that if creditors do not like
    the assignment, bankruptcy proceedings
    can be initiated.

5. Appointment of a trustee or a receiver
    while insolvent. While insolvent, the
    company appoints a trustee or a receiver
    to take charge of its assets.

6. Written admission of insolvency. The
    company admits in writing that it is
    unable to pay debts and that it is
    willing to be adjudged bankrupt.

272

Priority of Claims   The trustee would first convert all of the assets into cash and then distribute the proceeds according to the following schedule:

1. Court costs incurred in administering the bankrupt estate.

2. Employee wages up to $600 per worker if earned within three months prior to the filing of the petition in bankruptcy.

3. Payment of local, state, and federal taxes.

4. Certain debts that have been given special priority. Unpaid rent within three months prior to bankruptcy falls in this category.

5. Claims of secured creditors who have collateral pledged by the company to secure the debt. If the liquidation value of the collateral is not sufficient to cover the secured claims, the secured creditors become general creditors for the unpaid amount.

6. Claims of general creditors. The claims of unsecured creditors, the unsatisfied portion of secured creditors' claims, and the claims of subordinated creditors are all treated equally.

7. Preferred stockholders, who receive an amount up to the par or stated value of the preferred stock.

8. Common stockholders, who are last in line; they are the residual claimants.

Example 15-2   Table 15-1 shows the balance sheet of a bankrupt firm.

Table 15-1   The Bankrupt Firm's Balance Sheet

Assets		Liabilities and Net Worth	
Current assets	$ 8,420	Accounts payable	$ 400
Net property	7,780	Notes payable (bank)	2,000

Assets		Liabilities and Net Worth	
		Accrued wages	$ 800
		Accrued rent	200
		Taxes payable	600
		Current liabilities	$ 4,000
		First mortgage a/	3,600
		Second mortgage a/	2,000
		Subordinated deben-	
		tures b/	1,600
		Long-term debt	$ 7,200
		Preferred stock	800
		Common stock	1,000
		Capital surplus	3,000
		Retained earnings	200
		Net Worth	$ 5,000
Total	$16,200	Total	$16,200

a/ Secured by all the firm's plant and equipment.
b/ Subordinated to $2,000 notes payable to the bank.

Now assume that the trustee has liquidated the firm's assets and realized the following amounts:

Current assets	$4,600
Net property	4,000
Total	$8,600

How should the trustee distribute the proceeds to the various creditors?

Table 15-2 shows the distribution of $8,600 to the various creditors on the basis of the absolute priority rule. A total of $3,200 is used to satisfy such priority claims as bankrupt costs, accrued wages, accrued taxes, and accrued rent. The net proceeds of $4,000 from the sale of the fixed property are then used to pay the first mortgage of $3,600 and the second mortgage of $400. Because the net proceeds from the collateral sale are insufficient to satisfy the second mortgage, the remaining portion of the second mortgage ($1,600 = $2,000 - $400) will go into the general creditors' claims. The claims of the general creditors total $5,600. Because only $1,400 is available for the general

274

Table 15-2 The Distribution of the Liquidation
Proceeds of the Bankrupt Firm

Proceeds of sale of assets	$8,600
-Bankruptcy cost	1,600
-Accrued wages	800
-Accrued taxes	600
-Accrued rent	200
Funds available for creditors	$5,400
-First mortgage, paid from the $4,000 proceeds from the sale of the fixed property	3,600
-Second mortgage, partially paid from the remaining $400 of the fixed asset proceeds	400
Funds available for general creditors	$1,400

Claims of General Creditors (1)	Amount (2)	Application of 25% (3)	After Subordination Adjustment (4)
Unpaid balance of second mortgage	$1,600	$ 400	$ 400
Accounts payable	400	100	100
Notes payable (bank)	2,000	500	900
Subordinated debentures	1,600	400	0
Total	$5,600	$1,400	$1,400

creditors, each claimant would receive 25 per cent of
his claim before the subordination adjustment. Because the claims of the unsecured creditors are not
fully satisfied, the preferred and common stockholders
receive nothing.

FOOTNOTES

1. The Failure Record, 1972 (New York: Dun &
    Bradstreet, Inc., 1973).

2. See James E. Walter, "Determination of Tech-
    nical Insolvency," Journal of Finance (Janu-
    ary 1957), pp. 30-43; and Edward I. Altman,
    "Financial Ratios, Discriminant Analysis and
    the Prediction of Corporate Bankruptcy,"
    Journal of Finance (September 1968), pp.
    589-609.

TABLE A   Compound Value of $1

Period	1%	2%	3%	4%	5%	6%	7%	8%	9%	10%
1	1.010	1.020	1.030	1.040	1.050	1.060	1.070	1.080	1.090	1.100
2	1.020	1.040	1.061	1.082	1.102	1.124	1.145	1.166	1.188	1.210
3	1.030	1.061	1.093	1.125	1.158	1.191	1.225	1.260	1.295	1.331
4	1.041	1.082	1.126	1.170	1.216	1.262	1.311	1.360	1.412	1.464
5	1.051	1.104	1.159	1.217	1.276	1.338	1.403	1.469	1.539	1.611
6	1.062	1.126	1.194	1.265	1.340	1.419	1.501	1.587	1.677	1.772
7	1.072	1.149	1.230	1.316	1.407	1.504	1.606	1.714	1.828	1.949
8	1.083	1.172	1.267	1.369	1.477	1.594	1.718	1.851	1.993	2.144
9	1.094	1.195	1.305	1.423	1.551	1.689	1.838	1.999	2.172	2.358
10	1.105	1.219	1.344	1.480	1.629	1.791	1.967	2.159	2.367	2.594
11	1.116	1.243	1.384	1.539	1.710	1.898	2.105	2.332	2.580	2.853
12	1.127	1.268	1.426	1.601	1.796	2.012	2.252	2.518	2.813	3.138
13	1.138	1.294	1.469	1.665	1.886	2.133	2.410	2.720	3.066	3.452
14	1.149	1.319	1.513	1.732	1.980	2.261	2.579	2.937	3.342	3.797
15	1.161	1.346	1.558	1.801	2.079	2.397	2.759	3.172	3.642	4.177
16	1.173	1.373	1.605	1.873	2.183	2.540	2.952	3.426	3.970	4.595
17	1.184	1.400	1.653	1.948	2.292	2.693	3.159	3.700	4.328	5.054
18	1.196	1.428	1.702	2.026	2.407	2.854	3.380	3.996	4.717	5.560
19	1.208	1.457	1.753	2.107	2.527	3.026	3.616	4.316	5.142	6.116
20	1.220	1.486	1.806	2.191	2.653	3.207	3.870	4.661	5.604	6.727
21	1.232	1.516	1.860	2.279	2.786	3.399	4.140	5.034	6.109	7.400
22	1.245	1.546	1.916	2.370	2.925	3.603	4.430	5.436	6.658	8.140
23	1.257	1.577	1.974	2.465	3.071	3.820	4.740	5.871	7.258	8.954
24	1.270	1.608	2.033	2.563	3.225	4.049	5.072	6.341	7.911	9.850
25	1.282	1.641	2.094	2.666	3.386	4.292	5.427	6.848	8.623	10.834
30	1.348	1.811	2.427	3.243	4.322	5.743	7.612	10.062	13.267	17.449
40	1.489	2.208	3.262	4.801	7.040	10.285	14.974	21.724	31.408	45.258

TABLE A Compound Value of $1 (continued)

Period	11%	12%	13%	14%	15%	16%	17%	18%	19%	20%
1	1.110	1.120	1.130	1.140	1.150	1.160	1.170	1.180	1.190	1.200
2	1.232	1.254	1.277	1.300	1.322	1.346	1.369	1.392	1.416	1.440
3	1.368	1.405	1.443	1.482	1.521	1.561	1.602	1.643	1.685	1.728
4	1.518	1.574	1.630	1.689	1.749	1.811	1.874	1.939	2.005	2.074
5	1.685	1.762	1.842	1.925	2.011	2.100	2.192	2.288	2.386	2.488
6	1.870	1.974	2.082	2.195	2.313	2.436	2.565	2.700	2.840	2.986
7	2.076	2.211	2.353	2.502	2.660	2.826	3.001	3.185	3.379	3.583
8	2.305	2.476	2.658	2.853	3.059	3.278	3.511	3.759	4.021	4.300
9	2.558	2.773	3.004	3.252	3.518	3.803	4.108	4.435	4.785	5.160
10	2.839	3.106	3.395	3.707	4.046	4.411	4.807	5.234	5.695	6.192
11	3.152	3.479	3.836	4.226	4.652	5.117	5.624	6.176	6.777	7.430
12	3.498	3.896	4.334	4.818	5.350	5.936	6.580	7.288	8.064	8.916
13	3.883	4.363	4.898	5.492	6.153	6.886	7.699	8.599	9.596	10.699
14	4.310	4.887	5.535	6.261	7.076	7.987	9.007	10.147	11.420	12.839
15	4.785	5.474	6.254	7.138	8.137	9.265	10.539	11.974	13.589	15.407
16	5.311	6.130	7.067	8.137	9.358	10.748	12.330	14.129	16.171	18.488
17	5.895	6.866	7.986	9.276	10.761	12.468	14.426	16.672	19.244	22.186
18	6.543	7.690	9.024	10.575	12.375	14.462	16.879	19.673	22.900	26.623
19	7.263	8.613	10.197	12.055	14.232	16.776	19.748	23.214	27.251	31.948
20	8.062	9.646	11.523	13.743	16.366	19.461	23.105	27.393	32.429	38.337
21	8.949	10.804	13.021	15.667	18.821	22.574	27.033	32.323	38.591	46.005
22	9.933	12.100	14.713	17.861	21.644	26.186	31.629	38.141	45.923	55.205
23	11.026	13.552	16.626	20.361	24.891	30.376	37.005	45.007	54.648	66.247
24	12.239	15.178	18.788	23.212	28.625	35.236	43.296	53.108	65.031	79.496
25	13.585	17.000	21.230	26.461	32.918	40.874	50.656	62.667	77.387	95.395
30	22.892	29.960	39.115	50.949	66.210	85.849	111.061	143.367	184.672	237.373
40	64.999	93.049	132.776	188.876	267.856	378.715	533.846	750.353	1051.642	1469.740

278

TABLE A   Compound Value of $1 (continued)

Period	21%	22%	23%	24%	25%	26%	27%	28%	29%	30%
1	1.210	1.220	1.230	1.240	1.250	1.260	1.270	1.280	1.290	1.300
2	1.464	1.488	1.513	1.538	1.562	1.588	1.613	1.638	1.664	1.690
3	1.772	1.816	1.861	1.907	1.953	2.000	2.048	2.097	2.147	2.197
4	2.144	2.215	2.289	2.364	2.441	2.520	2.601	2.684	2.769	2.856
5	2.594	2.703	2.815	2.932	3.052	3.176	3.304	3.436	3.572	3.713
6	3.138	3.297	3.463	3.635	3.815	4.001	4.196	4.398	4.608	4.827
7	3.797	4.023	4.259	4.508	4.768	5.042	5.329	5.629	5.945	6.275
8	4.595	4.908	5.239	5.589	5.960	6.353	6.767	7.206	7.669	8.157
9	5.560	5.987	6.444	6.931	7.451	8.004	8.595	9.223	9.893	10.604
10	6.727	7.305	7.926	8.594	9.313	10.086	10.915	11.806	12.761	13.786
11	8.140	8.912	9.749	10.657	11.642	12.708	13.862	15.112	16.462	17.921
12	9.850	10.872	11.991	13.215	14.552	16.012	17.605	19.343	21.236	23.298
13	11.918	13.264	14.749	16.386	18.190	20.175	22.359	24.759	27.395	30.287
14	14.421	16.182	18.141	20.319	22.737	25.420	28.395	31.691	35.339	39.373
15	17.449	19.742	22.314	25.195	28.422	32.030	36.062	40.565	45.587	51.185
16	21.113	24.085	27.446	31.242	35.527	40.357	45.799	51.923	58.808	66.541
17	25.547	29.384	33.758	38.740	44.409	50.850	58.165	66.461	75.862	86.503
18	30.912	35.848	41.523	48.038	55.511	64.071	73.869	85.070	97.862	112.454
19	37.404	43.735	51.073	59.567	69.389	80.730	93.813	108.890	126.242	146.190
20	45.258	53.357	62.820	73.863	86.736	101.720	119.143	139.379	162.852	190.047
21	54.762	65.095	77.268	91.591	108.420	128.167	151.312	178.405	210.079	247.061
22	66.262	79.416	95.040	113.572	135.525	161.490	192.165	228.358	271.002	321.178
23	80.178	96.887	116.899	140.829	169.407	203.477	244.050	292.298	349.592	417.531
24	97.015	118.203	143.786	174.628	211.758	256.381	309.943	374.141	450.974	542.791
25	117.388	144.207	176.857	216.539	264.698	323.040	393.628	478.901	581.756	705.627
30	304.471	389.748	497.904	634.810	807.793	1025.904	1300.477	1645.488	2078.208	2619.936
40	2048.309	2846.941	3946.340	5455.797	7523.156	10346.879	14195.051	19426.418	26520.723	36117.754

279

TABLE A Compound Value of $1 (continued)

Period	31%	32%	33%	34%	35%	36%	37%	38%	39%	40%
1	1.310	1.320	1.330	1.340	1.350	1.360	1.370	1.380	1.390	1.400
2	1.716	1.742	1.769	1.796	1.822	1.850	1.877	1.904	1.932	1.960
3	2.248	2.300	2.353	2.406	2.460	2.515	2.571	2.628	2.686	2.744
4	2.945	3.036	3.129	3.224	3.321	3.421	3.523	3.627	3.733	3.842
5	3.858	4.007	4.162	4.320	4.484	4.653	4.826	5.005	5.189	5.378
6	5.054	5.290	5.535	5.789	6.053	6.328	6.612	6.907	7.213	7.530
7	6.621	6.983	7.361	7.758	8.172	8.605	9.058	9.531	10.025	10.541
8	8.673	9.217	9.791	10.395	11.032	11.703	12.410	13.153	13.935	14.758
9	11.362	12.166	13.022	13.930	14.894	15.917	17.001	18.151	19.370	20.661
10	14.884	16.060	17.319	18.666	20.106	21.646	23.292	25.049	26.924	28.925
11	19.498	21.199	23.034	25.012	27.144	29.439	31.910	34.567	37.425	40.495
12	25.542	27.982	30.635	33.516	36.644	40.037	43.716	47.703	52.020	56.694
13	33.460	36.937	40.745	44.912	49.469	54.451	59.892	65.830	72.308	79.371
14	43.832	48.756	54.190	60.181	66.784	74.053	82.051	90.845	100.509	111.119
15	57.420	64.358	72.073	80.643	90.158	100.712	112.410	125.366	139.707	155.567
16	75.220	84.953	95.857	108.061	121.713	136.968	154.002	173.005	194.192	217.793
17	98.539	112.138	127.490	144.802	164.312	186.277	210.983	238.747	269.927	304.911
18	129.086	148.022	169.561	194.035	221.822	253.337	289.046	329.471	375.198	426.875
19	169.102	195.389	225.517	260.006	299.459	344.537	395.993	454.669	521.525	597.625
20	221.523	257.913	299.937	348.408	404.270	468.571	542.511	627.443	724.919	836.674
21	290.196	340.446	398.916	466.867	545.764	637.256	743.240	865.871	1007.637	1171.343
22	380.156	449.388	530.558	625.601	736.781	866.668	1018.238	1194.900	1400.615	1639.878
23	498.004	593.192	705.642	838.305	994.653	1178.668	1394.986	1648.961	1946.854	2295.829
24	652.385	783.013	938.504	1123.328	1342.781	1602.988	1911.129	2275.564	2706.125	3214.158
25	854.623	1033.577	1248.210	1505.258	1812.754	2180.063	2618.245	3140.275	3761.511	4499.816
30	3297.081	4142.008	5194.516	6503.285	8128.426	10142.914	12636.086	15716.703	19517.969	24201.043

TABLE B   Present Value of $1

Period	1%	2%	3%	4%	5%	6%	7%	8%	9%	10%
1	0.990	0.980	0.971	0.962	0.952	0.943	0.935	0.926	0.917	0.909
2	0.980	0.961	0.943	0.925	0.907	0.890	0.873	0.857	0.842	0.826
3	0.971	0.942	0.915	0.889	0.864	0.840	0.816	0.794	0.772	0.751
4	0.961	0.924	0.888	0.855	0.823	0.792	0.763	0.735	0.708	0.683
5	0.951	0.906	0.863	0.822	0.784	0.747	0.713	0.681	0.650	0.621
6	0.942	0.888	0.837	0.790	0.746	0.705	0.666	0.630	0.596	0.564
7	0.933	0.871	0.813	0.760	0.711	0.665	0.623	0.583	0.547	0.513
8	0.923	0.853	0.789	0.731	0.677	0.627	0.582	0.540	0.502	0.467
9	0.914	0.837	0.766	0.703	0.645	0.592	0.544	0.500	0.460	0.424
10	0.905	0.820	0.744	0.676	0.614	0.558	0.508	0.463	0.422	0.386
11	0.896	0.804	0.722	0.650	0.585	0.527	0.475	0.429	0.388	0.350
12	0.887	0.788	0.701	0.625	0.557	0.497	0.444	0.397	0.356	0.319
13	0.879	0.773	0.681	0.601	0.530	0.469	0.415	0.368	0.326	0.290
14	0.870	0.758	0.661	0.577	0.505	0.442	0.388	0.340	0.299	0.263
15	0.861	0.743	0.642	0.555	0.481	0.417	0.362	0.315	0.275	0.239
16	0.853	0.728	0.623	0.534	0.458	0.394	0.339	0.292	0.252	0.218
17	0.844	0.714	0.605	0.513	0.436	0.371	0.317	0.270	0.231	0.198
18	0.836	0.700	0.587	0.494	0.416	0.350	0.296	0.250	0.212	0.180
19	0.828	0.686	0.570	0.475	0.396	0.331	0.277	0.232	0.194	0.164
20	0.820	0.673	0.554	0.456	0.377	0.312	0.258	0.215	0.178	0.149
21	0.811	0.660	0.538	0.439	0.359	0.294	0.242	0.199	0.164	0.135
22	0.803	0.647	0.522	0.422	0.342	0.278	0.226	0.184	0.150	0.123
23	0.795	0.634	0.507	0.406	0.326	0.262	0.211	0.170	0.138	0.112
24	0.788	0.622	0.492	0.390	0.310	0.247	0.197	0.158	0.126	0.102
25	0.780	0.610	0.478	0.375	0.295	0.233	0.184	0.146	0.116	0.092
26	0.772	0.598	0.464	0.361	0.281	0.220	0.172	0.135	0.106	0.084
27	0.764	0.586	0.450	0.347	0.268	0.207	0.161	0.125	0.098	0.076
28	0.757	0.574	0.437	0.333	0.255	0.196	0.150	0.116	0.090	0.069
29	0.749	0.563	0.424	0.321	0.243	0.185	0.141	0.107	0.082	0.063
30	0.742	0.552	0.412	0.308	0.231	0.174	0.131	0.099	0.075	0.057
40	0.672	0.453	0.307	0.208	0.142	0.097	0.067	0.046	0.032	0.022
50	0.608	0.372	0.228	0.141	0.087	0.054	0.034	0.021	0.013	0.009

TABLE B Present Value of $1 (continued)

Period	11%	12%	13%	14%	15%	16%	17%	18%	19%	20%
1	0.901	0.893	0.885	0.877	0.870	0.862	0.855	0.847	0.840	0.833
2	0.812	0.797	0.783	0.769	0.756	0.743	0.731	0.718	0.706	0.694
3	0.731	0.712	0.693	0.675	0.658	0.641	0.624	0.609	0.593	0.579
4	0.659	0.636	0.613	0.592	0.572	0.552	0.534	0.516	0.499	0.482
5	0.593	0.567	0.543	0.519	0.497	0.476	0.456	0.437	0.419	0.402
6	0.535	0.507	0.480	0.456	0.432	0.410	0.390	0.370	0.352	0.335
7	0.482	0.452	0.425	0.400	0.376	0.354	0.333	0.314	0.296	0.279
8	0.434	0.404	0.376	0.351	0.327	0.305	0.285	0.266	0.249	0.233
9	0.391	0.361	0.333	0.308	0.284	0.263	0.243	0.225	0.209	0.194
10	0.352	0.322	0.295	0.270	0.247	0.227	0.208	0.191	0.176	0.162
11	0.317	0.287	0.261	0.237	0.215	0.195	0.178	0.162	0.148	0.135
12	0.286	0.257	0.231	0.208	0.187	0.168	0.152	0.137	0.124	0.112
13	0.258	0.229	0.204	0.182	0.163	0.145	0.130	0.116	0.104	0.093
14	0.232	0.205	0.181	0.160	0.141	0.125	0.111	0.099	0.088	0.078
15	0.209	0.183	0.160	0.140	0.123	0.108	0.095	0.084	0.074	0.065
16	0.188	0.163	0.141	0.123	0.107	0.093	0.081	0.071	0.062	0.054
17	0.170	0.146	0.125	0.108	0.093	0.080	0.069	0.060	0.052	0.045
18	0.153	0.130	0.111	0.095	0.081	0.069	0.059	0.051	0.044	0.038
19	0.138	0.116	0.098	0.083	0.070	0.060	0.051	0.043	0.037	0.031
20	0.124	0.104	0.087	0.073	0.061	0.051	0.043	0.037	0.031	0.026
21	0.112	0.093	0.077	0.064	0.053	0.044	0.037	0.031	0.026	0.022
22	0.101	0.083	0.068	0.056	0.046	0.038	0.032	0.026	0.022	0.018
23	0.091	0.074	0.060	0.049	0.040	0.033	0.027	0.022	0.018	0.015
24	0.082	0.066	0.053	0.043	0.035	0.028	0.023	0.019	0.015	0.013
25	0.074	0.059	0.047	0.038	0.030	0.024	0.020	0.016	0.013	0.010
26	0.066	0.053	0.042	0.033	0.026	0.021	0.017	0.014	0.011	0.009
27	0.060	0.047	0.037	0.029	0.023	0.018	0.014	0.011	0.009	0.007
28	0.054	0.042	0.033	0.026	0.020	0.016	0.012	0.010	0.008	0.006
29	0.048	0.037	0.029	0.022	0.017	0.014	0.011	0.008	0.006	0.005
30	0.044	0.033	0.026	0.020	0.015	0.012	0.009	0.007	0.005	0.004
40	0.015	0.011	0.008	0.005	0.004	0.003	0.002	0.001	0.001	0.001
50	0.005	0.003	0.002	0.001	0.001	0.001	0.000	0.000	0.000	0.000

TABLE B   Present Value of $1 (continued)

Period	21%	22%	23%	24%	25%	26%	27%	28%	29%	30%
1	0.826	0.820	0.813	0.806	0.800	0.794	0.787	0.781	0.775	0.769
2	0.683	0.672	0.661	0.650	0.640	0.630	0.620	0.610	0.601	0.592
3	0.564	0.551	0.537	0.524	0.512	0.500	0.488	0.477	0.466	0.455
4	0.467	0.451	0.437	0.423	0.410	0.397	0.384	0.373	0.361	0.350
5	0.386	0.370	0.355	0.341	0.328	0.315	0.303	0.291	0.280	0.269
6	0.319	0.303	0.289	0.275	0.262	0.250	0.238	0.227	0.217	0.207
7	0.263	0.249	0.235	0.222	0.210	0.198	0.188	0.178	0.168	0.159
8	0.218	0.204	0.191	0.179	0.168	0.157	0.148	0.139	0.130	0.123
9	0.180	0.167	0.155	0.144	0.134	0.125	0.116	0.108	0.101	0.094
10	0.149	0.137	0.126	0.116	0.107	0.099	0.092	0.085	0.078	0.073
11	0.123	0.112	0.103	0.094	0.086	0.079	0.072	0.066	0.061	0.056
12	0.102	0.092	0.083	0.076	0.069	0.062	0.057	0.052	0.047	0.043
13	0.084	0.075	0.068	0.061	0.055	0.050	0.045	0.040	0.037	0.033
14	0.069	0.062	0.055	0.049	0.044	0.039	0.035	0.032	0.028	0.025
15	0.057	0.051	0.045	0.040	0.035	0.031	0.028	0.025	0.022	0.020
16	0.047	0.042	0.036	0.032	0.028	0.025	0.022	0.019	0.017	0.015
17	0.039	0.034	0.030	0.026	0.023	0.020	0.017	0.015	0.013	0.012
18	0.032	0.028	0.024	0.021	0.018	0.016	0.014	0.012	0.010	0.009
19	0.027	0.023	0.020	0.017	0.014	0.012	0.011	0.009	0.008	0.007
20	0.022	0.019	0.016	0.014	0.012	0.010	0.008	0.007	0.006	0.005
21	0.018	0.015	0.013	0.011	0.009	0.008	0.007	0.006	0.005	0.004
22	0.015	0.013	0.011	0.009	0.007	0.006	0.005	0.004	0.004	0.003
23	0.012	0.010	0.009	0.007	0.006	0.005	0.004	0.003	0.003	0.002
24	0.010	0.008	0.007	0.006	0.005	0.004	0.003	0.003	0.002	0.002
25	0.009	0.007	0.006	0.005	0.004	0.003	0.003	0.002	0.002	0.001
26	0.007	0.006	0.005	0.004	0.003	0.002	0.002	0.002	0.001	0.001
27	0.006	0.005	0.004	0.003	0.002	0.002	0.002	0.001	0.001	0.001
28	0.005	0.004	0.003	0.002	0.002	0.002	0.001	0.001	0.001	0.001
29	0.004	0.003	0.002	0.002	0.002	0.001	0.001	0.001	0.001	0.000
30	0.003	0.003	0.002	0.002	0.001	0.001	0.001	0.001	0.000	0.000
40	0.000	0.000	0.000	0.000	0.000	0.000	0.000	0.000	0.000	0.000
50	0.000	0.000	0.000	0.000	0.000	0.000	0.000	0.000	0.000	0.000

283

TABLE B   Present Value of $1 (continued)

Period	31%	32%	33%	34%	35%	36%	37%	38%	39%	40%
1	0.763	0.758	0.752	0.746	0.741	0.735	0.730	0.725	0.719	0.714
2	0.583	0.574	0.565	0.557	0.549	0.541	0.533	0.525	0.518	0.510
3	0.445	0.435	0.425	0.416	0.406	0.398	0.389	0.381	0.372	0.364
4	0.340	0.329	0.320	0.310	0.301	0.292	0.284	0.276	0.268	0.260
5	0.259	0.250	0.240	0.231	0.223	0.215	0.207	0.200	0.193	0.186
6	0.198	0.189	0.181	0.173	0.165	0.158	0.151	0.145	0.139	0.133
7	0.151	0.143	0.136	0.129	0.122	0.116	0.110	0.105	0.100	0.095
8	0.115	0.108	0.102	0.096	0.091	0.085	0.081	0.076	0.072	0.068
9	0.088	0.082	0.077	0.072	0.067	0.063	0.059	0.055	0.052	0.048
10	0.067	0.062	0.058	0.054	0.050	0.046	0.043	0.040	0.037	0.035
11	0.051	0.047	0.043	0.040	0.037	0.034	0.031	0.029	0.027	0.025
12	0.039	0.036	0.033	0.030	0.027	0.025	0.023	0.021	0.019	0.018
13	0.030	0.027	0.025	0.022	0.020	0.018	0.017	0.015	0.014	0.013
14	0.023	0.021	0.018	0.017	0.015	0.014	0.012	0.011	0.010	0.009
15	0.017	0.016	0.014	0.012	0.011	0.010	0.009	0.008	0.007	0.006
16	0.013	0.012	0.010	0.009	0.008	0.007	0.006	0.006	0.005	0.005
17	0.010	0.009	0.008	0.007	0.006	0.005	0.005	0.004	0.004	0.003
18	0.008	0.007	0.006	0.005	0.005	0.004	0.003	0.003	0.003	0.002
19	0.006	0.005	0.004	0.004	0.003	0.003	0.003	0.002	0.002	0.002
20	0.005	0.004	0.003	0.003	0.002	0.002	0.002	0.002	0.001	0.001
21	0.003	0.003	0.003	0.002	0.002	0.002	0.001	0.001	0.001	0.001
22	0.003	0.002	0.002	0.002	0.001	0.001	0.001	0.001	0.001	0.001
23	0.002	0.002	0.001	0.001	0.001	0.001	0.001	0.001	0.001	0.000
24	0.002	0.001	0.001	0.001	0.001	0.001	0.001	0.000	0.000	0.000
25	0.001	0.001	0.001	0.001	0.001	0.000	0.000	0.000	0.000	0.000
26	0.001	0.001	0.001	0.000	0.000	0.000	0.000	0.000	0.000	0.000
27	0.001	0.001	0.000	0.000	0.000	0.000	0.000	0.000	0.000	0.000
28	0.001	0.000	0.000	0.000	0.000	0.000	0.000	0.000	0.000	0.000
29	0.000	0.000	0.000	0.000	0.000	0.000	0.000	0.000	0.000	0.000
30	0.000	0.000	0.000	0.000	0.000	0.000	0.000	0.000	0.000	0.000
40	0.000	0.000	0.000	0.000	0.000	0.000	0.000	0.000	0.000	0.000
50	0.000	0.000	0.000	0.000	0.000	0.000	0.000	0.000	0.000	0.000

284

TABLE B   Present Value of $1 (continued)

Period	41%	42%	43%	44%	45%	46%	47%	48%	49%	50%
1	0.709	0.704	0.699	0.694	0.690	0.685	0.680	0.676	0.671	0.667
2	0.503	0.496	0.489	0.482	0.476	0.469	0.463	0.457	0.450	0.444
3	0.357	0.349	0.342	0.335	0.328	0.321	0.315	0.308	0.302	0.296
4	0.253	0.246	0.239	0.233	0.226	0.220	0.214	0.208	0.203	0.198
5	0.179	0.173	0.167	0.162	0.156	0.151	0.146	0.141	0.136	0.132
6	0.127	0.122	0.117	0.112	0.108	0.103	0.099	0.095	0.091	0.088
7	0.090	0.086	0.082	0.078	0.074	0.071	0.067	0.064	0.061	0.059
8	0.064	0.060	0.057	0.054	0.051	0.048	0.046	0.043	0.041	0.039
9	0.045	0.043	0.040	0.038	0.035	0.033	0.031	0.029	0.028	0.026
10	0.032	0.030	0.028	0.026	0.024	0.023	0.021	0.020	0.019	0.017
11	0.023	0.021	0.020	0.018	0.017	0.016	0.014	0.013	0.012	0.012
12	0.016	0.015	0.014	0.013	0.012	0.011	0.010	0.009	0.008	0.008
13	0.011	0.010	0.010	0.009	0.008	0.007	0.007	0.006	0.006	0.005
14	0.008	0.007	0.007	0.006	0.006	0.005	0.005	0.004	0.004	0.003
15	0.006	0.005	0.005	0.004	0.004	0.003	0.003	0.003	0.003	0.002
16	0.004	0.004	0.003	0.003	0.003	0.002	0.002	0.002	0.002	0.002
17	0.003	0.003	0.002	0.002	0.002	0.002	0.001	0.001	0.001	0.001
18	0.002	0.002	0.002	0.001	0.001	0.001	0.001	0.001	0.001	0.001
19	0.001	0.001	0.001	0.001	0.001	0.001	0.001	0.001	0.001	0.000
20	0.001	0.001	0.001	0.001	0.001	0.001	0.000	0.000	0.000	0.000
21	0.001	0.001	0.001	0.000	0.000	0.000	0.000	0.000	0.000	0.000
22	0.001	0.000	0.000	0.000	0.000	0.000	0.000	0.000	0.000	0.000
23	0.000	0.000	0.000	0.000	0.000	0.000	0.000	0.000	0.000	0.000
24	0.000	0.000	0.000	0.000	0.000	0.000	0.000	0.000	0.000	0.000
25	0.000	0.000	0.000	0.000	0.000	0.000	0.000	0.000	0.000	0.000
26	0.000	0.000	0.000	0.000	0.000	0.000	0.000	0.000	0.000	0.000
27	0.000	0.000	0.000	0.000	0.000	0.000	0.000	0.000	0.000	0.000
28	0.000	0.000	0.000	0.000	0.000	0.000	0.000	0.000	0.000	0.000
29	0.000	0.000	0.000	0.000	0.000	0.000	0.000	0.000	0.000	0.000
30	0.000	0.000	0.000	0.000	0.000	0.000	0.000	0.000	0.000	0.000
40	0.000	0.000	0.000	0.000	0.000	0.000	0.000	0.000	0.000	0.000
50	0.000	0.000	0.000	0.000	0.000	0.000	0.000	0.000	0.000	0.000

285

TABLE C Present Value of an Annuity of $1

Period	1%	2%	3%	4%	5%	6%	7%	8%	9%	10%
1	0.990	0.980	0.971	0.962	0.952	0.943	0.935	0.926	0.917	0.909
2	1.970	1.942	1.913	1.886	1.859	1.833	1.808	1.783	1.759	1.736
3	2.941	2.884	2.829	2.775	2.723	2.673	2.624	2.577	2.531	2.487
4	3.902	3.808	3.717	3.630	3.546	3.465	3.387	3.312	3.240	3.170
5	4.853	4.713	4.580	4.452	4.329	4.212	4.100	3.993	3.890	3.791
6	5.795	5.601	5.417	5.242	5.076	4.917	4.767	4.623	4.486	4.355
7	6.728	6.472	6.230	6.002	5.786	5.582	5.389	5.206	5.033	4.868
8	7.652	7.325	7.020	6.733	6.463	6.210	5.971	5.747	5.535	5.335
9	8.566	8.162	7.786	7.435	7.108	6.802	6.515	6.247	5.995	5.759
10	9.471	8.983	8.530	8.111	7.722	7.360	7.024	6.710	6.418	6.145
11	10.368	9.787	9.253	8.760	8.306	7.887	7.499	7.139	6.805	6.495
12	11.255	10.575	9.954	9.385	8.863	8.384	7.943	7.536	7.161	6.814
13	12.134	11.348	10.635	9.986	9.394	8.853	8.358	7.904	7.487	7.103
14	13.004	12.106	11.296	10.563	9.899	9.295	8.745	8.244	7.786	7.367
15	13.865	12.849	11.938	11.118	10.380	9.712	9.108	8.559	8.061	7.606
16	14.718	13.578	12.561	11.652	10.838	10.106	9.447	8.851	8.313	7.824
17	15.562	14.292	13.166	12.166	11.274	10.477	9.763	9.122	8.544	8.022
18	16.398	14.992	13.754	12.659	11.690	10.828	10.059	9.372	8.756	8.201
19	17.226	15.678	14.324	13.134	12.085	11.158	10.336	9.604	8.950	8.365
20	18.046	16.351	14.877	13.590	12.462	11.470	10.594	9.818	9.129	8.514
21	18.857	17.011	15.415	14.029	12.821	11.764	10.836	10.017	9.292	8.649
22	19.660	17.658	15.837	14.451	13.163	12.042	11.061	10.201	9.442	8.772
23	20.456	18.292	16.444	14.857	13.489	12.303	11.272	10.371	9.580	8.883
24	21.243	18.914	16.936	15.247	13.799	12.550	11.469	10.529	9.707	8.985
25	22.023	19.523	17.413	15.622	14.094	12.783	11.654	10.675	9.823	9.077
26	22.795	20.121	17.877	15.983	14.375	13.003	11.826	10.810	9.929	9.161
27	23.560	20.707	18.327	16.330	14.643	13.211	11.987	10.935	10.027	9.237
28	24.316	21.281	18.764	16.663	14.898	13.406	12.137	11.051	10.116	9.307
29	25.066	21.844	19.188	16.984	15.141	13.591	12.278	11.158	10.198	9.370
30	25.808	22.396	19.600	17.292	15.372	13.765	12.409	11.258	10.274	9.427
40	32.835	27.355	23.115	19.793	17.159	15.046	13.332	11.925	10.757	9.779
50	39.196	31.424	25.730	21.482	18.256	15.762	13.801	12.233	10.962	9.915

TABLE C Present Value of an Annuity of $1 (continued)

Period	11%	12%	13%	14%	15%	16%	17%	18%	19%	20%
1	0.901	0.893	0.885	0.877	0.870	0.862	0.855	0.847	0.840	0.833
2	1.713	1.690	1.668	1.647	1.626	1.605	1.585	1.566	1.547	1.528
3	2.444	2.402	2.361	2.322	2.283	2.246	2.210	2.174	2.140	2.106
4	3.102	3.037	2.974	2.914	2.855	2.798	2.743	2.690	2.639	2.589
5	3.696	3.605	3.517	3.433	3.352	3.274	3.199	3.127	3.058	2.991
6	4.231	4.111	3.998	3.889	3.784	3.685	3.589	3.498	3.410	3.326
7	4.712	4.564	4.423	4.288	4.160	4.039	3.922	3.812	3.706	3.605
8	5.146	4.968	4.799	4.639	4.487	4.344	4.207	4.078	3.954	3.837
9	5.537	5.328	5.132	4.946	4.772	4.607	4.451	4.303	4.163	4.031
10	5.889	5.650	5.426	5.216	5.019	4.833	4.659	4.494	4.339	4.129
11	6.207	5.938	5.687	5.453	5.234	5.029	4.836	4.656	4.486	4.327
12	6.492	6.194	5.918	5.660	5.421	5.197	4.988	4.793	4.611	4.439
13	6.750	6.424	6.122	5.842	5.583	5.342	5.118	4.910	4.715	4.533
14	6.982	6.628	6.302	6.002	5.724	5.468	5.229	5.008	4.802	4.611
15	7.191	6.811	6.462	6.142	5.847	5.575	5.324	5.092	4.876	4.675
16	7.379	6.974	6.604	6.265	5.954	5.668	5.405	5.162	4.938	4.730
17	7.549	7.120	6.729	6.373	6.047	5.749	5.475	5.222	4.990	4.775
18	7.702	7.250	6.840	6.467	6.128	5.818	5.534	5.273	5.033	4.812
19	7.839	7.366	6.938	6.550	6.198	5.877	5.584	5.316	5.070	4.843
20	7.963	7.469	7.025	6.623	6.259	5.929	5.628	5.353	5.101	4.870
21	8.075	7.562	7.102	6.687	6.312	5.973	5.665	5.384	5.127	4.891
22	8.176	7.645	7.170	6.743	6.359	6.011	5.696	5.410	5.149	4.909
23	8.266	7.718	7.230	6.792	6.399	6.044	5.723	5.432	5.167	4.925
24	8.348	7.784	7.283	6.835	6.434	6.073	5.746	5.451	5.182	4.937
25	8.422	7.843	7.330	6.873	6.464	6.097	5.766	5.467	5.195	4.948
26	8.488	7.896	7.372	6.906	6.491	6.118	5.783	5.480	5.206	4.956
27	8.548	7.943	7.409	6.935	6.514	6.136	5.798	5.492	5.215	4.964
28	8.602	7.984	7.441	6.961	6.534	6.152	5.810	5.502	5.223	4.970
29	8.650	8.022	7.470	6.983	6.551	6.166	5.820	5.510	5.229	4.975
30	8.694	8.055	7.496	7.003	6.566	6.177	5.829	5.517	5.235	4.979
40	8.951	8.244	7.634	7.105	6.642	6.233	5.871	5.548	5.258	4.997
50	9.042	8.304	7.675	7.133	6.661	6.246	5.880	5.554	5.262	4.999

TABLE C   Present Value of an Annuity of $1 (continued)

Period	21%	22%	23%	24%	25%	26%	27%	28%	29%	30%
1	0.826	0.820	0.813	0.806	0.800	0.794	0.787	0.781	0.775	0.769
2	1.509	1.492	1.474	1.457	1.440	1.424	1.407	1.392	1.376	1.361
3	2.074	2.042	2.011	1.981	1.952	1.923	1.896	1.868	1.842	1.816
4	2.540	2.494	2.448	2.404	2.362	2.320	2.280	2.241	2.203	2.166
5	2.926	2.864	2.803	2.745	2.689	2.635	2.583	2.532	2.483	2.436
6	3.245	3.167	3.092	3.020	2.951	2.885	2.821	2.759	2.700	2.643
7	3.508	3.416	3.327	3.242	3.161	3.083	3.009	2.937	2.868	2.802
8	3.726	3.619	3.518	3.421	3.329	3.241	3.156	3.076	2.999	2.925
9	3.905	3.786	3.673	3.566	3.463	3.366	3.273	3.184	3.100	3.019
10	4.054	3.923	3.799	3.682	3.571	3.465	3.364	3.269	3.178	3.092
11	4.177	4.035	3.902	3.776	3.656	3.543	3.437	3.335	3.239	3.147
12	4.278	4.127	3.985	3.851	3.725	3.606	3.493	3.387	3.286	3.190
13	4.362	4.203	4.053	3.912	3.780	3.656	3.538	3.427	3.322	3.223
14	4.432	4.265	4.108	3.962	3.824	3.695	3.573	3.459	3.351	3.249
15	4.489	4.315	4.153	4.001	3.859	3.726	3.601	3.483	3.373	3.268
16	4.536	4.357	4.189	4.033	3.887	3.751	3.623	3.503	3.390	3.283
17	4.576	4.391	4.219	4.059	3.910	3.771	3.640	3.518	3.403	3.295
18	4.608	4.419	4.243	4.080	3.928	3.786	3.654	3.529	3.413	3.304
19	4.635	4.442	4.263	4.097	3.942	3.799	3.664	3.539	3.421	3.311
20	4.657	4.460	4.279	4.110	3.954	3.808	3.673	3.546	3.427	3.316
21	4.675	4.476	4.292	4.121	3.963	3.816	3.679	3.551	3.432	3.320
22	4.690	4.488	4.302	4.130	3.970	3.822	3.684	3.556	3.436	3.323
23	4.703	4.499	4.311	4.137	3.976	3.827	3.689	3.559	3.438	3.325
24	4.713	4.507	4.318	4.143	3.981	3.831	3.692	3.562	3.441	3.327
25	4.721	4.514	4.323	4.147	3.985	3.834	3.694	3.564	3.442	3.329
26	4.728	4.520	4.328	4.151	3.988	3.837	3.696	3.566	3.444	3.330
27	4.734	4.524	4.332	4.154	3.990	3.839	3.698	3.567	3.445	3.330
28	4.739	4.528	4.335	4.157	3.992	3.840	3.699	3.568	3.446	3.331
29	4.743	4.531	4.337	4.158	3.994	3.841	3.700	3.569	3.446	3.332
30	4.746	4.534	4.339	4.160	3.995	3.842	3.701	3.570	3.447	3.332
40	4.760	4.544	4.347	4.166	3.910	3.846	3.703	3.571	3.448	3.333
50	4.762	4.545	4.348	4.167	3.910	3.846	3.703	3.571	3.448	3.333

TABLE C   Present Value of an Annuity of $1 (continued)

Period	31%	32%	33%	34%	35%	36%	37%	38%	39%	40%
1	0.763	0.758	0.752	0.746	0.741	0.735	0.730	0.725	0.719	0.714
2	1.346	1.331	1.317	1.303	1.289	1.276	1.263	1.250	1.237	1.224
3	1.791	1.766	1.742	1.719	1.696	1.673	1.652	1.630	1.609	1.589
4	2.130	2.096	2.062	2.029	1.997	1.966	1.935	1.906	1.877	1.849
5	2.390	2.345	2.302	2.260	2.220	2.181	2.143	2.106	2.070	2.035
6	2.588	2.534	2.483	2.433	2.385	2.339	2.294	2.251	2.209	2.168
7	2.739	2.677	2.619	2.562	2.508	2.455	2.404	2.355	2.308	2.263
8	2.854	2.786	2.721	2.658	2.598	2.540	2.485	2.432	2.380	2.331
9	2.942	2.868	2.798	2.730	2.665	2.603	2.544	2.487	2.432	2.379
10	3.009	2.930	2.855	2.784	2.715	2.649	2.587	2.527	2.469	2.414
11	3.060	2.978	2.899	2.824	2.752	2.683	2.618	2.555	2.496	2.438
12	3.100	3.013	2.931	2.853	2.779	2.708	2.641	2.576	2.515	2.456
13	3.129	3.040	2.956	2.876	2.799	2.727	2.658	2.592	2.529	2.469
14	3.152	3.061	2.974	2.892	2.814	2.740	2.670	2.603	2.539	2.478
15	3.170	3.076	2.988	2.905	2.825	2.750	2.679	2.611	2.546	2.484
16	3.183	3.088	2.999	2.914	2.834	2.757	2.685	2.616	2.551	2.489
17	3.193	3.097	3.007	2.921	2.840	2.763	2.690	2.621	2.555	2.492
18	3.201	3.104	3.012	2.926	2.844	2.767	2.693	2.624	2.557	2.494
19	3.207	3.109	3.017	2.930	2.848	2.770	2.696	2.626	2.559	2.496
20	3.211	3.113	3.020	2.933	2.850	2.772	2.698	2.627	2.561	2.497
21	3.215	3.116	3.023	2.935	2.852	2.773	2.699	2.629	2.562	2.498
22	3.217	3.118	3.025	2.936	2.853	2.775	2.700	2.629	2.562	2.498
23	3.219	3.120	3.026	2.938	2.854	2.775	2.701	2.630	2.563	2.499
24	3.221	3.121	3.027	2.939	2.855	2.776	2.701	2.630	2.563	2.499
25	3.222	3.122	3.028	2.939	2.856	2.777	2.702	2.631	2.563	2.499
26	3.223	3.123	3.028	2.940	2.856	2.777	2.702	2.631	2.564	2.500
27	3.224	3.123	3.029	2.940	2.856	2.777	2.702	2.631	2.564	2.500
28	3.224	3.124	3.029	2.940	2.857	2.777	2.702	2.631	2.564	2.500
29	3.225	3.124	3.030	2.941	2.857	2.777	2.702	2.631	2.564	2.500
30	3.225	3.124	3.030	2.941	2.857	2.778	2.702	2.631	2.564	2.500
40	3.226	3.125	3.030	2.941	2.857	2.778	2.703	2.632	2.564	2.500
50	3.226	3.125	3.030	2.941	2.857	2.778	2.703	2.632	2.564	2.500

TABLE C Present Value of an Annuity of $1 (continued)

Period	41%	42%	43%	44%	45%	46%	47%	48%	49%	50%
1	0.709	0.704	0.699	0.694	0.690	0.685	0.680	0.676	0.671	0.667
2	1.212	1.200	1.188	1.177	1.165	1.154	1.143	1.132	1.122	1.111
3	1.569	1.549	1.530	1.512	1.493	1.475	1.458	1.441	1.424	1.407
4	1.822	1.795	1.769	1.744	1.720	1.695	1.672	1.649	1.627	1.605
5	2.001	1.969	1.937	1.906	1.876	1.846	1.818	1.790	1.763	1.737
6	2.129	2.091	2.054	2.018	1.983	1.949	1.917	1.885	1.854	1.824
7	2.219	2.176	2.135	2.096	2.057	2.020	1.984	1.949	1.916	1.883
8	2.283	2.237	2.193	2.150	2.109	2.069	2.030	1.993	1.957	1.922
9	2.328	2.280	2.233	2.187	2.144	2.102	2.061	2.022	1.984	1.948
10	2.360	2.310	2.261	2.213	2.168	2.125	2.083	2.042	2.003	1.965
11	2.383	2.331	2.280	2.232	2.185	2.140	2.097	2.055	2.015	1.977
12	2.400	2.346	2.294	2.244	2.196	2.151	2.107	2.064	2.024	1.985
13	2.411	2.356	2.303	2.253	2.204	2.158	2.113	2.071	2.029	1.990
14	2.419	2.363	2.310	2.259	2.210	2.163	2.118	2.075	2.033	1.993
15	2.425	2.369	2.315	2.263	2.214	2.166	2.121	2.078	2.036	1.995
16	2.429	2.372	2.318	2.266	2.216	2.169	2.123	2.079	2.037	1.997
17	2.432	2.375	2.320	2.268	2.218	2.170	2.125	2.081	2.038	1.998
18	2.434	2.377	2.322	2.270	2.219	2.172	2.126	2.082	2.039	1.999
19	2.435	2.378	2.323	2.271	2.220	2.172	2.126	2.082	2.040	1.999
20	2.436	2.379	2.324	2.271	2.221	2.173	2.127	2.083	2.040	1.999
21	2.437	2.379	2.324	2.272	2.221	2.173	2.127	2.083	2.040	2.000
22	2.438	2.380	2.325	2.272	2.222	2.173	2.127	2.083	2.041	2.000
23	2.438	2.380	2.325	2.272	2.222	2.174	2.127	2.083	2.041	2.000
24	2.438	2.380	2.325	2.272	2.222	2.174	2.127	2.083	2.041	2.000
25	2.439	2.381	2.325	2.272	2.222	2.174	2.128	2.083	2.041	2.000
26	2.439	2.381	2.325	2.273	2.222	2.174	2.128	2.083	2.041	2.000
27	2.439	2.381	2.325	2.273	2.222	2.174	2.128	2.083	2.041	2.000
28	2.439	2.381	2.325	2.273	2.222	2.174	2.128	2.083	2.041	2.000
29	2.439	2.381	2.326	2.273	2.222	2.174	2.128	2.083	2.041	2.000
30	2.439	2.381	2.326	2.273	2.222	2.174	2.128	2.083	2.041	2.000
40	2.439	2.381	2.326	2.273	2.222	2.174	2.128	2.083	2.041	2.000
50	2.439	2.381	2.326	2.273	2.222	2.174	2.128	2.083	2.041	2.000

INDEX

292

293

END-OF-CHAPTER PROBLEMS

2-1 The City Plastic Company wants to replace an old equipment with a new one. The company purchased the old equipment for $9,000 four years ago and its current market value is $2,000. At the time of purchase, the equipment had an expected life of nine years and had no expected salvage value on retirement. It has been depreciated on a straight-line basis. The firm wishes to buy a new equipment with a cost of $20,000 and an expected salvage value of $400. The new equipment is expected to reduce operating costs by $2,000 a year and to increase sales by $4,000 per year. It has an estimated useful life of five years and is expected to be depreciated on a straight-line basis. Assume that the firm's marginal tax rate is 46 per cent.

    (a) Determine the net cash investment of the new machine.
    (b) Determine the project's incremental net cash flows.

2-2 A net cash investment of a new machine is $9,000 and it is expected to have no salvage value on retirement. The machine can be depreciated for tax purposes in three years, and the firm has decided to use the sum-of-years-digits method. It is expected to generate an annual revenue of $20,000 for three years and to require an annual operating cost of $4,500 (excluding the depreciation of the machine). The firm's marginal tax rate is 40 per cent.

    (a) Compute the net cash flows of each year.
    (b) How would the net cash flows of each year be changed if the firm uses the double-declining-balance method?

2-3 The Utica Machine Tool Company desires to replace an existing machine with a new one. The old machine has a book value of $5,000 and a market value of $4,000. The new machine costs $9,000. It has an expected economic life of six years but can be depreciated for tax purposes in five years. The freight and installation costs will be $2,000. The new machine is expected to have a salvage value of $1,000 on retirement. The two machines have the following revenues and operating costs:

	Year 1	Year 2	Year 3	Year 4	Year 5	Year 6
Old Machine						
Revenues	$ 2,000	$2,000	$2,000	$2,000	$2,000	
Costs	500	500	500	500	500	
New Machine						
Revenues	$10,000	$9,000	$8,000	$7,000	$6,000	$5,500
Costs	3,500	3,500	3,500	3,500	3,500	3,500

Additional assumptions are: (1) The firm's marginal tax rate is 40 per cent. (2) Use the straight-line depreciation method for both machines. (3) Ignore the investment tax credit.

(a) Determine the net cash investment of the project.
(b) Determine the project's incremental net cash flows.

3-1 Find the compound value when $10,000 is invested at 9 per cent compounded continuously for five years.

3-2 Find the present value of $20,000 to be received at the end of four years with a discount rate of 10 per cent compounded continuously.

3-3 Exactly 15 years from now Mr. Smith will start receiving a pension of $20,000 per year. The pension payments will continue for 10 years. How much is the pension worth now if money is worth 10 per cent per year?

3-4 How long does it take $1 to triple if money grows at 6 per cent compounded annually?

3-5 The present value of a five-year annuity is $20,000. What is each quarterly payment if the interest rate is 8 per cent compounded quarterly?

3-6 A four-year note promises to pay $3,000 at the end of each year for four years. What is the implicit interest rate if the price of the note is $10,161?

3-7 The cash price of a small building is $190,000. The owner of the building agrees to sell you the building in return for your promise to pay $40,000 down and $3,826.9 at the end of each month. If money is worth 12 per cent compounded monthly, how long will it take you to pay off the balance and the interest?

3-8 A 20-year bond promises to pay $60 interest at the end of every six months. The bond has a maturity value of $1,000 and its appropriate yield rate is 10 per cent. What is the value of the bond?

3-9 If you decide to buy a house, you have to pay $10,000 per year for nine years. What is the price of the house if paid in a lump sum today? Assume that the interest rate is 10 per cent.

3-10 Assume that you are given the choice between $20,000 in cash and $2,000 per year for perpetuity. If money is worth 10 per cent, which would you prefer?

4-1   The Brown Company wishes to replace a current
      operation with a more efficient and reliable
      automatic process. This plan requires the
      purchase of a machine with a net cost of $35,000
      and an estimated useful life of seven years. It
      will be depreciated over a seven-year period on
      a straight-line basis for tax purposes. The ma-
      chine is expected to have no salvage value at
      the end of seven years and to reduce operating
      costs by $8,000 per year. The firm's marginal
      tax rate is 46 per cent and its cost of capital
      is 5 per cent.

      Determine (a) the payback period, (b) the aver-
      age rate of return, (c) the net present value,
      (d) the profitability index, and (e) the in-
      ternal rate of return.

4-2   A large company is considering the purchase of
      a new computer. Two types of computers are
      currently under consideration. The two com-
      puters are expected to do the job satisfactorily
      and have an equal life of ten years. Computer
      C would require an initial cash outlay of
      $300,000 and an operating cost of $60,000 per
      year. Computer D would require an initial out-
      lay of $200,000 and an operating cost of
      $80,000 per year. Both computers have no ex-
      pected salvage value on retirement and would
      be depreciated on a straight-line basis. The
      company's marginal tax rate is 50 per cent and
      its cost of capital is 10 per cent.

      (a)   What is the present value of the total
            after-tax cost for each computer?
      (b)   Which computer would the company purchase?

4-3   Problem 4-2 shows that Computer C is more ex-
      pensive than Computer D, but the former re-
      quires less operating expenses.

      (a)   Determine the incremental after-tax operat-
            ing costs of Computer D over Computer C
            and the present value of these extra costs
            at each of the following discount rates:
            5%, 10%, and 20%.
      (b)   Compare the present value of the additional
            after-tax operating costs for Computer D
            with the additional investment for Computer C.

4-4 Two mutually exclusive projects have the following cash flows:

Project	Year 0	Year 1	Year 2	Year 3	Year 4	Year 5
E	-$3,200	$1,600	$1,600	$ 800	$ 400	$ 0
F	- 3,200	400	800	800	800	2,455

Rank the projects by the following methods: (a)
the payback period, (b) the average rate of return (average annual net cash flow/investment),
(c) the net present value at 10 per cent discount rate, and (d) the internal rate of return.

4-5 Two mutually exclusive projects have the following characteristics:

Project	Year 0	Year 1	Year 2	Year 3	Year 4
G	-$30,000	$15,000	$10,000	$20,000	$5,000
H	-20,000	18,000	10,000		

The cost of capital is 10 per cent. Choose
the more desirable project on the basis of
the annualized net present value.

5-1 The ABC Corporation has two mutually exclusive
projects, A and B. The company's cost of
capital is 10 per cent. These two projects
have the following cash flows:

Project	Year 0	Year 1	Year 2	Year 3	Year 4
A	-$17,500	$7,000	$7,000	$7,000	$ 7,000
B	-17,500	0	3,500	7,000	21,000

(a) Compute the net present value for each
     project.
(b) Compute the internal rate of return for
     each project.
(c) Determine the terminal value for each
     project at a reinvestment rate of 7
     per cent.
(d) Determine the modified net present value
     and the modified internal rate of return
     for each project, assuming that the re-
     investment rate is 7 per cent and the
     cost of capital is 10 per cent.
(e) If the cost of capital is indeed 10 per
     cent, which project would you choose
     and why?
(f) Use Project A to confirm the reinvestment
     assumption under each of the two dis-
     counted cash-flow approaches.

5-2 The XYZ Corporation is faced with two mutually
exclusive projects, C and D. The expected cash
flows are as follows:

Project	Year 0	Year 1
C	-$40,000	$48,000
D	-60,000	70,800

(a) Determine the Fisher's intersection.
(b) Compute the net present values of Proj-
     ects C and D at each of the following
     discount rates: 0%, 5%, 10%, 14%, 18%,
     and 20%.
(c) Use the data obtained in (b) to con-
     struct a graph such as Figure 5-1.

(d)   Determine the terminal value for each
      project at a reinvestment rate of
      8 per cent.
(e)   If the cost of capital is indeed 10 per
      cent, which project would you prefer
      and why?

5-3   Project E requires an outlay in year 0 of
      $3,200 followed by a positive $20,000 inflow
      in year 1 and a -$20,000 in year 2.

(a)   Determine the two internal rates of re-
      turn for Project E. (Hint: Reduce the
      equation for the internal rate of return
      to ax^2 + bx + c and then use the clas-
      sic quadratic formula):

$$x = \frac{-b \pm \sqrt{b^2 - 4ac}}{2a}$$

(b)   Construct a graph such as 5-3.
(c)   Adjust the cash flows at 30 per cent
      in a way that the possibility of
      double rates will be eliminated and
      then determine the internal rate of
      return for Project E.

6-1 Mr. Eric Mulroy and Mrs. Susan Mulroy have two small children. Because they have a limited income, they are forced to live frugally. One day Susan decides to make a beef and potato stew for herself and three other family members. Because she knows something about dietary requirements, she stipulates that the stew must yield at least 8,000 calories and at least 350 grams of protein. Her decision problem is to buy the combination of beef and potatoes that would yield the minimum food requirements at minimum cost. She knows that beef yields 2,500 calories and 180 grams of protein per pound. The cost of beef is $1.85 per pound. She also knows that potatoes yield 600 calories and 15 grams of protein per pound. Potatoes cost only 35 cents.

(a) Set up the primal linear programming problem.
(b) Formulate the dual for Susan's diet problem.

6-2 Solve the following linear programming problem using the graphic method.

maximize $50x_1 + 80x_2$

subject to $5x_1 + 6x_2 \leq 600$

$x_1 + 2x_2 \leq 160$

$x_1 \leq 80$

$x_2 \leq 60$

and $x_1 \geq 0, \; x_2 \geq 0$

6-3 The Ace Rubber and Tire Corporation is examining the feasibility of six projects. There are limitations imposed on budget ($950 in period 1 and $300 in period 2), managerial supervision of the projects (90 hours), and working-capital requirements for all projects ($500) over their useful lives. These six projects have the following features:

302

Proj-ect	NPV	Budget in Period 1	Budget in Period 2	Managerial Supervision	Working-Capital Requirement
1	$85	$250	$150	15 hours	$100
2	60	300	170	12	80
3	75	300	150	10	200
4	40	400	120	40	50
5	75	100	200	20	150
6	90	150	110	30	100
Constraint		950	300	90	500

Formulate the LP model to maximize the total net present value of accepted projects.

6-4 Assume that the solution of a four-project problem is as follows:

Basic Variable	x_1	x_4	s_2	s_3	RHS
x_2	1.0			0.4	1.0
x_3			1.0	0.7	0.9
s_1		1.0		1.5	150
	2.1	4.5	4.8	0.8	549

Slack variables s_1, s_2, and s_3 are defined as the number of excess budget dollars in periods 1, 2, and 3.

Interpret the solution table in some detail.

6-5 Assume that a company has $1,000 to invest in period 1 and $1,500 in period 2. It has the following four indivisible projects:

Project	NPV	Cost in Period 1	Cost in Period 2
1	$250	$500	$350
2	150	750	250
3	100	500	250
4	300	500	750

303

(a) Write out the integer programming problem
     formulation of this problem.
(b) Solve the problem using implicit enumera-
     tion.

6-6 Assume that a company has the following six
     individual projects:

Project	NPV	Cost in Period 1	Cost in Period 2
1	$80	$300	$250
2	50	225	225
3	95	400	150
4	90	200	150
5	75	250	100
6	75	175	175

The following additional assumptions exist:
(1) The company has $1,000 to invest in period
1 and $800 in period 2.   (2) Projects 3 and 4
are mutually exclusive.   (3) If project 3 is
accepted, project 1 must be rejected.   (4) If
project 4 is accepted, project 5 must be accepted.   (5) If projects 1 and 2 are accepted
in combination, the combined NPV of these two
projects will increase to 120 per cent and
their combined cost will decrease to 85 per
cent of the combined cost for the two projects
separately.

(a) Formulate the problem as an integer
     programming model.
(b) Solve the problem using implicit
     enumeration.

7-1 A company produces calculators and radios.
The average production rates for both products are identical: 2,000 units per hour.
The company's operating capacity is 160 hours
per week. The marketing department expects
the minimum weekly sales to be 140,000 calculators and 90,000 radios. The accounting
department expects profits to be $5 per cal-
culator and $3 per radio. The company has
set the following four goals in order of
their importance:

P_1 is to avoid any underutilization of normal
production capacity.
P_2 is to limit the overtime operation of the
plant to 20 hours.
P_3 is to achieve the sales goals of 140,000
calculators and 90,000 radios.
P_4 is to minimize the overtime operation of the
plant as much as possible.

(a) Write out the goal programming formulation of this problem.
(b) Solve the problem using the graphic
method.

7-2 The following problem is adopted from: Arthur
J. Kewn and John D. Martin, "An Integer Programming Model for Capital Budgeting in Hos-
pitals," Financial Management (Autumn 1976),
pp. 28-35. The problem involves the availability of 14 hospital improvement projects.
The following table shows the costs and technical coefficients associated with the func-
tional performance improvement goals. Additional assumptions are: (1) Projects 3 and
4 are mutually exclusive. (2) Project 12 cannot be accepted unless project 7 is also accepted. (3) The first goal is to invest a
maximum of $250,000 for all projects. (4) The
second goal is to accept at least two of the
following seven projects: 3, 5, 8, 10, 11,
12, and 13. (5) The third goal is to spend
at least $100,000 on projects 1, 3, 4, 6, 7,
and 8. (6) The fourth goal is to accept at
least one of projects 5, 10, and 11. (7)
The fifth goal is to increase the performance
measure in the blood diagnosis area by 260

Project Description	CO_1	Blood (QAPDs)	Respiratory (QAPDs)	Coronary (QAPDs)	Cancer (QAPDs)
x_1 Radio-isotope scanner	$80,000	40			100
x_2 Zero-radiography/mammography	37,000				70
x_3 Automated chemistry analyzer	75,000	140	20	30	
x_4 Coulter-S analyzer	70,000	100	10	60	
x_5 Pulmonary function machine	30,000		70	10	
x_6 Additional monitor with central systems reporter	35,000			40	
x_7 Blood gas analyzer	45,000	110	30	10	
x_8 EKG machine	60,000			70	
x_9 Defibulator	60,000		20	50	
x_{10} Bennet respirator	60,000		80	10	
x_{11} 37° incubator	25,000	110			
x_{12} Flame photometer	30,000	120			
x_{13} Portable X-ray	25,000		10	50	10
x_{14} Nebulizer	35,000		60		

quality adjusted patient days. (8) The sixth
goal is to increase the performance measure
in the respiratory diagnosis area by 150
quality adjusted patient days. (9) The
seventh goal is to increase the performance
measure in the coronary diagnosis area by
150 quality adjusted patient days. (10) The
eighth goal is to increase the performance in
the cancer diagnosis area by 100 quality adjusted patient days.

(a)   Set up this problem as an integer goal
      programming model.
(b)   Solve the problem and discuss the results.

7-3   Solve Example 7-2 assuming that the multiple
      goals of net present value, average rate of
      return, and payback period are weighted as
      40%, 30%, and 30%, respectively.

8-1   A company has two investment projects under
      the three different states of the economy:
      above normal, normal, below normal. The
      probabilities of these states of the economy
      and their corresponding net cash flows are
      as follows:

| State of | | Net Cash Flows | |
Economy	Probability	Project A	Project B
Above normal	0.50	$900	$700
Normal	0.30	500	700
Below normal	0.20	350	550

    (a)   Determine the following: expected value,
          variance, standard deviation, semi-
          variance, and coefficient of variation.
    (b)   Interpret the measures.

8-2   A project has an initial cost of $2,800 and the
      firm's cost of capital is 10 per cent. The
      project has the following probability distribu-
      tion of expected net cash flows in each of the
      next three years:

Probability	Net Cash Flow
0.20	$1,000
0.10	2,000
0.30	3,000
0.40	4,000

    (a)   Determine the expected value of net cash
          flows in each of the next three years
          for the project.
    (b)   Determine the net present value of the
          project.
    (c)   Determine the standard deviation of the
          project under the assumption of mutual
          independence of net cash flows over time.
    (d)   Determine the standard deviation of the
          project under the assumption of mutual
          dependence of net cash flows over time.

8-3   Assume that in year 1, a project with a cost
       of $200 has a 0.4 chance to earn $200 and a
       0.6 chance to earn $100. Given a net cash
       flow of $200 in year 1, the probabilities are
       0.5 that the project will earn $400 in year 2
       and 0.5 that it will yield $300. If a net
       cash flow of $100 is given in year 1, the
       probabilities are 0.5 that the project will
       produce $200 in year 2 and 0.5 that it will
       produce $100. The firm's cost of capital is
       10 per cent and the net cash flows of the proj-
       ect are mixed correlated over time.

       (a)   Prepare the conditional probability
             distribution such as Table 8-1.
       (b)   Compute the expected net present value
             of the project.
       (c)   Compute the standard deviation of the
             project.

8-4   A project has an expected net present value of
       $2,000 and a standard deviation of $1,000.
       The returns from this project are normally
       distributed.

       (a)   What is the probability that the actual
             net present value of the project will
             be greater than $0?
       (b)   What is the probability that the actual
             net present value of the project will
             be between $500 and $3,000?

8-5   A project with an initial cost of $15,000 is
       expected to produce net cash flows of $8,000,
       $9,000, $10,000, and $11,000 for each of the
       next four years. The firm's cost of capital
       is 12 per cent, but the financial manager
       perceives the risk of this particular project
       to be much higher than 12 per cent. The
       financial manager feels that a 20 per cent
       discount rate would be appropriate for the
       project.

       (a)   Compute the net present value of the
             project at the firm's cost of capital.
       (b)   Compute the risk-adjusted net present
             value of the project.

8-6   A project has a cost of $1,400. Its net cash
       flows are expected to be $900, $1,000, and
       $1,400 for each of the next three years. The
       respective certainty-equivalent coefficients
       are estimated to be 0.75, 0.55, and 0.35.
       With a 6 per cent risk-free discount rate,
       determine the certain net present value of
       the project.

8-7   Two mutually exclusive projects have an equal
       cost of $1,200 and an equal expected life of
       two years. For the first year, project A has
       a .50 chance to obtain a net cash flow of $800
       and a .5 chance to produce a net cash flow of
       $400. Given a net cash flow of $800 in year
       1, the probabilities are .4 that the project
       will yield $1,600 in year 2 and .6 that it
       will yield $1,200. If a net cash flow of
       $400 is given in year 1, the probabilities
       are .4 that the project will earn $800 in year
       2 and .6 that it will earn $400. On the other
       hand, project B has a .5 chance to earn $400
       in year 1 and a .5 chance to earn $800.
       Given a net cash flow of $400 in year 1, the
       probabilities are .4 that project B will pro-
       duce $2,000 in year 2 and .6 that it will
       produce $1,500. Given a net cash flow of $800
       in year 1, the probabilities are .4 that proj-
       ect B will yield $1,000 in year 2 and .6 that
       it will yield $500.

       (a)   Construct a decision tree in a tabular
             form so that management can use it in
             evaluating the two projects.
       (b)   With a 5 per cent cost of capital, deter-
             mine the expected value, the standard de-
             viation, and the coefficient of variation
             for each project.
       (c)   Which project would you choose?

8-8   An investment project has a cost of $200 and
       an estimated life of one year. It has only
       two uncertain variables: the unit sales
       volume and the variable cost per unit. The
       estimates for these two variables are given
       as the probability distributions as follows:

310

Vari-able Cost	Proba-bility	Identication Number	Unit Sales	Proba-bility	Identication Number
$2	.2	a	100	.1	x
3	.6	b	200	.8	y
4	.2	c	300	.1	z

Sales volume and variable cost are independent of each other, and the sales price per unit is a known $5. To simplify the matter, ignore taxes, the time value of money, and depreciation. The profit is:

$$\text{Profit} = S(\$5 - V) - \$200$$

where S = unit sales volume and V = variable cost per unit.

(a) Determine the various profit levels for sales and variable cost.

(b) Construct a frequency table of these profits such as Table 8-3 with the following classes: -$300 to $0; $1 to $300; $301 to $600; and $601 to $900.

(c) Determine the expected profit and the standard deviation.

8-9 In Problem 8-8, the expected variable cost per unit is $3 = $2 x .2 + $3 x .6 + $4 x .2. The expected sales are 200 units = 100 x .1 + 200 x .8 + 300 x .1. The profit for these two specific values is $200 = 200(5-3)-200.

(a) Determine the effect of a 10 per cent increase in the sales volume on the computed profit.

(b) Measure the effect of a 10 per cent increase in the variable cost per unit on the computed profit.

(c) Which variable is more critical?

9-1 Projects A and B are under consideration by a company. The following contingency table shows the characteristics of these two projects:

Returns of Project B		Returns of Project A		
	e_i / e_{i+2}	e_1 $100	e_2 $200	Column Totals
$200	e_3	0.00	0.40	0.40
$100	e_4	0.40	0.20	0.60
Row Totals		0.40	0.60	1.00

(a) Compute the expected return of the two-project portfolio.
(b) Compute the variance of each project.
(c) Compute the covariance of these two projects.
(d) Compute the portfolio variance.

9-2 Assume: $\bar{R}_Y = 32\%$; $\bar{R}_Z = 35\%$; $\sigma_Y = 0.07$; $\sigma_Z = 0.007$;

$x_Y = 0.5$; $x_Z = 0.5$ and $r_{YZ} = -0.32$.

(a) Compute the portfolio return.
(b) Compute the portfolio standard deviation.

9-3 Security j and Market Portfolio m have the following characteristics: $R_f = 0.10$; $\sigma_j = 0.20$; $\sigma_m = 0.13$; $\bar{R}_m = 0.15$; and $r_{jm} = 0.40$.

(a) Determine the beta coefficient of security j.
(b) Determine the required rate of return on security j.
(c) Do you think that security j should be accepted if the expected return of security j is 12 per cent?

9-4 The following table shows the percentage returns of a security and a market portfolio over a 10-year period:

Year	Security (R_{jt})	Market Portfolio (R_{mt})
19-0	0.401	0.298
19-1	0.426	0.303
19-2	0.297	0.251
19-3	0.052	0.074
19-4	0.073	0.082
19-5	0.101	0.123
19-6	0.154	0.169
19-7	0.198	0.191
19-8	0.249	0.225
19-9	0.352	0.264

(a) Determine the parameters ∂_j and β_j.
(b) Determine the regression equation for security j.
(c) Determine the coefficient of determination.

10-1 A company is planning to launch a major expansion program which will require $1 million. The firm wants to maintain its current capital structure: debt = 30%, preferred stock = 20%, and common equity = 50%. New bonds will have an after-tax cost of 4.74 per cent. New preferred stock will have a 9 per cent dividend rate and will be sold at par. Common stock with a current market price of $50 can be sold to net the firm $40 per share. The firm currently pays a $2 dividend and plans to increase its dividend at the rate of 5 per cent per year. The retained earnings available to the expansion program are estimated to be $200,000.

   (a) To maintain the current capital structure, how much of the capital budget should be financed by external equity?
   (b) Determine the cost of each individual component. (Use Equation (10-7) to compute the cost of the retained earnings.)
   (c) Compute the weighted average cost of incremental capital.

10-2 A company has the historical pattern of dividend payments as follows:

1976	$1.50
1977	1.48
1978	1.64
1979	1.87
1980	2.00

The firm expects to pay a $2.10 dividend per share at the end of 1981. Dividends are expected to grow at the five-year average (1976-1980) per year. Common stock currently selling for $25 per share can be sold to net the firm $20.

   (a) Compute the growth rate of dividends.
   (b) Compute the cost of existing common equity.
   (c) Compute the floatation cost percentage of market price. (Ignore the underpricing of new common stock.)
   (d) Compute the cost of new common stock.

314

10-3 The current capital structure of a firm is con-
      sidered to be optimal. It has $5,000 in debt
      at 8 per cent interest. The firm is expected
      to earn $1,500 before taxes of 50 per cent per
      year, all of which will be paid in dividends.
      The cost of equity capital is 10 per cent.

      (a) Determine the total market value of the
           firm.
      (b) Determine the overall cost of capital.

10-4 Determine the value of the following:

      (a) A bond with a yield rate of 10 per cent
           and an annual interest of $80 for
           perpetuity.
      (b) A common stock with the following charac-
           teristics: a current dividend of $4 per
           share, an expected growth rate of 5 per
           cent, and a 10 per cent required rate
           of return.

10-5 Assume the riskless rate of return is 10 per
      cent. Possible returns for market portfolio
      m and security D are as follows:

State of the Economy	Associated Probability	Possible Returns	
		Market Portfolio m	Security D
Recession	0.20	0.10	0.05
Normal	0.60	0.15	0.20
Prosperity	0.20	0.20	0.30

      (a) Determine the variance of the market portfolio.
      (b) Determine the covariance between the returns
           on security D and market portfolio m.
      (c) Determine beta for security D.
      (d) Determine whether security D should be
           accepted or rejected.

10-6 At present, the riskless rate of return is 10
      per cent and the expected rate of return on the
      market portfolio is 15 per cent. The expected
      returns for five stocks are listed below, to-
      gether with their expected betas:

315

Stock	Expected Return	Expected Beta
A	0.22	1.5
B	0.30	1.3
C	0.12	0.8
D	0.15	0.7
E	0.14	1.1

On the basis of these expectations, which stocks are overvalued? Which stocks are undervalued?

10-7   A machine tool company is an all-equity company. It is considering the purchase of a new machine for $130,000. The machine is expected to produce annual net cash flows of $35,000, $32,000, $28,000, $25,000, $22,000, $18,000, $15,000, $12,000, $10,000, and $8,000 for the next 10 years. The company has bought similar machines in the past and feels appropriate to use past behavior as a proxy for the future. A comparable machine produced annual net cash flows of $7,060, $3,400, $5,700, $3,550, $4,220, $3,860, $2,200, $2,540, $3,000, and $5,710 for its 10-year life. Its external market value was $22,000 in year 0, $20,000 in year 1, $18,000 in year 2, $15,000 in year 3, $14,000 in year 4, $13,000 in year 5, $12,000 in year 6, $11,000 in year 7, $10,000 in year 8, $9,0000 in year 9, and $5,000 in year 10. The one-year returns of Standard and Poor's 500-stock index were 10%, 2%, 4%, 6%, 8%, 7%, 4%, 6%, 7%, and 6% during the same 10-year period.

(a)   Compute the annual percentage returns of the comparable machine.
(b)   Compute beta for the comparable machine.
(c)   Compute the required rate of return for the new machine assuming that the riskless rate of return is 4.16%.
(d)   Determine the net present value of the new machine.

11-1   The Zero Company wants to acquire a machine
       with a cost of $30,000 and an estimated eco-
       nomic life of five years. The machine is ex-
       pected to have no salvage value at the end of
       five years. If the company decides to buy the
       machine, it can finance the project with a loan
       at an interest rate of 10 per cent. The ma-
       chine is to be depreciated on the basis of the
       sum-years-digits method. An investment tax
       credit of 7 per cent is available in year 1.
       The lender requires the company to repay its
       loan in five annual installments. The com-
       pany's tax rate is 50 per cent. By compari-
       son, if the company decides to lease the ma-
       chine, it will have the following character-
       istics: (1) The lease has a fixed noncancel-
       able term of five years with a return of 14
       per cent per year on the $30,000 investment.
       (2) Annual lease payments are made at the
       beginning of each year.

       (a)   Compute the present value of the after-
             tax cash outflows for the buying al-
             ternative.
       (b)   Compute the present value of the after-
             tax cash outflows for the leasing al-
             ternative.
       (c)   Determine the internal rate of return for
             the leasing alternative.

11-2   Two pieces of equipment under consideration
       for leasing are expected to achieve the same
       task. These two alternatives have the fol-
       lowing characteristics:

	Option A	Option B
Value of asset and basis of lease	$20,000	$60,000
Implicit interest rate on lease	10%	9%
Annual maintenance operating cost	4,000	3,000
Expected life of lease	3 years	8 years

       Additional assumptions are: (1) Both options
       are operating leases in nature.   (2) The firm
       will be able to release assets of exactly the
       same characteristics as those currently being
       used.

(a) Determine the annualized cost (annualized lease cost plus annualized maintenance-operating cost) for both lease options.

(b) Assume that Option B's maintenance-operating costs are a part of the lease contract, while Option A requires the lessee to pay all maintenance-operating costs. How large should A's annual maintenance-operating costs be before B is preferred to A?

(c) If the company really preferred the operating and other characteristics of B over A, how low should B's implicit interest rate be for the total costs of both leases to become equal?

12-1   Assume that the American Electrical Corpora-
        tion (AEC) is considering the establishment
        of a freezer manufacturing plant in Spain.
        AEC wants to invest a total of 10,000 Spanish
        pesetas in the proposed plant. The Pts10,000
        will be financed with only common stock, all
        of which will be owned by the parent company.
        The plant is to be depreciated over a five-
        year period on a straight-line basis for tax
        purposes. It is expected to have a salvage
        value of Pts5,000 at the end of five years.
        Spain has 35 per cent corporate income tax
        and no withholding taxes on dividend paid.
        The United States has 50 per cent corporate
        income tax with direct credit for Spanish taxes.
        Spain does not impose any restrictions on divi-
        dend repatriation, but it does not allow the
        parent company to repatriate depreciation cash
        flows until the plant is liquidated. These
        depreciation cash flows may be reinvested in
        Spanish government bonds to earn 8 per cent
        tax exempt interest. The cost of capital used
        to analyze the project is 15 per cent. The
        current exchange rate of Pts5.00 per U.S. dol-
        lar is expected to hold during year 1, but the
        Spanish peseta is expected to depreciate there-
        after at a rate of 5 per cent per year. Assume
        the following revenues and operating costs in
        terms of Spanish pesetas:

	Year 1	Year 2	Year 3	Year 4	Year 5
Revenues	10,000	11,000	12,000	13,000	14,000
O.C.	6,000	6,000	7,000	7,000	8,000

        (a) Determine the projected earnings after taxes
             for the proposed plant.
        (b) Determine the interest-compounded depreciation
             cash flows at the end of five years.
        (c) Determine the net present value of the
             plant, the profitability index, and the
             internal rate of return for the plant
             in terms of the U.S. dollar.

12-2   The Wayne Company currently exports 500 cal-
        culators per month to Jordan at a price of $60
        and the variable cost per calculator is $40.

319

In May 1980, the company was approached by the government of Jordan with a request that it establish a small manufacturing plant in Jordan. After a careful analysis the company decided to make an equity investment of $1 million, half of which would represent working capital and the other half fixed assets. The company would sell the plant to a local investor for the sum of $1 at the end of five years and the central bank of Jordan would repay the company for the working capital of $500,000. In return for an increase in tariffs against other companies, the Wayne Company is willing to sell its calculators in Jordan for $50 per unit. In addition, the company will have to buy certain raw materials from local suppliers and to use local managers. Total costs of local managers and materials would be $15 per calculator. Other materials would be purchased from the parent at $10 and the parent would receive a direct contribution to overhead after variable costs of $5 per unit sold. Under this arrangement, the company expects that it can sell 1,000 calculators per month. The fixed assets are to be depreciated on a straight-line basis over a five-year period. The company will have to pay income taxes at 50 per cent on profits earned in Jordan. The United States also has a 50 per cent tax rate with direct credit for Jordanian taxes. The current exchange rate is 10 Jordanian dinars per dollar and it is expected to stay the same for the next five years. There is no restriction on cash flow repatriation.

(a)   Determine the net present value of the project at 10 per cent.
(b)   The Wayne Company has been informed that, if it decides to reject the project, it would lose its entire export sales. How does this affect the decision by the Wayne Company?

12-3   Problems 12-1 and 12-2 highlight the complexities involved in foreign investment decisions. Identify these problems.

13-1 The four callable bonds have the following
call prices and issue sizes:

Bond	Size of Issue	Call Price
A	50,000 bonds	$1,050
B	10,000	1,030
C	25,000	1,100
D	15,000	1,040

Additional assumptions are: (1) Each bond has
a face value of $1,000. (2) The firm's mar-
ginal tax rate is 40 per cent. What is the
after-tax cost of calling the issue for each
of these callable bonds?

13-2 The Park Company issued $1.5 million of 30-
year, $1,000 bonds with a coupon rate of 9
per cent five years ago. The bonds with a
call price of $1,050 were sold at a discount
of $30 per bond or with a total discount of
$45,000. The initial flotation cost was
$18,000. The company wishes to sell a $1.5
million new issue of 7 per cent, 25-year bonds
in order to retire its existing bonds. The
company intends to sell its new bonds at
their face value of $1,000 per bond. The
flotation costs of the new issue are estimated to be $22,000. The company's marginal
tax rate is 50 per cent. The new bonds are
sold four months before the old bonds are
called.

(a) Determine the net cash outflow of the
refunding operation.
(b) Determine the annual interest savings
of the refunding operation.
(c) Determine the present value of the interest savings over a 25-year period at
5 per cent discount rate.
(d) Should the company refund its old bonds?
(e) Use the internal rate of return approach
to determine whether the company should
refund its old bonds or not.

13-3 A project with a cost of $7,500 is expected
to produce a net cash flow of $2,000 in each
of the next five years. The salvage values
of the project at the end of each year are
estimated to be $6,200, $5,200, $4,000, $2,200,
and $0 for the next five years. The firm's
cost of capital is 10 per cent. Determine
the optimal time for the project to be
retired.